Leadership Assessment for Talent Development

PRAISE FOR *LEADERSHIP ASSESSMENT AND TALENT DEVELOPMENT*

'A 'child in their favourite toy store'... that is how this book will make any inquisitive HR Executive or Business Leader feel when they delve into the rich insights, learnings and opportunities it provides! For any 'self-aware, development-hungry leader' who strives to be successful, this provides both immediate and long-term direction on how to excel as a business and a leader whilst encouraging us to become exceptional role models for future generations.' **Peter Collyer, Senior Vice President, Global Human Resources, Claire's Stores Inc.**

'Leadership capabilities at all levels have never been more important in times of great change and uncertainty, and most CEOs will cite leadership as one of their most critical areas of concern. So how do we make sure we are assessing and developing leaders in the best way? Much is changing in this field and this book brings together some of the best thinking, case studies and ideas that help us all better understand and develop leaders for the future.' **Peter Cheese, CEO, CIPD (Chartered Institute of Personal Development)**

'Without leadership, organizations (and nations) perish; this is why this book is so timely, and important. Full of interesting research, practical examples, and insightful advice. An excellent contemporary resource for developing leadership talents; invaluable at both an individual and organizational level.' **Dr Barry Z. Posner, Accolti Professor of Leadership, Santa Clara University and co-author of *The Leadership Challenge*, selected as one of the top ten leadership books of all time**

'Tomorrow's leadership will face far greater challenges than today's privileged generation. We need to be developing tomorrow's leadership now and this book provides many tools, approaches and case studies that can help us with that urgent task.' **Professor Peter Hawkins, Henley Business School, author of *Leadership Team Coaching***

'A timely and insightful treatise on a subject of central importance to every organization today. Essential learning for all professionals engaged in leadership and talent development.' **Shubhro Sen, Director, TATA Management Training Centre**

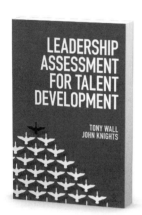

Leadership Assessment for Talent Development

Edited by
Tony Wall and
John Knights

KoganPage

LONDON PHILADELPHIA NEW DELHI

First published in Great Britain and the United States in 2013 by Kogan Page Limited

120 Pentonville Road	1518 Walnut Street, Suite 1100	4737/23 Ansari Road
London N1 9JN	Philadelphia PA 19102	Daryaganj
United Kingdom	USA	New Delhi 110002
www.koganpage.com		India

© Tony Wall, John Knights and individual contributors

The right of Tony Wall, John Knights and individual contributors to be identified as the authors of this work has been asserted by them in accordance with the Copyright, Designs and Patents Act 1988.

ISBN   978 0 7494 6860 6
E-ISBN   978 0 7494 6861 3

British Library Cataloguing-in-Publication Data

A CIP record for this book is available from the British Library.

Library of Congress Cataloging-in-Publication Data

Leadership assessment for talent development / [edited by] Tony Wall, John Knights.
    pages cm
  Includes bibliographical references.
    ISBN 978-0-7494-6860-6 – ISBN 978-0-7494-6861-3 1. Leadership. 2. Executive ability.
3. Personnel management. 4. Leadership–Case studies. 5. Executive ability–Case studies.
6. Personnel management–Case studies. I. Wall, Tony, 1979- II. Knights, John, 1946-
    HD57.7.L43166 2013
    658.4'092–dc23
                                                                                    2013015901

Typeset by Graphicraft Limited, Hong Kong
Printed and bound in India by Replika Press Pvt Ltd

CONTENTS

ABOUT THE EDITORS

Tony Wall has a passion for facilitating personal and organizational transformation with CEOs, entrepreneurs, small businesses, governments and education across the globe. As senior lecturer, action-researcher and international work-based learning consultant at the Centre for Work Related Studies, University of Chester, he uses applied psychologies and organizational development methodologies to facilitate behavioural change and impact. In addition to international journal articles, he is the author of *Learning through Work, Transforming Prior Learning Policy & Practice* and *Making Employer and University Partnerships Work*.

http://www.linkedin.com/in/cwrstony
http://www.cwrs.eu

John Knights' business life changed when in 1998 he had the serendipitous opportunity to learn to coach other Chief Executives and started to understand the real issues around leadership. Developing 'excellent leaders' became and remains his passion. John, chairman of LeaderShape, is an experienced senior executive coach and facilitator, and an expert in emotional intelligence, transpersonal leadership and neuro-leadership. He has been a senior executive in major international corporations, a serial entrepreneur and lecturer at Oxford University. He is author of *The Invisible Elephant* & *The Pyramid Treasure* and has written for *HR Magazine*.

www.leadershape.biz
https://twitter.com/leadershapejohn
https://leadershape.wordpress.com
http://www.speakingtree.in/public/john.knights/blog
http://www.linkedin.com/in/johnknights

Introduction

TONY WALL

The three jewels in the crown of sustainable performance

Do you ever find yourself wondering why things happen? Do you ever wonder how we seem to be witnessing a number of occurrences that are unusual in our lifetime? How did that corporate giant collapse? How did that bank become so weak and so quickly come to depend on the government and the taxpayer? How could 'rate fixing' happen within that bank, given such high levels of regulation? How could the behaviour of a relatively small group of people lead to such a global economic crisis? How can the behaviours of a relatively few news reporters create the collapse of a giant newspaper? What happened for that newspaper to allow the listening in to those personal voice messages? What has happened in the supply chain to allow the alleged inclusion of horse meat in beef burgers in a large chain store?

These are complex questions, but *perhaps* they are indicators of what can happen when we, as a human race, constantly strive for personal gain over all else. That is not to say that striving for personal gain is wrong – nor is it saying that all those who strive for personal gain create such catastrophic consequences. Indeed, all of the authors of this book devote their lives to helping professionals improve themselves. But *perhaps* when the personal gain overpowers and outweighs the wider gain of stakeholders, this creates an environment for such catastrophe to become possible – perhaps more possible. In the examples referred to above, the banking, news and retail industries, organizational performance was not only negatively affected but, in some cases, organizations were killed off.

Thinking and acting beyond profit to think of people and the planet, remains a hot topic. So too, as part of this debate, does sustainable organizational performance. For example, the Chartered Institute for Personnel and Development (CIPD) reported the outcomes of an action research project in 2011, which identified the key drivers for sustainable organizational performance (CIPD, 2011). Within the research eight themes were high-lighted. Interestingly, five of them can be directly linked to leadership.

First, the research identified that leaders at all levels need a future-oriented vision to help inform decision making, and use appropriate styles to help others achieve. Let's emphasize two points here – leaders are at *all levels*, and *help others* achieve. Second, the research identified that a shared purpose must be created and maintained; where purpose is the 'golden thread' that runs throughout an organization, like a collective but flexible glue holding direction together. A leader has a key role in weaving this thread or making the glue. A key way of doing this was through the third driver of sustainable performance: engaging others. Enabling others at different levels through-out the organization to be involved and inform decision making was a key factor in sustainable organizational performance. Again, this was about facilitating others rather than directing and instructing. Yet this was done with alignment of values and purpose, whereby there was an awareness and facilitation of the consistency and fit between the values, behaviours or pur-poses of the different stakeholders.

There appears to be nothing surprising or shocking here – there isn't. These are the messages coming from leadership theory and practice for many years, particularly creating shared purpose and aligning values and purpose. Yet there are indicators of subtle difference here, perhaps most significant in the enabling and engagement of others for their achievement (rather than the leader's gain). The fifth driver of sustainable performance sheds more light on this subtly different form of leadership: the ability to balance short- and long-term outcomes. This is the ability to be aware of the shorter-term effects on other people, communities, shareholders, the planet – and the longer-term effects. This balancing is a sensitive juggling act that is part of what might be called 'transpersonal leadership' – thinking and acting beyond the leader's own personal gain, and paying attention to those around them now and in the future (discussed in more depth in Chapters 2 and 5). A type of leadership that is emotionally aware and connected to those around them. A type of leadership that is still absent in today's organ-izations and corporations – indeed, some high profile cases were alluded to at the start of this introduction.

So this type of leadership is a jewel in the crown of sustainable perform-ance, and can be seen to link to five of the eight themes of the CIPD's re-search into the drivers of sustainable organizational performance, but there are other important drivers. The next two drivers relate to talent develop-ment. The sixth driver of organizational performance was capacity building, or equipping people with the skills and knowledge they need today *and* in the future. But the research highlighted that it wasn't just about having the skills for tomorrow, but also having an agility, or readiness for change – the seventh driver. Together, these position talent development as a continually forming strategic resource that not only enables people to do their job today, to potentially do a job tomorrow, but be ready for the change of what else might need to be done. It is dynamic, not static. So talent development is another jewel in the crown for sustainable development.

The final jewel in the crown is perhaps not as obvious as leadership and talent development. According to the research, it was important to assess and evaluate where we are up to, where we are going, and how far we are in reaching our goals. This was at different levels, and in different areas – to learn, to inform decisions, like a learning organization. Assessment, the eighth driver of sustainable performance, is therefore a strategic activity that helps inform what happens next – the crux of the sustainability of an organization. This book is not a general book about the three jewels, but drills deep in to the jewels to look at the specific practice of using assessments for the development of leadership talents. Our collective experience tells us that doing so is an effective and efficient way to develop leadership behaviours, to expand both leadership talent and the wider talent pool through these leadership talents. And in doing so, we are polishing the three leadership jewels of leadership, talent and assessment.

We also know that these jewels do need to be deep cleaned; in a recent survey (CIPD, 2013), 41 per cent of HR professionals were kept awake at night thinking about their organization's future leadership capability, and 27 per cent were kept awake thinking about whether they had the right talent. We know from our consulting experience that many contemporary organizations continue to create a management elite (rather than multi-level leaders), cut back training and development and cut many forms of assessment. Within difficult economic times, there are keen budgeters who want to cut rather than invest, to balance the books. Balancing the books is a traditional management strategy to focus on profit at the expense of wider performance, not to mention people or the planet. Some research even suggests that less than half of organizations deploy talent management, and there is little awareness of some of the emerging models from neuroscience, cognitive research and behavioural science (CIPD, 2012). The CIPD's research gives us glimpses, or reminders of the glimpses we've had for some time, into a different form of leadership, one we refer to in this book as 'transpersonal' leadership, or leading beyond one's own personal gain (ego), and acting with others' stakes in heart and mind.

The importance of the transpersonal also featured in an earlier CIPD report, pressing for a next generation of HR (CIPD, 2010). In this thought piece, there were three key ideas. First, we need to future-proof our organizations towards sustainable performance – drawing on the eight drivers discussed above, specifically through future-fit leaders (what we call transpersonal leaders here). Second, we need to create an environment to enable an insight-driven HR, whereby business, organizational and contextual savvies, in a supportive culture, nourish new insights to be generated. The transpersonal leader, as presented through this book, understands insight, learns to trust it, and uses it to inform his or her decision making. And finally, we need the next-generation HR leaders, who act as partners and provocateurs in insight generation and decision making. Many of the chapters and tools in this book use the power of the incisive and open question to move understanding or thinking to a new place without direct instruction.

Indeed, leadership assessment for talent development is not presented as an approach to leadership or talent development. It is presented as a strong, high-value, high-impact part of the strategy jigsaw. It can form a talent management strategy (if there is an explicit one), or directly align and feed in to the corporate strategy. This is where it can make most impact for an organization, whether the talent management strategy adopted is an exclusive approach (say just for leaders) or an inclusive approach (for everyone). Leadership assessment can and is being used for selecting talent, for example through assessment centres, or for managing talent, say through successful planning. Yet the key premise of this book is that there is a huge amount of additional value potential in another area – developing talent. When used carefully in ways to develop talent (through assessment), major strides in performance can be achieved and sustained, because the developmental actions are credible, evidenced and owned. Yet there are subtle strategies to enable this, sometimes counter-intuitive, which enters the realms of coaching, mentoring, experiential and action learning facilitation. This book aims to offer practical strategies, tried and tested in practice, with explanations linking to neuroscience, cognitive research and behavioural science.

A bird's eye view of the book

The main thrust of the book starts in Chapter 2, which argues the case for why the 21st century needs transpersonal leaders with emotional intelligence. The chapter discusses how business environments are unstable from a multitude of movements in technology, politics, economics and the environment

– and how within such change, it is essential to become a transpersonal leader who thinks and acts beyond his or her own gain. Emotional intelligence has a core role as the connecting force or resonance between people, scientifically supported by neuroscience research.

In Chapters 3 and 4, we report some unique but powerful research using a contemporary leadership assessment tool to identify needs (discussed in more detail in Chapter 5). Unlike much research in leadership talent development, this is based on real, authentic leadership development work with organizations. The research highlights some very interesting core findings that will be of interest to all responsible for talent development – even if it is simply to help better target investment in talent development activity.

From the research, Chapter 3 analyses recurring leadership development needs across a variety of organizations and leadership levels. The most common development needs include empathy, developing others and conflict management. Similarly, in Chapter 4, common leadership blind spots and hidden strengths are analysed. The most common blind spots were capabilities to be a change catalyst, emotional self-awareness and accurate self-assessment, whereas the most common hidden strengths were emotional self-control, building bonds and organizational awareness. Both sets are important to acknowledge and deal with to maximize the talent development within any organization.

Chapter 5 presents leadership development as a journey, which passes through particular stages and steps; from a rational, ego-based as-usual leadership, to a type of leadership that is radically ethical, authentic leadership – essentially led by the interests of others rather than personal gain. Using these ideas, the chapter explains how assessment can help develop transpersonal leadership journeys, and presents two key leadership assessment tools and processes to do this. The outcome of using these leadership assessment tools is the identification of development needs – which form the starting point of the following talent development methods, ranging from giving feedback through to team interventions.

Once needs have been identified, delivering that communication in a way that stimulates motivated development with a forward focus, rather than creating stunted and resentful action on previous performance, is the focus of Chapter 6. Feeding back/forward for talent development is an important skill for all leaders and HR practitioners, as it can provide such immediate but long-lasting effects. Strategies and tactics for delivering messages using neuroscience are shared, with a working example. The case study provides another example of how feedback can be given in team contexts. Feeding forward is essential to the success of using leadership assessment for talent development.

Delivering messages for development is often done through one-to-one coaching, and so is particularly relevant to Chapter 7, coaching for talent development. Yet coaching is much more purposively about helping the individual develop awareness, and identifying and overcoming blockages to talent development. Such awareness and blockages might be beliefs or particular interpretations of the behaviours of others, in relation to the leadership assessments undertaken. Coaching has a powerful role in positively moving people forward.

Another way of positively developing long-lasting behavioural change is through real workplace projects. Chapter 8 explains how to design workplace projects for talent development. Here, helping individuals design a project to specifically address their development needs creates a high level of ownership, but also adds a level of authenticity to the learning that cannot be replicated through training. Thorough workplace projects that require individuals to investigate how to undertake them, and how to reflect on their experience, can also be rewarded through university credits – adding a higher level of credibility and performance.

For the talent development of senior leaders, Chapter 9 discusses director peer groups (DPGs). After a leadership assessment, or as part of one, DPGs can be used for highly relevant, deep impact learning using action learning processes. Here, executives share a real-life issue with peers that is constructively explored and challenged, leading to action points/plans. Over time, the outcomes of these plans are also shared for an ongoing cycle of collaborative sharing, constructive challenge, and essentially experiential learning alongside strategic problem solving.

Chapter 10 shares another way of developing talents with teams or whole organizations: leadership storytelling. The power of stories works through the architecture of the brain to create a connection (limbic resonance) to stimulate developmental thoughts or actions – often metaphorically rather than via a direct communication. A key message from neuroscience, introduced in Chapter 2, is that allowing people to make their own decisions can have a longer lasting impact on learning and engagement.

Whichever talent development strategies are chosen to supplement leadership assessments, it is important to know the fruits of that investment. In contemporary organizations, expenditure is closely monitored and, for many, budgets are reducing. Being more strategic about where to place talent development or indeed leadership assessment is the focus of Chapter 11. This chapter is about improving results through measuring the 'return on investment' of the decisions you make on leadership talent development. A key advantage of the type of leadership assessments discussed in this book is that they are a cost-effective way of developing leadership talent. So this final chapter is crucial in ensuring you gain and continue to gain that added value not just for your current leadership, but more important, the future sustainability of your organization.

Ways to read this book

This book was designed for practitioners in different contexts, with different experience levels, so we present a variety of ideas of how to use this book.

Dipping in to chapters, case studies and tools: though there will be some who might want to read this book from cover to cover, we expect most will want to focus on the areas that are most relevant to their particular context or pressing concern – and so we encourage you to dip in to each of the chapters, case studies and tools. If you decide to dip in to a case study, we would encourage you to get a fuller context of the main learning and action points of the chapter – and perhaps consider some of the tools to help you. If you decide to dip in to the tools, we strongly encourage you to get a fuller context of the main learning and action points of the chapter. The tools are designed with the chapters in mind.

Research update on leadership: Chapters 2 and 5 provide an accessible update on the scientific and theoretical developments in leadership talent development. Many leadership assessments reflect these updates, so it is useful for all readers to catch up on these ideas.

Research update on needs/strengths/blind spots: Chapters 3 and 4 summarize research that analyses leadership needs/strengths/blind spots across a variety of organizations. This is useful for all organizations to become aware of and consider for their own leadership talent development investment.

Beyond this, you might want to select specific areas of development, such as individual talent development – Chapters 6 (feeding back/forward), 7 (coaching), 8 (workplace projects) and 10 (storytelling); or for team talent development – Chapters 6 (feeding back/forward), 9 (director peer groups) and 10 (storytelling). In both cases, Chapter 11 provides insights into how to measure (and therefore improve) the impact of your leadership talent development activity.

A reminder: this is a unique collection of chapters but you will be able to explore and expand your reading in the specialist application areas such as coaching or storytelling. As you extend your reading, we encourage you to remember that other texts may be written for a context other than leadership assessment – so it is important to be aware of this in any actions they recommend. The principles in Chapter 5 are particularly helpful to keep in mind as you develop your own learning and practice.

We wish you well in your own leadership journey.

References

CIPD (2010) *Next Generation HR: Time for change*, The Chartered Institute of Personnel and Development, London

CIPD (2011) *Shaping the Future*, The Chartered Institute of Personnel and Development, London

CIPD (2012) *The CIPD 2012 Learning and Talent Development Survey*, The Chartered Institute of Personnel and Development, London

CIPD (2013) *HR Outlook: Winter 2012–13: A variety of leader perspectives*, The Chartered Institute of Personnel and Development, London

Twenty-first century needs transpersonal leaders with emotional intelligence

JOHN KNIGHTS

EXECUTIVE SUMMARY

The world is changing at an ever increasing rate, fuelled mainly by the widespread availability and distribution of information as a result of the invention of the internet and the mobile phone. This in turn is rapidly changing society and technology which, when added to the financial and economic crises, globalization, the awareness that resources are finite, and the shift in world economic power, positions us on the edge of chaos.

At the same time the present day human brain at birth is virtually the same as that of stone-age man, more than 250,000 years ago. Fortunately, at the dawn of the 21st century, neuroscience research took a leap forward with the invention of hi-tech scanners that could investigate the minute actions of the brain in real time so we now understand much more about how the brain works, and perhaps most important, how the brain prefers to learn.

A transpersonal leader is one who thinks beyond his or her ego and focuses on the needs of all the stakeholders of the organization, from client, shareholder and employees, the community and... the planet. Our research and experience show that to develop as a transpersonal leader one has to change oneself first before one can change the world (ie be transformational). This means learning to proactively reconfigure the neural connections in our brains to change our behaviours and even attitudes rather than letting it happen as a result of traditional teaching and random experiences.

To develop and improve these behaviours we need to raise our emotional intelligence. This means being aware of our emotions in real time and managing them effectively so that they do not hijack us into reacting instinctively and displaying our stone-age default. As a leader it also means being aware of the emotions of others and using that knowledge to effectively manage relationships.

Twenty-first century leaders

To understand the kind of leadership we need in the 21st century and to develop appropriate capabilities in our leaders, we need first to look at how the world has changed and is continuing to change. Then we need to understand why traditional leadership just won't work effectively any more, and to learn how the human brain can best cope with this fundamental change to enable the development of the leaders the world needs.

It is not that the characteristics of excellent leadership have changed, it is just that the default stereotype 'alpha-male' leadership style of 'I know everything and I'll tell people what to do' that goes back to stone-age man and is still predominant in organizational leadership, does not work in our new world. It is also a fact that there has never been a recognized best practice of what excellent leadership was or how to become one. So we finish up getting whichever leaders rise to the top for whatever reasons.

The world is changing... faster than ever

I am not going to provide here a chronicle of the increasing speed of change in the world but it is important to highlight that until the mid-1990s everyone accepted that the Industrial Revolution that began in the mid-1700s changed the world faster and more fundamentally than any previous period in history. And then in the mid-1980s we had the development of the mobile phone, which became generally available in the industrialized world in the mid-1990s – at the same time as the beginnings of the general availability of the internet and the ever increasing speed of computers. To think that as I write this it is only 16 years since e-mails became generally available and accessible in the UK!

In my view, this fundamental revolution in global communication and access to information is having a greater impact on the world we know and will continue to live in than any invention in history. And these changes have spawned many other inventions and developments that are changing the way we live our lives, such as smart phones, social networks, information gathering technologies (eg barcodes and radio frequency tags), medical technology, global travel, globalization of business, new emerging economic powers, reducing influence of the United States, rights vs responsibilities, flexible working structures, global terrorism, global drugs, diversity and human rights, the changing face of religion, an increasingly 'rule bound' society and the age of celebrity.

Then we have the issues of climate change and limitation of natural resources, and the attempts to respond through corporate governance, social responsibility and sustainability all while there is a deep financial and economic crisis caused by both bad leadership and pure greed... and we have no idea of the outcome. We are in many ways on the edge of chaos and are likely to continue surfing on the wave of uncertainty and increasing change. I am completely agnostic about astrology but the 'dawning age of Aquarius' does have a ring to it!

Leadership needs to catch up

We have always been taught that 'knowledge is power' (in Sir Francis Bacon's *Religious Meditations, of Heresies*, 1597) and in a way that is still true. But knowledge is not now the domain of leaders of organizations as it was in the past; knowledge is increasingly available to everyone. Whereas in 1985 executives could retain 85 per cent of the information they needed to do their job in their head, by 2005 it had reduced to less than 10 per cent (Kelley, 2008) and given the rate of increase in availability of information this is likely to soon be below 1 per cent. So the 'know everything and tell people what to do' approach, which we all tend to default to when we are stressed even if we have learnt more progressive behaviours, is just not effective in this new world. But it is not only that our brain cannot hold sufficient information to know everything, it is also that our brains don't like being told what to do and are ineffective in that mode! Our brain is much more effective at learning from insights (Rock and Schwartz, 2006).

So we have this conundrum. Society and the world are changing at an ever faster pace and our brains are changing at a Darwinian speed – glacial by comparison to society. In other words our brain is changing minutely in each human generation whereas over the same period society is changing at an enormous rate. This means the human brain at birth today is very similar to that of stone-age man. It is only how the brain changes through the life of the human that enables it to cope with a changing world. We have a whole range of educational interventions to help the brain to reconfigure, some of which are more effective than others, but when it comes to leadership much of this reconfiguring has been left to experience, serendipity and pure chance.

Traditional leadership development has been about how leaders change other things (organizations, their people, strategies, the world!) rather than how they proactively change themselves. As Tolstoy, the Russian novelist and social reformer wrote: 'Everyone thinks of changing the world, but no one thinks of changing himself.' Now it is time for leaders to focus on how to change themselves – how they can proactively reconfigure their brains to become more effective. As leaders we can only keep up with change by using our 'personal choice' and 'intense will' to make the effort to reconfigure our neural circuits to a non-default state, and embed that change so they become new habits.

Finally, we need to understand that 'leadership' is not the same as 'management'. Management is about planning, organizing, staffing, controlling and problem solving whereas leadership is about establishing direction, aligning people, motivating and inspiring. Management produces key results – leadership produces change and transformation (see Covey, 1992; Landsberg, 2001). Try the quiz 'Management vs Leadership' at **www.leadershape.biz** to check your own understanding of the difference and receive a detailed report.

Considering the management-type tasks listed above it becomes apparent that most people in leadership positions spend most of their time 'managing'. Leadership is about vision, direction and people; management is about process. But even with vision and direction you have to engage people to achieve it. So in the end leadership is about people.

The neuroscience of leadership

By understanding how the brain works we can improve our personal performance and leadership. Fortunately, one of the other great developments since the change of the century was neuroscience research enabled by the development of hi-powered brain scanners, especially the invention of the magnetoencephalograph (MEG), which allows 3-D, real-time brain mapping in great detail (Zohar and Marshall, 2000). Some people are content to accept the latest psychological theories and research on behaviour whereas others will be given comfort that neuroscience actually supports most of those theories and gives them even greater credence. In turn this may provide leaders with greater insights into why they need to change their behaviour.

The human brain has developed genetically at a much slower pace than society, which provides a behavioural conflict. Genetically, how the brain works is all about the inter-relationships between energy, memory and neural wiring, which defaults the brain to resist change while at the same time wanting to be creative. There are three kinds of neural connections (Zohar and Marshall, 2000):

1 Serial connections (like a row of Christmas tree lights) provide our IQ, instinct and learnt habits and are more or less fixed.

2 Associative connections, which enable our emotional intelligence and conceptual thinking where bundles of brain cells can connect with each other apparently at random but which can be reconfigured through practising and focusing on specific behaviours. This is where new wiring can become stabilized and embedded and thus is more like serial connections.

3 Synchronous neural oscillations are where wave motions form in all the parts of a brain that relate to a particular event, providing unitive, holistic and transpersonal thinking, which ranges from the relative simplicity of understanding the totality of a coffee mug to the high order of things such as spirituality.

However, the brain also resists being told what to do (it takes so much of the brain's energy, which in our stone-age brain is needed to be preserved for 'fight or flight') and therefore any change is most effectively implemented by the individual having an insight and thus developing his or her own solution. Insights also use up a lot of energy but the process simultaneously releases adrenaline-like chemicals that sustain the energy for a longer period of time.

Continued focus and attention opens up associative neural circuits and then stabilizes the new neural connections (created by insights) until they become a new habit. This is how behavioural change occurs. Finally, we know from research in positive psychology and neuroscience that happy people are more effective and learn better (Seligman, 2002).

Enabling leaders to become more competent

So what can we learn from all this to enable leaders to be more competent and effective in this new world? Here are a few things we have learnt from our work in developing leaders over more than a decade, which is confirmed by Rock and Schwartz (2006):

- Leaders need to understand the changes in behaviour that will have the most impact on their own performance and how they affect the performance of others.

- They then need to focus on and practise these new behaviours and get feedback as to how they are succeeding with the new behaviours and what else they could do to implement the identified behaviours.

- For this to be effective leaders need to think beyond their ego; that is, not just what is best for 'me' but what is best for the people around me and the organization as a whole.

- One of the most important and often forgotten roles of leaders is developing their followers, especially those reporting directly to them. A few key activities are:
  - Provide them with the right environment to allow them to reach their own solutions through insights.
  - Don't tell people what to do, except as a last resort, as it does not provide sustainable effective change.
  - To learn new behaviours, leaders must provide the opportunity and environment for their people to focus on and spend time learning new behaviours in order to sustain change.
  - Involve their people in the development of 'vision' at an early stage so that everyone can contribute through their own insights and feel ownership to the vision of the organization.
  - Provide an open, no-blame culture that helps people perform from a basis of opportunity rather than threat.

- Coaching, group facilitation, reflection, action learning and experiential learning, as well as contemplation and meditation are all excellent techniques to support people in finding their own solutions, embedding change into habits and sustaining new behaviour (Raelin, 2008).

The importance and role of emotional intelligence

Most leaders try to improve organizational performance by implementing new processes and structures and by developing their people through the learning of 'hard skills'. This manifests itself by changing the organizational structure, implementing a change programme or introducing a new process such as 'lean' (a recent buzz word). They send their staff to learn about project management and strategic planning but rarely about how to understand themselves or deal effectively with each other. In general, the methods normally used do not work (Beer *et al*, 1990). Although processes and structures are necessary, a fundamental premise of this book is that they only work when the people involved (and especially the leaders) develop and use behaviours that provide for high levels of awareness of self and others, self-management and relationship management (Carnell, 2007). This is called 'emotional intelligence' (EI), first defined as the 'ability to monitor one's own and others' feelings and emotions, to discriminate among them and to use this information to guide one's own thinking and actions' (Salovey and Mayer, 1990).

However, it is not possible to embed these new EI behaviours using traditional teaching methods as it requires learning through insight, practice, reflection and time, and to be directly related to the context of the workplace (see Chapter 8 for more details). Even for people who have the right behaviours (either inherent or developed), it is not natural for them to manage themselves in a way that is most conducive to maximizing personal and organizational performance.

While some of us may be born with greater natural leadership abilities than others, there is now no doubt that leadership skills can be built through practice and that each individual's leadership potential can be realized through effective development. Anyone in a senior position requires both management and leadership skills – and the more senior the role, the more time needs to be spent operating as a leader than as a manager. Leadership development should be an ongoing journey towards excellence, with the indispensable ingredients of continually increasing self-awareness and inner self-confidence.

The approach we use is centred on the Goleman, Boyatzis and McKee model of emotional intelligence (Goleman *et al*, 2002). This model proposes that successful leaders require something beyond intellectual ability – they need also to be able to understand and manage their own and others' emotions. Goleman (1996) tells us that the basis of EI is self-awareness, an understanding of our personality and our emotions and the ability to notice how we react emotionally to events and individuals. This self-awareness provides the underpinning for both the ability to manage our own emotions and to understand those of others. The fourth element of EI is the ability to effectively manage relationships with others, in particular to be able to develop and lead them.

The main reason for using this model is that, uniquely, it relates specific EI capabilities to particular leadership styles and then compares the impact of various styles on the performance of an organization and explains when the various styles should be used. In connecting EI capabilities to leadership styles to be used in a specific context, they have provided leaders with a valuable route to leadership excellence. We need to build on this though by providing specific methodologies on 'how' the leader can actually develop and improve their emotional intelligence.

Developing emotional intelligence

The first step in developing EI is to understand a little about emotions and how they work. It is generally agreed there are six primary emotions (Ekman, 1992): anger, fear, disgust, joy (or happiness), sadness and surprise. More recently 'contempt' has been suggested as the seventh (Ekman, 2003) but some believe it is just a mixture of anger and disgust. Whatever is the case, it is worth noting that of these six or seven primary emotions, only one is positive (joy), one is neutral (surprise) and all the others are negative. It is said that primary emotions are emotions that have been scientifically proven to have a certain facial expression associated with them, but there are over 600 words in the English language to describe emotions and we use 42 muscles in our faces to express them (see the Science Museum website).

What is most important about emotions is they are initiated outside our conscious control. In other words, we cannot stop an emotion happening! We can only decide how to respond to the emotion once we are aware of it. But how often are we hi-jacked by our emotions and taken over by our instinctive stone-age default – and then live to regret it?

Emotions have information, energy and influence and they can trigger behaviours, feelings and actions. Emotions are felt in response to a situation (real or imagined) and prepare us to take action. We should not submit to them or pretend they are not there. To manage emotions effectively we first have to acknowledge them and then respond, as follows:

1 What am I beginning to feel (our own subjective representation of the emotion)?

2 What do I feel compelled to do (what would be my default behaviour in response)?

3 What do I need to be aware of (what would be the consequence of that default)?

4 What important goal of mine is involved (what do I really want to achieve)?

5 What is the key issue and which response shall I choose (choosing a behaviour that will have the most positive outcome)?

6 Am I going to achieve my goal or just be frustrated (success or failure)?

Even more difficult is that a good leader must be sensitive to the emotions of others and be able to use that knowledge to manage relationships and help people be more effective.

To learn this process of increasing emotional intelligence takes dedication, time, practice and focus. Various interventions such as coaching, reflective practice, mindfulness (we prefer the term 'full consciousness') and action learning/science can all be of great help. However, the single most effective intervention to help leaders increase their competence is, in our experience, the use of an effective 360° assessment tool that can identify the two or three key behaviours that will have the greatest impact in the context of their role. It is also important that the implementation of the process follows best practice (CIPD, 2003).

Chapters 3, 4 and 6 describe this process and the outcomes in more detail based on LeaderShape's unique LEIPA® (Leadership and Emotional Intelligence Profile Assessment) 360° tool, which not only assesses granular behavioural traits of emotional intelligence but also compares the candidate's competence in six leadership styles to the importance of those styles in their current role. By doing this, it is possible to identify the two or three key granular behaviours that will have the greatest impact on an individual's leadership performance as well as providing a personal development manual for continued reference and improvement.

A word of warning

Organizations must realize that once they have gone down the route of developing the EI of their people and thus providing them with more effective, sophisticated styles of leadership and behaviour than our default, which creates a higher performing culture, there is no turning back! We have witnessed occasions where either in the middle of or at the end of a leadership programme, a new chief executive has been introduced (say because of retirement or an acquisition) who is lacking either EI or the right values, or both. Because of the new awareness of everyone in the organization, poor behaviour and lack of true engagement and authenticity were not acceptable, resulting in the loss of the best people who went elsewhere to utilize their new found skills.

An issue can emerge when those who made the new appointment focus on experience (often in a different context) and formal qualifications rather than more carefully assessing the soft competencies that are required in the new culture that has been created. It is imperative that the selection and interview process of any new recruits (especially the top leadership) is consistent with the transpersonal leadership programmes that have been implemented and that any development needs are discussed and committed to before employment.

Emotional intelligence is only the first step towards transpersonal leadership

EI is, however, not sufficient on its own. Unfortunately it is possible to combine some great EI capabilities with poor values, so EI is just an important stepping stone in moving towards transpersonal leadership, which we believe is the natural progression (Knights, 2012) as described in Chapter 5. EI provides a foundation of awareness and managing one's feeling and behaviour to improve performance, but it is only the first stage to enable leaders to become ethically authentic and act beyond their ego – to become 'transpersonal'.

To be organizationally useful, EI and leadership need to be connected to the development of the ideal culture of an organization. We have found that having identified the ideal culture of the organization according to its leaders and staff (LeaderShape, 2012), we know the leadership styles the leaders need to use. Once the key leadership styles are known we can work backwards to which EI capabilities are core and which granular behaviours they need to develop.

We define a 'transpersonal leader' (Knights, 2012) as one who 'thinks beyond his or her ego' and is a 'radical, ethical and authentic leader'. A more complete definition is:

> possesses the values, attitudes and behaviours necessary to intrinsically motivate oneself and others so all have a genuine desire to *serve others* – and in so doing deriving purpose and meaning in life, and *establish an organizational culture* whereby leaders have genuine care and concern together with appreciation and understanding for self and others (that is, all stakeholders), while having the will, energy, aspiration and sense of doing one's best (excellence) to achieve the highest level of performance to fulfil the organization's vision.

SPECIFIC ACTION POINTS

This chapter suggests that there needs to be a fundamentally different approach to developing and assessing leaders if we are to get the leaders we need in the 21st century to run our organizations successfully and sustainably. The key action points are:

- Differentiate between leadership and management development and ensure talent gets 'leadership' development. Learning business skills is not leadership development.

- Use or develop leadership programmes that are going to enable leaders and future leaders (talent) to change how they themselves behave in order to improve their own performance and those around them.

- Develop programmes that are a journey, which allow regular small doses of connected learning.

- Provide the time, space, environment and work-based interventions that allow talent to practise, focus and embed learning.

- Provide talent with a mixture of facilitated group and coached one-to-one learning opportunities.

- Within this framework use EI-based assessment tools similar to LEIPA® that help candidates identify those behaviours they need to develop and embed in order to get the biggest positive impact on their leadership competence.

- Make sure that once the 360° report is complete there is accredited feedback and follow-up to ensure an action plan is developed and implemented (see Chapter 6).

- Conventional consultants don't have the skills to provide leadership development – they usually tell or advise what to do. Coaches who can work with individuals *and* groups are more likely to be successful by helping talent find their own solutions. Coaches with business experience can more quickly connect to the contextual issues.

FURTHER RESOURCES

LeaderShape Resources: **www.leadershape.biz** provides a broad and open resource to leadership development. In particular for this chapter see **http://www.leadershape.biz/emotional-intelligence** and **http://www.leadershape.biz/transpersonal-leadership**. To find more information about the unique LEIPA® 360° assessment, go to **http://www.leadershape.biz/leipa** which provides all the details.

EI Consortium: **www.eiconsortium.org**: Its mission is 'to advance research and practice of emotional and social intelligence in organizations through the generation and exchange of knowledge'. The Consortium for Research on Emotional Intelligence in Organizations is currently made up of eight core members and 75 additional members who are individuals with a strong record of accomplishment as applied researchers in the field. There are also six organizational and corporate members. The Consortium was founded in the spring of 1996 with the support of the Fetzer Institute. Its initial mandate was to study all that is known about EI in the workplace. The website provides a range of case studies, development programmes, methodologies and tools for measuring emotional intelligence.

David Rock Net: **http://www.davidrock.net**: this website provides many links for more information about the applications of neuroscience to leadership development.

Wikipedia webpage on the Stone Age: there are numerous references to the development of the brain before during and after the Stone Age. A good place to start is **http://en.wikipedia.org/wiki/Stone_Age**. The Stone Age Institute website: **http://www.stoneageinstitute.org/** is another good general reference for further information about the Stone Age.

References

Beer, M, Eisenstat, R A and Spector, B (1990) Why change programmes don't produce change, *Harvard Business Review*, November-December

Carnell, C (2007) *A Strategic Convergence Model for Change Management*, C and R Carnell and Associates

CIPD (2003) *360 Degree Feedback – Best practice guidelines*, Chartered Institute of Personnel and Development, British Psychological Society, Department of Trade and Industry, University of Roehampton, London

Covey, S R (1992) *The Seven Habits of Highly Effective People*, Free Press, New York

Ekman, P (1992) An argument for basic emotions, *Cognition & Emotion*, 6, pp 169–200

Ekman, P (2003) *Emotions Revealed: Understanding faces and feelings*, Times Books, Henry Holt, New York

Goleman, D (1996) *Emotional Intelligence*, Bloomsbury, London

Goleman, D, Boyatzis, R and McKee, A (2002) *Primal Leadership*, Harvard Business School Press, Harvard, MA (published in the UK as *The New Leaders*)

Kelley, R (2008) *Longitudinal Study with Knowledge Workers*, Carnegie-Mellon University, Pittsburgh, PA

Knights, J (2012) *The Invisible Elephant and The Pyramid Treasure*, Tomorrows Company, London, available at http://www.leadershape.biz/

Landsberg, M (2001) *The Tools of Leadership*, HarperCollins Business, London

LeaderShape, (2012) Culture Change – LOCs Survey, http://www.leadershape.biz/locs-culture-survey

Raelin, J E (2008) *Work-based Learning: Bridging knowledge and action in the workplace*, 2nd edn, Jossey-Bass, San Francisco, CA

Rock, D and Schwartz, D (2006) The neuroscience of leadership, *Strategy and Business*, 43

Salovey, P and Mayer, J D (1990) *Emotional Intelligence*, Baywood Publishing, Amityville, NY

Science Museum, http://www.sciencemuseum.org.uk/WhoAmI/FindOutMore/Yourbrain/Whatareemotions.aspx

Seligman, M (2002) *Authentic Happiness: Using the new positive psychology to realize your potential for lasting fulfillment*, Simon & Schuster, New York

Zohar, D and Marshall, I (2000) *Spiritual Intelligence: The ultimate intelligence*, Bloomsbury, London

CASE STUDY   Increasing the emotional intelligence of Poolia

John Knights

It is always a difficult time for staff when their company is acquired by another. Leadership styles may be different and objectives may be changed. How do you quickly bring the team together under new ownership?

Poolia AB is a successful European recruitment agency, quoted on the Swedish Stock Exchange, which specializes in the recruitment of professionals for the accounting, finance and banking sectors.

Background

In 2004, Poolia, with ambitions of becoming the leading recruiter of professionals throughout Europe, acquired Parker Bridge Recruitment (later re-branded Poolia UK). It was chosen because of its reputation of providing a quality service to its clients and its strong ethos of high standards and good financial controls.

The leadership style of the previous owners had been to instil high standards through direct control, rigorous procedures and financial incentives for reward. In contrast, Poolia had a more participative style of leadership with a national culture reflecting the importance of respect and social responsibility. The challenge was to retain the best of the UK company style while introducing the core values of Poolia. Another key objective was to develop leadership excellence amongst its managers, creating a culture that would produce sustainable growth and profitability.

Method

When the former owner-managers departed at the end of February 2005, a new senior management structure was put in place by promoting from within, headed by Mark Widnall as Acting MD. At the same time, a search was instigated for a new chief executive who Poolia insisted should not only have a strong industry background at the top level but also have the people skills to drive the business forward in a way consistent with Poolia's values and culture.

Increasing the emotional intelligence of an organization

Initially, the LeaderShape facilitator interviewed each member of the new senior management team in strict confidence to understand what each thought the key issues and opportunities were, the relationships between each of the members, and their view of the new owners. The facilitator also interviewed the chief executive and the chairman of the holding Swedish company. This was followed up by a facilitated workshop for the senior management team to openly discuss the major issues facing the business, which resulted in:

1   An immediate realization that everyone in the team wished to change the style of the company by opening up communication throughout the organization, empowering individuals to take initiative and decisions, to support individuals in their development and to enable people to maximize their potential.

2   A real gelling of the team and a meeting of minds.

3   Consensus agreement for all managers in the company to receive leadership development training to enable them to develop EI behavioural competencies consistent with the style desired.

4   Immediate commitment to live the new approach that created a new climate – one in which a performance enhancing culture could begin to be developed.

A voluntary culture survey among all employees was undertaken – 85 per cent responded indicating a good buy-in and overwhelming support for the newly created management team.

A customized leadership programme developed by LeaderShape was rolled out, which focused on EI and its relationship to leadership styles in the context of real issues in the business (Figure 2.1 in the Tools section describes the steps). During this time, planned and intentionally ad hoc coaching sessions were also held and were integrated with workshops on vision and strategy development.

LEIPA 360° assessments were undertaken to identify the contextual leadership performance of the 22 managers and their further development needs towards leadership excellence. Each was provided with coaching support to enable them to work effectively on embedding the new behaviours that had been identified.

At the same time, training, recruitment and personal development plans were overhauled to incorporate aspects of EI. The purpose of this was to create the link between employing the right people, then developing and retaining them to provide an orderly career development programme and succession.

Results at the end of the programme

- The budget was 60 per cent up on the profit for the previous year. Q1 exceeded budget.

- Workforce stability increased with turnover of staff reducing from 48 per cent to just 23 per cent by the end of the year against an industry norm of 50 per cent.

- Sales team efficiency increased, with improvement of between 5 and 10 per cent in individual gross profit of consultants with the same experience factor.

- The time that temporary consultants take to create sustainable earnings has been reduced by one third.

- More sales consultants are reaching their monthly targets than ever before.

The leadership development programme has not only helped me to become a better, more confident leader it has also facilitated the changes in climate and culture that the business needed to move forward. We now have team managers who are better equipped to make decisions and who understand the changes we are trying to implement.

(Mark Widnall, Acting MD)

Learning points

Even today, several years after this programme was completed, many of the managers have kept contact with LeaderShape and often remark on the value of the programme and in particular the LEIPA 360° assessment. Without exception they refer to it as the best programme they have participated in in terms of developing their leadership capability and even improving relationships in their private lives. The difference was that this programme was not just about transferring information and knowledge it was about getting each individual to work on changing his or her own behaviour and embedding new habits that improved his or her leadership.

The keys to the success were getting the senior management team to discuss openly their issues and through that building a strong interdependent team, and supporting managers in learning the coaching style of leadership that enabled a complete change in the culture of the organization.

CASE STUDY   Leadership assessment in a Japanese logistics company

Dr Kate Julian

'Company X' runs a large logistics operation in Japan. Recently, facing increased competition and difficult domestic economic conditions in Japan, the company recognized that it needed to grow by launching subsidiary operations overseas. Early efforts to enter overseas markets, by hiring local staff led by Japanese managers on international postings, had been difficult, however. The managers on the international postings lacked the experience needed to successfully pursue the company's strategies in a foreign environment with more culturally diverse teams.

Top management at the company realized that it needed a planned approach to support its internal talent in developing this cultural awareness and flexibility. They enlisted the help of the University of Chester in the UK to create a bespoke talent development programme for its candidate-managers, which included taught accredited elements and an internship placement in a host organization in the UK. The programme was designed using the university's work-based learning framework, with the results of two leadership assessment tools helping the candidate managers and the university to focus the specific development activities provided on the taught and experiential parts of this work-based programme.

How did the organization use assessments for developing leadership talent?

A number of key middle managers in the Japanese company had been identified as high-potential staff and earmarked for roles in the new overseas operations. These managers had held a number of different roles in several functional areas of the domestic business, involving sideways as well as vertical moves. They therefore had a breadth of knowledge and experience, good technical skills and good management skills in the domestic context. What they lacked was the cultural awareness and flexibility to survive and thrive in an overseas posting in a senior leadership position. So the question facing the company was:

'How can we further develop the talent of the managers we have and release their full potential as international managers?'

The top managers at the company sought the help of the University of Chester to devise a bespoke talent development programme, which included taught accredited elements and an internship placement in a host organization. Awareness of intercultural difference was crucial for the individuals who were going to be working with people from other cultural backgrounds. Therefore, the programme began by helping the candidate-managers understand their cultural 'orientation' and their 'readiness' for the different cultural experience. Each candidate-manager had carried out project work in overseas environments previously and had some self-awareness already. However, two self-assessment tools were used to make this more explicit to candidates and to the university tutors – the PICO profiler and the Cultural Orientations Framework (COF) Assessment tool.

The PICO profiler (Shaules, 2006) is an online instrument used to inform managers who live or work in an unfamiliar cultural environment, or who plan to do so. It is used to create a PICO Profile, an individualized analysis of how one deals with the challenges of interacting with people from other cultural backgrounds. Two dimensions are measured. The first is an individual's tendency to be change-oriented or stability-oriented; the second is an individual's tendency to be inner-directed (relying on oneself when faced with uncertainty) or outer-directed (relying on others). These two dimensions combine to provide four different orientations: adaptive, proactive, attentive and protective. Managers who succeed in international or multicultural environments tend to be those who can switch successfully between these orientations. (Further information on the PICO profile can be found at **http://www.pico-global.com/**.)

The Cultural Orientations Framework (COF) Assessment tool provides greater awareness and clarity about a manager's own cultural assumptions arising from culturally-driven values and beliefs. There are 17 cultural dimensions assessed and they are grouped into seven categories of critical challenges: sense of power and responsibility; time management approaches; definitions of identity and purpose; organizational arrangements; notions of territory and boundaries; communication patterns; and modes of thinking. The COF assessment tool assesses the individual's cultural *abilities* as well as his or her cultural orientations. Further explanation of the research underpinning the COF and more detail on the seven critical challenges can be found in Rosinski's *Coaching Across Cultures* (2003).

In this particular case, the candidate-manager completed both the PICO profiler and the COF assessment before starting the talent development programme. The results of these two leadership assessment tools helped the candidate-manager and the university to plan the specific development activities the manager would undertake on the taught (university programme) and experiential part (internship) of this work based programme.

What were the benefits?

The COF assessment and the PICO profile were used as self-assessment activities to help the candidate-manager prepare for the opportunity to study and carry out an internship and a university programme in an unfamiliar cultural environment. The candidate-manager completed both the PICO profiler and the COF assessment at the beginning of the talent development programme. The following benefits were identified:

1   The candidate discussed the results of the self-assessments with the university lecturer responsible for programme design (a qualified coach) and together they developed a personal development plan for the candidate manager to carry out.

2 Having the assessment tool information meant that the university had a far greater understanding of a candidate's individual needs than is usual with new students. It meant that the university tutors were able to tailor the content of the taught seminars to support the development plan, and offer a truly bespoke programme, specific to each individual participant.

3 Undertaking the assessments helped a candidate-manager prepare for the work experience element of the programme. For example, understanding his orientation towards power and his approach to time management (from the COF assessment) and his orientation towards collaboration (from the PICO profiler) allowed a Japanese candidate-manager to better prepare for a (Western) team meeting at the host workplace.

4 Our experience indicates that international students sometimes have different expectations of their university tutors than do domestic students . These expectations may be driven in part by national cultural preferences. However, it is very easy to make assumptions about people's needs based on stereotypes of national identity. The COF assessment goes further than national focus and allows the manager to surface other cultural influences that make up his or her identity including gender, ethnicity, profession, generation (Rosinski, 2003). Having the COF assessment and a picture of the particular rather than the stereotype international student was hugely important to the university team from a teaching and learning perspective.

What were the learning points?

First, both the COF assessment and the PICO Profiler provide feedback to the respondent across a wide range of cultural dimensions or orientations. It would be easy for a respondent to feel overwhelmed by the sheer volume of feedback. Discussing the results with a critical friend, or a coach, can help put the feedback into perspective and can help the respondent chose just one or two key development areas to work on.

Secondly, having done the assessments, it is important for the individual manager (and other interested parties) to be realistic about the 'what now?' For example, the PICO Profiler information suggests that managers who can switch between cultural orientations are the most successful. However, this flexibility may be too great a stretch for some managers. They may not have the personal capability to learn the new orientation, or they may have the potential capability but not have enough time in the new environment to do so. Therefore managers need to be realistic and ask themselves whether their aim should be to develop true cultural *flexibility* or whether cultural *awareness* alone would be enough.

The PICO Profiler is available free-of-charge to individual managers at **http://www. pico-global.com**, and the Cultural Orientations Framework (COF) Assessment is available free of charge to individual managers at **www.philrosinski.com and www.COFassessment.com**.

References

Rosinski, P (2003) *Coaching across Cultures: New tools for leveraging national, corporate and professional differences*, Nicholas Brealey, London

Shaules, J (2006) Assessing intercultural learning strategies with Personal Intercultural Change Orientation (PICO) profiles, *Intercultural Communication Review*, 4

TOOL   Emotion check questions

John Knights and Tony Wall

What it is and when to use it

The emotion check questions tool is a list of questions that enable us or our colleagues to become aware of our default responses to a situation and make a decision about an alternative response, should one be useful for the context.

Every item in the list, shown in Table 2.1 is not meant to be used in every situation, and all of the questions may not be appropriate for every case. Rather, certain questions can provide major insights into awareness of auto-pilot responses – and facilitate the consideration of other responses. Within EI, this predominantly focuses on self-awareness and self-regulation (Goleman *et al*, 2002)

Emotion check questions – example

In this example, a manager of a sales department does not get a sales update report from one of his team leaders who reports to him. The manager would normally get irate and send an e-mail requesting it – which would be interpreted as 'angry' and 'aggressive' by his sales team leaders. Key thoughts based on using the questions are jotted down; see Table 2.2.

TABLE 2.1   Emotion check questions

Question	Explanation
What am I beginning to feel?	This question brings a focus and structure to our own subjective representation of the emotion.
What do I feel compelled to do? What would be my default behaviour in response?	These questions bring awareness of what we would normally do – the emphasis is on 'the prior' with no assumption that a prior behaviour needs to continue.
What do I need to be aware of?	This question encourages key knowledge from our subconscious or unconscious awareness to our conscious awareness.
What would be the consequence of that default?	This question encourages us to think about the outcome or knock-on effects of the default behaviour.
What important goal of mine is involved? What do I really want to achieve?	These questions check that there is alignment with what we are striving for – *really* striving for.
What is the key issue and which response shall I choose?	(Choosing a behaviour that will have the most positive outcome.)
Am I going to achieve my goal or just be frustrated?	This is a check about whether we are heading for an outcome that we would consider as a 'success' or 'failure'.

TABLE 2.2 Emotion check questions – example

Question	Key thoughts
What am I beginning to feel?	*I can feel my fuse about to blow. I'm angry!*
What do I feel compelled to do?	*I feel compelled to shout at the team leader – why does he always do this?!*
What would be my default behaviour in response?	*My default... to get angry! Then send an email demanding the report immediately.*
What do I need to be aware of?	*I need to be aware of the cause of the delay before getting angry. Making him get upset also may affect his performance further and could even lead to taking time off sick.*
What would be the consequence of that default?	*And this team leader can make mistakes when he doesn't have the time to do it right.*
What important goal of mine is involved?	*I just need them in on time so I can get an accurate report in to head office.*
What do I really want to achieve?	*The key issue is getting this team leader's report in before I put my report together. This makes our department look good in relation to other countries.*
What is the key issue and which response shall I choose?	*I shall contact him and ask him why he is delayed and whether he needs any support.*
	I can discuss with him calmly any dissatisfaction of his behaviour and the necessary remedies later after the crisis for the report is over.
Am I going to achieve my goal or just be frustrated?	*I don't want to continue to be frustrated! I could do various other inputs into the report while I wait for this person's response.*

The example shows how the questions have slowed down the manager's reactive thinking and he has become more aware of his default response, the consequences of his default, and what he actually needs and why. A template is provided in Table 2.3.

TABLE 2.3 Emotion check questions – template

Question	Key thoughts
What am I beginning to feel?	
What do I feel compelled to do?	
What would be my default behaviour in response?	
What do I need to be aware of?	
What would be the consequence of that default?	
What important goal of mine is involved?	
What do I really want to achieve?	
What is the key issue and which response shall I choose?	
Am I going to achieve my goal or just be frustrated?	

Reference

Goleman, D, Boyatzis, R and McKee, A (2002) *Primal Leadership*, Harvard Business School Press, Boston, MA

TOOL   EI self-assessment questionnaire

John Knights

What it is and when to use it

An appropriate 360° assessment tool can be one of the most valuable and effective ways of developing current senior leaders, the next generation of senior leaders (High Potentials – HiPos) and in fact anyone with a supervisory role. However, as a first step it can be very useful for participants to carry out a confidential self-assessment as a taster.

Figure 2.1 shows a programme that takes leaders through the development of emotional intelligence, culminating in a LEIPA 360° assessment at step 7. (More details can be found in Knights, 2012.) Although there is no substitute for a complete 360° assessment, during step 3 of the transpersonal leadership development journey, participants are provided with a self-assessment taster so they begin to understand the benefits of granular behavioural change and how it can affect their own leadership competence.

FIGURE 2.1   EI development programme

REAL Transpersonal leadership development journey to excellence

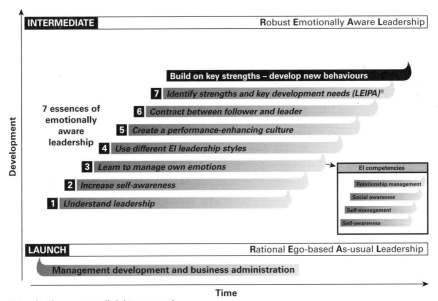

Using the EI self-assessment questionnaire

The process is to ask participants to complete the questionnaire shown in Figure 2.2, giving them the following instructions.

FIGURE 2.2   EI self-assessment questionnaire

EMOTIONAL INTELLIGENCE SELF-ASSESSMENT			
X			
A			
1	Know which emotions I am feeling and why		
2	Realise the links between feelings and what I think, say and do		
3	Recognise how feelings affect performance		
4	Take time to understand my own feelings		Sub-Total
B			
5	Listen attentively to what people say		
6	Demonstrate an awareness of how others are feeling		
7	Accurately identify the underlying cause of other person's perspective		
8	Express an understanding of other person's perspective		Sub-Total
C			
9	Give personal recognition to the accomplishments and achievements of others		
10	Offer useful feedback and help others to identify their personal needs for further growth		
11	Identify opportunities and stimulate individuals to develop to their full potential		
12	Involve individuals in the process of making decisions that will affect them		Sub-Total
			Total A – C
Y			
D			
13	Present myself with self-assurance and have 'presence'		
14	Go out on a limb for what is right including voicing unpopular views		
15	Decisive, able to make sound decisions despite uncertainties and pressures		
16	Confident in my own abilities		Sub-Total
E			
17	Effectively communicate and arouse enthusiasm for a shared vision and mission		
18	Step forward to lead as needed, regardless of position		
19	Lead by example and set standards		
20	Make considered decisions based on both logic and intuition		Sub-Total
F			
21	Recognise the need for change and proactively remove barriers		
22	Challenge the status quo to acknowledge the need for change		
23	Champion change and enlist others in its pursuit		
24	Demonstrate by my actions the change expected of others		Sub-Total
G			
25	Always do what I say I will do		
26	Ready to acknowledge own mistakes or error of judgement		
27	Actions reflect personal values		
28	Believe honesty is always the best policy whatever the consequences		Sub-Total
			Total D – G

Against each statement score yourself from 1 to 5 according the listing below as to how often you perform/achieve the behaviours described in the questionnaire:

1 Never or almost never

2 Occasionally

3 Quite often

4 Usually

5 Always

To get the full value from this exercise try to be honest and objective. The completed forms will be retained by you, and you only share the information you wish to.

Complete the sub-totals and totals for each section as marked.

Now complete the blank rows as follows:

X = Coaching Style Leadership

A = Emotional Self-awareness

B = Empathy

C = Developing Others

Y = Visionary Style Leadership

D = Self Confidence

E = Inspirational Leadership

F = Change Catalyst

G = Transparency

You now have a complete picture of your own assessment of your competence in seven EI Capabilities but also the two most impactful leadership styles, Visionary and Coaching (Goleman *et al*, 2002).

You can rate your competence in the Coaching Style as follows:

The maximum score is 60.

If you have 48 or above, you are a natural at the coaching style but may still need to learn specific techniques.

If you have 36–48, you are good but may need some further development.

If you score 24–36, some improvement is probably needed.

If you scored less than 24, a significant improvement is needed.

You can also rate your competence in the Visionary Style as follows:

The maximum score is 80.

If you have 64 or above, you are a natural at the visionary style but may still need to learn specific techniques.

If you have 48–64, you are good but may need some further development.

If you score 32–48, some improvement is probably needed.

If you scored less than 32, a significant improvement is needed.

(Note: Most leaders in our experience will have a better rating, eg, 'natural', 'good', 'some improvement', 'significant improvement', in the visionary style than in the coaching style.)

Finally, take a look at the granular behaviours where you scored lowest compared to your other scores. What would it take for you to improve these scores? Choose one to three granular behaviours to work on to improve your leadership.

Most will agree that it is much easier to work on improving a specific granular behaviour than something as broad as say 'empathy' where most would ask, 'What does this mean and where would I start?'

Depending on the situation and how open your organization is, candidates can discuss the results with colleagues, with their mentor, or perhaps best of all with their coach. Our experience is that this exercise creates real insights even though the candidates are assessing themselves. One should of course make the point that the result of the questionnaire is only their view – what would the people they work with say?

This process often encourages leaders to be more accepting of the full 360° assessment but occasionally leaders are in denial or fear admitting a failing, and then the question has to be asked whether they have what it takes to develop as transpersonal leaders.

References

Goleman, D, Boyatzis, R and McKee, A (2002) *Primal Leadership*, Harvard Business School Press, Boston, MA

Knights, J (2012) *The Invisible Elephant and The Pyramid Treasure*, Tomorrows Company, London

Recurring leadership development needs: findings from research

ETUKUDO ODUNGIDE and JOHN KNIGHTS

EXECUTIVE SUMMARY

As today's business climate becomes more challenging and dynamic, leadership in organizations has also taken a different shape. An increasing number of leaders now agree with the need for training and development in order to effectively manage the workforce. Since it is now more widely accepted that leadership competencies and skills can be learnt, developed and improved upon, business leaders have started to place emphasis on behavioural leadership training and development. A logical and measurable approach to leadership development is to discover the 'leadership gap' and then equip the organization and everyone within it a leadership role to fill that gap. This book shares strategies and actions to achieve such an approach.

The 360° feedback method, when good practice is used, has proven to be one of the best ways to assess leadership capabilities because it provides leaders with feedback from those they work with, including their peers, their managers and the people they lead. An analysis of 95 leaders from 21 different organizations in the UK using a leadership assessment tool reveals a pattern in terms of leadership development needs. While the development needs vary from one leader to another and from one organization to another, certain capabilities reoccur in the majority of the leaders assessed. This research shows that a high proportion of leaders need development in capabilities like empathy, developing others and in conflict management.

Empathy involves sensing and understanding other people's feeling and taking an interest in their concerns. This ability to work through emotions and use them to bring out the best in organizations creates resonance. *Developing others* involves identifying development needs and potential in others and supporting them. This is the basis for talent development, and where this is neglected it can lead to a shortfall of talent, increased staff turnover and a loss of core contributors. A high proportion of the leaders studied also had *conflict management* as one of their top development needs. Although managers have tended to shift this responsibility on to HR practitioners, this should be the task of leaders at all levels to ensure increased performance.

The starting point for developing leadership skills is an awareness of the specific competencies that need developing, and the research presented here reveals a pattern that serves as a pathway in terms of personal and organizational development.

Leadership gaps

We have seen from the previous chapter that leadership skills can be developed to increase effectiveness and that leaders are increasingly aware of this. As Kouzes and Posner (2007) put it, leadership development is about an inner quest to discover oneself. Once a leader recognizes his or her strengths and weaknesses, a need arises to work on and improve the latter.

Awareness of the specific leadership competencies and capabilities needed for improved performance is the starting point to leadership development (Goleman *et al*, 2002), and this can be achieved by assessing oneself against the competencies and capabilities required for a particular role. Byham *et al* (2002) calls this a 'diagnosis of development needs'.

Leadership strengths and development needs vary from one individual to another. Previous research has shown that no leader, no matter how talented, has strength in all leadership capabilities such that they do not need improvement or development (Goleman *et al*, 2002). Since leadership is about inspiring people to do their best through a shared vision, which ideally involves a process of mutual influence (Armstrong, 2009), development and continuous improvement must be taken seriously to achieve the desired results. Martin and Schmidt (2010) agree that 21st century leaders need to pay attention to leadership development due to the changing nature of the business environment.

To be more efficient and effective in terms of leadership development, leaders and organizations can assess their leadership skills to discover the specific capabilities that require attention. Where specific capabilities are lacking, the gap can negatively affect the performance of an organization. Put another way, a leadership gap is the vacuum created as a consequence or lack of certain leadership skills (Weiss and Molinaro, 2005). Once the skills shortfall is identified as a development need and is addressed, the organization has more effective and productive leaders. The next section identifies the gaps in leadership capabilities that reoccur among senior level leaders.

Research into gaps

Research has shown that certain capabilities lead to leadership effectiveness (Goleman *et al*, 2002). Many scholars have grouped these competencies and capabilities into what is widely known today as emotional intelligence (EI) competencies (see Table 3.1). It should be noted that the main competencies in this table are self-awareness, self-management, social awareness and relationship management, where the sub-competencies listed are referred to in this book as 'capabilities'.

A total of 95 senior level leaders from 21 different organizations (public and private sector) were studied. The leaders were assessed in terms of the specific leadership competencies listed in Table 3.1. The assessment of the leaders utilized a proprietary 360° assessment tool; LeaderShape's Leadership and Emotional Intelligence Profile Assessment (LEIPA®). This tool measures leadership competencies in the context of a leader's current role and the culture of that organization, and identifies a set of granular behaviours that reflect the competencies listed in Table 3.1. Four behaviours represent each competency, creating a total list of 76 behaviours for the 19 emotional intelligence capabilities.

The leaders were rated by the people who knew them fairly well, usually for at least six months. This consisted of their boss, their peers, their direct reports and others with whom they worked. To get honest feedback, all participants (leaders and raters) were briefed on the concept of EI and informed that the exercise was clearly a development tool and not a performance

TABLE 3.1   El competency and capability chart

Competencies (and capabilities)	Definition
Self-awareness	
Emotional self-awareness	Being aware of one's emotion and the effects it has
Accurate self-assessment	Being aware of strengths and limits
Self-confidence	A good sense of self-worth and capabilities
Self-management	
Emotional self-control	Controlling disruptive emotions and impulses
Transparency	Maintaining integrity and honesty; trustworthiness
Adaptability	Flexibility in adapting to change
Achievement	The desire to improve and meet standards of excellence
Initiative	Readiness to act on opportunities
Optimism	Pursuing goals despite the obstacles
Social awareness	
Empathy	Sensing others' feelings, their perspectives, and taking interest in their concerns
Organizational awareness	Reading a group's *emotional currents*, social networks, power structure and politics
Service orientation	Recognizing and meeting the needs of others
Relationship management	
Inspirational leadership	Inspiring, guiding and motivating others
Influence	Exercising effective skills for persuasion
Developing others	Sensing development needs in others and supporting their abilities
Change catalyst	Initiating and managing change
Conflict management	Resolving disagreements
Building bonds	Cultivating and maintaining relationships
Team work and collaboration	Working with others toward a goal, cooperating and building teams

PERSONAL COMPETENCE (Self-awareness, Self-management)
SOCIAL COMPETENCE (Social awareness, Relationship management)

Adapted from Goleman *et al* (2002)

appraisal tool, so the result would not be fed back to their respective HR departments or managers. The input from all raters (except their manager) was kept anonymous. The ratings were based on observed and desired behaviours. Raters were asked to give numerical values to reflect the observed or desired behaviours shown in Table 3.2.

TABLE 3.2 Rated 'desired' and 'observed' behaviours

Numerical value	'Observed' or 'desired' level
1	Never or almost never
2	Occasionally
3	Quite often
4	Usually
5	Always

Raters were asked to rate leaders on particular EI behaviours, for example, 'demonstrates an awareness of how others are feeling'. They then used the values in Table 3.2 to describe what was observed and what was desired. If a rater's response was that he or she observed this behaviour 'quite often' that would translate as an 'observed' score of '3'. If he or she would like this behaviour to occur 'always', the 'desired' score would be '5'. In this case the difference between 'desired vs observed' is '2'. However, if he or she believed that the desired frequency was also 'quite often', it would score '3' and the difference would be '0'. This value thus shows the difference between the observed and desired results.

This difference figure is called the 'difference index'. The difference index was classified to point out areas where the leader was performing at expectation, close to expectation and also areas that needed improvement. The lower the difference index the better, as it shows that the leaders were performing close to expectation (signifying an area of strength); see Table 3.3 for the difference index classification.

The data were then analysed to find the average difference index achieved by each leader for each of the EI competencies and capabilities. The higher the numerical value of the difference index, the greater the need for development. This is a much more meaningful way to score competence than just

TABLE 3.3   Difference index classification

Numerical difference	Performance level and development need
< 0	Performing beyond expectation
0.	Performing at expectation
between 0 and 0.5	Performing close to expectation
between 0.5 and 1.0	May need improvement
between 1.0 and 1.5	Indicates need for change
greater than 1.5	May indicate significant shortfall

an absolute value as it takes into consideration the context of the role and environment of the organization.

The initial results were compiled from all raters excluding the leader themselves to reduce the effect of negative or inflated self-reporting. Reports from the leaders when compared with other raters revealed blind spots and hidden strengths as some leaders overrate and others underrate themselves. This aspect is discussed in more detail in Chapter 4 of this book.

The LEIPA® assessment tool also collects the raters' view of the order of importance of six leadership styles (Goleman *et al*, 2002) in a particular role. The styles are visionary, coaching, affiliative, democratic, pace-setting and commanding. In addition, as each leadership style is made up of various specific EI capabilities, by aggregating the scores of these appropriate capabilities we can measure the competence on a particular leadership style. For example, the dominant capabilities that make up the coaching style of leadership are emotional self-awareness, empathy and developing others. This then provides for a comparison between the competence in different leadership styles and the importance of the different leadership style in a particular role. The report is organized to reflect:

1 Leadership styles: the order of importance in the context of current role.

2 Observed vs desired competency of each leadership style.

3 Observed vs desired competency of each EI capability.

4 Overview of each leader's main strengths and areas for development.

5 Blind spots and hidden strengths.

To ensure the report is understood and acted upon, each leader receives at least one coaching-style feedback session so they can identify the areas on which they wish to focus. The strategies and actions developed are discussed in more detail in Chapters 6 (Feeding (back and) forwards for talent development) and 7 (Coaching for talent development) of this book.

These data varied because of the differences between the types of people, the organizations they worked in and the different job duties and expectations. The analysis comprised sorting out the top five scores of each leader, which represent the leader's development needs, and the bottom five scores, which represent the leader's strengths. These top five development needs were further analysed to find the most frequent in the 95 leaders studied.

Top three EI capability gaps

After analysing the top five development needs for each of the 95 leaders and carrying out a frequency analysis, the analysis showed that *empathy* was the most frequently occurring development need (62 per cent of executives had this within their top five development needs), followed by developing others (55 per cent). Conflict management was the third most frequent development need (see Table 3.4).

But how *much* development was needed in these areas? Or, put another way, how big was the difference index? Considering the difference indexes for each of the capabilities shows us which of them needed the most development. Figure 3.1 shows the full list of capabilities that needed the most development, from the most (highest index) to the least (lowest index).

TABLE 3.4 Most common development needs

Capability	Percentage of leaders in study with need
Empathy	62
Developing others	55
Conflict management	46

FIGURE 3.1 Capabilities needing the most development (most-to-least)

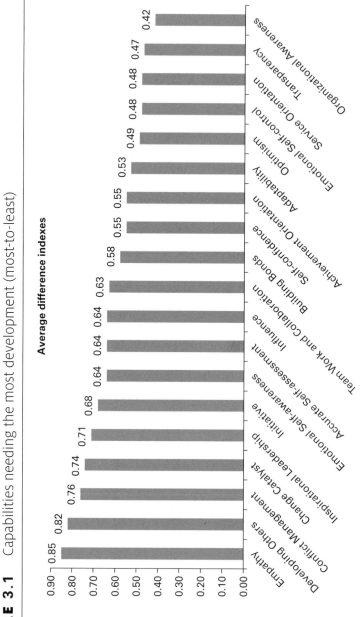

Average difference indexes

Being empathetic

Empathy was the capability with the most common need amongst the leaders undertaking LEIPA®, and was the need that required most development. Goleman *et al* (2002) define this capability as sensing other people's emotions, looking at things from their perspective and making appropriate decisions while taking into consideration their different feelings. This is what Maguire (2002) called the 'relational aspect' of leadership, which must be in balance with the transactional aspect for a healthy working relationship to thrive. This means that leaders must pay attention to people's feelings, and in essence relationships, as well as the core functions of the business.

Martin and Schmidt (2010) note that since the economic downturn around 2007, companies have adjusted their strategy, which is now characterized by the curbing of spending, mergers, forced redundancy, job insecurity and pay cuts. Some of these business survival measures and other HR policies like the 'best fit' approach of people management make business growth rather than employees their core focus (Marchington and Wilkinson, 2008).

Leadership is about the emotional connection between leaders and their reports and other people they have influence over, and previous research has shown that there is a relationship between the display of empathy and people's perceptions of leaders (Kellett *et al*, 2006). In other words, when leaders are empathetic they win the trust of their people, who feel they are understood and valued. This ability to work through emotions and use them to bring out the best in organizations is what Goleman *et al* (2002) call 'resonance'. They stress that empathy makes resonance possible; leaders who lack empathy act in ways that create dissonance. Dissonance is a feeling of detachment that leads to lack of trust and ultimately reduces performance.

1. The behaviours of empathy

Empathy as a word can be ambiguous with different meanings according to the context it is being applied. This competency can be better understood when viewed as a set of behaviours that leaders display. The leadership assessment tool used in the research above, LEIPA®, identifies four behaviours that make this competency simpler to understand in work environments. These are:

a Listening attentively to what people say.

b Demonstrating an awareness of how people are feeling.

   c Accurately identifying the underlying causes of another person's perspective.

   d Expressing an understanding of another person's perspective.

Since empathy was seen as the competency with the most common and greatest development need, further analysis was carried out to find which granular behaviours had the greatest development need. The results are shown in Figure 3.2. The analysis shows that the behaviour, 'demonstrates an awareness of how others are feeling' was the one with the biggest need in the majority of the leaders (in terms of the difference index). This was closely followed by 'accurately identifies the underlying causes of other person's perspective'. The percentages shown in Figure 3.2 reflect the proportion of leaders (among the 62 per cent who had empathy in their top five development needs) who had the highest difference index in each of the four behaviours relating to empathy.

Goleman *et al* (2002) clarify that being skilled in this competence does not mean that leaders must agree with everyone's view or try to please everybody. Rather, they consider other people's feelings and other factors while making important decisions. If leaders are seen to genuinely appreciate the other person's point of view, influence becomes much easier (Whitelaw, 2012) and the other person is also more likely to accept a decision in good grace even if he or she does not agree with it.

FIGURE 3.2 Proportion of leaders with specific behavioural development needs (empathy)

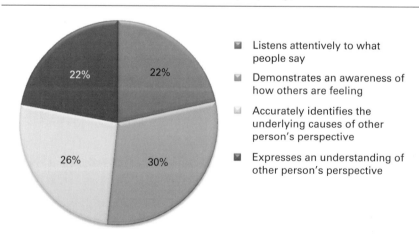

This is a significant finding. It has become a generally accepted fact that leaders increase their effectiveness by listening more and telling less. This research, however, shows that the most important development needed to improve empathy is for the leader to feed back that they are aware of how others are feeling. It is also interesting that the difference between the men and women in this study was less significant than expected. From the practical experience of facilitating the feedback from these LEIPA® reports, it is believed that, in general, men lack empathy because their default state is often not in tune with understanding emotions. For women, the lack of empathy is usually because it is confused with sympathy and therefore, as a default, they are more likely to share the feelings than voice awareness or understanding of them.

2. Developing others

The next most common development need is 'developing others'. This involves sensing development needs in others and supporting their abilities. Perhaps the current business trend characterized by budget reductions as described by Martin and Schmidt (2010) can be a factor in some organizations not investing more in developing talent or in training and development.

The behaviours of developing others

LEIPA® identifies four core behaviours that make up this capability:

a Gives personal recognition to the accomplishments and achievements of others.

b Offers useful feedback and helps others to identify their personal needs for further growth.

c Identifies opportunities and stimulates individuals to develop to their full potential.

d Involves individuals in the process of making decisions that will affect them.

The leaders involved in the LEIPA® assessments were rated against these behaviours and further analysis was undertaken to determine the behaviour with the most common development need. The analysis shows that 'identifying opportunities and stimulating individuals to develop to their full potential' was the behaviour that was most often (33 per cent) the greatest development need (or highest difference index) in this capability. This was followed by 'offering useful feedback and helping others to identify their personal needs

FIGURE 3.3   Proportion of leaders with specific behavioural development needs (developing others)

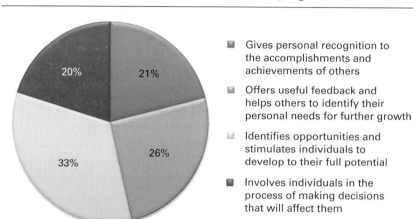

Gives personal recognition to the accomplishments and achievements of others

Offers useful feedback and helps others to identify their personal needs for further growth

Identifies opportunities and stimulates individuals to develop to their full potential

Involves individuals in the process of making decisions that will affect them

for further growth' (26 per cent). The percentages shown in Figure 3.3 reflect the proportion of leaders (amongst the 55 per cent who had 'developing others' in their five top development needs) who had the highest difference index in each of the four behaviours relating to this capability.

Discussions with leaders during the LEIPA® feedback process reveal that the most common reason for 'developing others' being such a high priority for personal development is that many leaders just do not recognize their role in the development of the people who report to them and are unaware of the expectations of their direct reports.

Martin and Schmidt (2010) believe that this competency is the basis for talent development, and the lack of it is the reason why some organizations experience a talent shortfall. Employees respond well to the leaders they feel are interested in their development as this is part of their expectation, perception and informal obligation (the psychological contract). Where this is lacking, there is a potential breach of contract, and trust can be negatively affected (Atkinson, 2007). This in essence means that when leaders are not interested in developing others, recognizing achievement and involving employees, staff turnover can increase and there can be a reduction in core performers.

Many job roles are filled with people whose expertise and knowledge sustain the organization – core assets and the key to achieving competitive advantage (Allen and Wright, 2008). Twenty-first century leaders have to change to properly manage this workforce – a key message of Chapter 2.

A direct result of this neglect is what Martin and Schmidt (2010) call 'disengagement', or when core contributors feel they, or their development, are no longer important to the organization personified by their leader. The result is a reduced effort and performance.

Martin and Schmidt's (2010) research shows an increasing number of disengaged employees since the economic downturn around 2007, and warn that one great mistake leaders make is to assume that 'high potential' staff are fully engaged. It is therefore important for leaders to reposition themselves and take developing others seriously so as to attract and keep the right workforce.

3. Conflict management

The third most common development need was conflict management. This competency involves the ability to manage and resolve disagreements (Goleman *et al*, 2002). Disagreements and conflict at work are an integral part of the working relationship and it takes a competent leader to manage them and maintain focus at work (CIPD, 2007).

The LEIPA® assessment tool identifies four behaviours that make up this competency:

a Handles difficult people and tense situations with diplomacy and tact.

b Spots potential conflict, brings disagreements into the open and helps de-escalate.

c Encourages debate and open discussion.

d Orchestrates win-win solutions.

Further analysis of these four behaviours reveals that among the 46 per cent of leaders who have conflict management in their top five development needs, 'spotting potential conflict, bringing disagreements into the open and helping to de-escalate them' was most commonly the greatest development need (had the highest difference index). Figure 3.4 shows the relevant percentage for each of the behaviours.

A survey into leadership and conflict management (CIPD, 2008) shows that many leaders are aware of the disruptive effects that conflict can have in the workplace. It also shows that more than 80 per cent of HR professionals cite 'identifying and addressing underlying tensions more effectively before things start going wrong' as key to helping managers become more effective in managing conflict at work. Interestingly this same behaviour was

FIGURE 3.4   Proportion of leaders with specific behavioural development needs (conflict management)

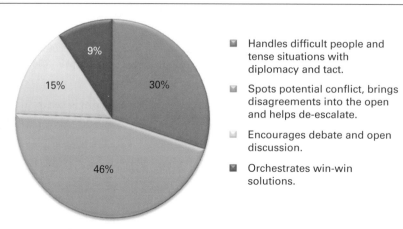

- Handles difficult people and tense situations with diplomacy and tact.
- Spots potential conflict, brings disagreements into the open and helps de-escalate.
- Encourages debate and open discussion.
- Orchestrates win-win solutions.

seen as the greatest development need out of the four behaviours that make up conflict management. This suggests that although many leaders are aware of the need to identify and address conflicts before things go wrong, this behaviour was still lacking in the leaders studied.

The CIPD's (2008) survey identifies that, on average, HR practitioners spend three and a half hours every week managing conflict at work; this was higher for public sector respondents. As a result of this, it becomes an integral part of most HR practitioners' work on a daily basis. If conflict management is not handled properly it will affect employee morale, increase absence levels and reduce employee performance.

In a different study (CIPD, 2007), it was found that many organizations rely on their HR department to manage and resolve conflict. Some managers shy away from this responsibility in case they do or say something that might be held against them during formal proceedings. This approach was seen as counterproductive as it only makes matters worse by prolonging the effect of conflict. To prevent this, a recommendation was put forward that *all* HR practitioners should ensure that managers at *all* levels are trained and well equipped with the skills and knowledge needed to manage workplace conflicts at an early stage. This supports addressing this common leadership development area.

Facilitators of the LEIPA® tool found that the most common cause for conflict management being a high development need is that many leaders avoid addressing conflict until it becomes so serious that it is an emotive issue and as a result is not handled well. The lesson is that leaders should address issues in a constructive way when they are first identified and not just hope they will 'go away'.

Conclusion

Assessing and discovering the leadership gap in individuals and in organizations is an effective first step in leadership talent development. Once the specific capabilities and behaviours are identified, leadership development programmes can be more tailored and focused in order to achieve the desired results.

SPECIFIC ACTION POINTS

What this research shows is that to improve leadership in general, organizations (both HR departments and line managers) should be focusing on identifying 'behaviours' for further development as well as the traditional management skills related to strategy, processes and structures. Although it is critical to the integrity and effectiveness of a 360° development tool that the report is confidential to the individual, people are expected to share the development areas they have chosen to work on with all of their raters, including their line manager (see Chapters 5 and 7 for more details).

Support for the improvement of behaviours that have been identified as critical for more competent leadership can be effected through one-to-one coaching (see Chapter 7). Yet there is also the opportunity here to provide support for teams of leaders to work together to improve, because according to the analysis presented in this chapter, many have similar behavioural development areas. A programme that engages complete leadership teams in the development of specific behaviours works as follows:

● From the individual 360° assessment of each member of a leadership team (eg the board of directors, the senior management team, or a group of middle managers), identify the most common behavioural development needs across the team. With the LEIPA® tool it is possible to produce a 'Team LEIPA'. As shown in

Figure 3.1, empathy, developing others, conflict management, change catalyst and inspirational leadership are the five EI capabilities most needing development. Our experience is that at least three of those five are seen in almost all organizations, with differences usually related to the culture of the organization and the type of leaders it attracts/promotes.

- Once the major capabilities and granular behaviours that the team need to develop have been identified, it is possible to plan a specific programme. Ideally, these 360° assessments will have been part of a behavioural leadership programme where the participants will have learnt the coaching style of leadership and have developed reasonable competence in coaching as line managers. With this skill in place, a facilitator organizes the team into groups of three where in turn they act as coach, coachee and observer. Each individual spends 20–30 minutes coaching. The coachee has as the topic, or focus, how he or she can improve a specific behaviour. If possible, coachees can take examples from their discussions with raters or the verbatim comments they received in the 360° report.

- The outcomes from these coaching sessions can then be presented to the entire team and further discussion can ensue.

- Each member of the team or group declares their key learning from the session and then commits to one or more specific actions they will practise before the next team session.

- At the next team session (perhaps at three- or four-week intervals – so as to have sufficient time to practise but not too long to have started to forget the original learning) each team member explains what they have done and what they learnt. This is not primarily to demonstrate success but to show that real learning has taken place.

- These kind of workshops can continue indefinitely, and after a while when the original identified behaviours have been brought up to an acceptable standard, other EI capabilities can be worked on. Initially, it is advisable to have an external facilitator to bring his or her expertise and discipline to the meetings but over time members can share the facilitation role and use that as an opportunity to learn another skill.

FURTHER RESOURCES

LeaderShape website: **www.leadershape.biz** provides a broad and open resource to leadership development. In particular for this chapter see **http://www.leadershape.biz/emotional-intelligence,** **http://www.leadershape.biz/locs-culture-survey** and **http://www.leadershape.biz/transpersonal-leadership.**

Chartered institute of Personnel Development resources website: **http://www.cipd.co.uk/hr-resources/** provides a wide range of HR resources, training programmes, survey reports, etc.

EI Consortium: **http://www.eiconsortium.org/** contains articles, videos, podcasts, updates and research on EI; it also has recommended books on leadership and EI.

References

Allen, M R and Wright, P (2008) Strategic management in HRM in (eds) P Boxall, J Purcell and P Wright, *The Oxford Handbook of Human Resource Management*, pp 88–107, Oxford University Press, Oxford

Armstrong, M (2009) *A Handbook of Human Resource Management Practice*, 11th edn, Kogan Page, London

Atkinson, C (2007) Trust and the psychological contract, *Employee Relations*, **29** (3), pp 227–46, retrieved from www.emeraldinsight.com/0142-5455.htm

Byham, W, Smith, A and Paese, M (2002) *Grow Your Own Leaders: How to identify, develop and retain leadership talent*, Pearson Education, New Jersey

CIPD (2007) *Managing Conflict at Work Survey Report*, retrieved from http://www.cipd.co.uk/hr-resources/survey-reports/managing-conflict-work.aspx

CIPD (2008) *Leadership and the Management of Conflict at Work Survey Report*, retrieved from http://www.cipd.co.uk/NR/rdonlyres/E426E492-7AED-46A6-B8F5-92B9CF9725C5/0/4545Leadershipconflict.pdf

Goleman, D, Boyatzis, R and McKee, A (2002) *The New Leaders: Transforming the art of leadership into the science of results*, Time Warner, London

Kellett, J B, Humphrey, R H and Sleeth, R G (2006) Empathy and the emergence of task and relations leaders, *Leadership Quarterly*, **17**, pp 146–62

Kouzes, J M and Posner, B Z (2007) *The Leadership Challenge*, 4th edn, John Wiley, Chichester

Maguire, H (2002) Psychological contracts: are they still relevant? *Career Development International*, **7** (3), pp 167–80, retrieved on 08/08/2010 from www.emeraldinsight.com/1362-0436.htm

Marchington, M and Wilkinson, A (2008) *Human Resource Management at Work: People management and development*, 4th edn, CIPD, London

Martin, J, and Schmidt, C (2010) How to keep your top talent, *Harvard Business Review*, pp 54–61

Weiss, D S and Molinaro, V (2005) *The Leadership Gap: Building leadership capacity for competitive advantage*, John Wiley, Chichester

Whitelaw, G (2012) *The Zen Leader: 10 ways to go from barely managing to leading fearlessly*, Career Press, New York

Blind spots and hidden strengths: findings from research

ETUKUDO ODUNGIDE and JOHN KNIGHTS

EXECUTIVE SUMMARY

Leaders are seen as individuals who possess the abilities and competencies needed to get the right things done in an effective way. The problem is that some leaders underestimate their competence in some of their skills and behaviours, but also overestimate others. This can lead to issues of underperforming people and organizations in that they are held back or do not realize their full potential. It is therefore important for leaders to understand the areas where their performance is perceived by the people they work with to be at a higher level than their own view of themselves (hidden strengths). It is equally important for leaders to understand where their performance is seen by the people around them to be at a lower level than their own opinion (blind spots).

The danger of not recognizing and working on hidden strengths and blind spots is that it can cause a disconnect between the leader and the people they are leading. Leaders who do not recognize their hidden strengths can spend time, energy and money developing areas that do not need development while underutilizing core strengths. This can impair decision making and ultimately reduce effectiveness. At the same time leaders who are not aware of their blind spots are missing an opportunity to improve their own performance and that of the organization.

The research presented in this chapter shows that among the 95 leaders in the study, the most common hidden strengths were 'emotional self-control', 'building bonds' and 'organizational awareness'. In other words, the people leaders worked with thought they did better in these areas than they thought themselves. In terms of blind spots, the research reveals that the ability to be an effective 'change catalyst' was the most common. While the leaders thought they were good at initiating and managing change, the people they worked with thought otherwise. The other most common blind spots were 'emotional self-awareness' and 'accurate self-assessment'. Paying attention to blind spots and hidden strengths is an effective approach to professional development and can help improve leadership performance.

The danger in blind spots and hidden strengths

While there are different schools of thought about whether individuals are born with leadership skills or they are learnt, the fact is there are certain skills and competencies that are indispensable to becoming an effective leader. We have seen from previous chapters that people respond more positively and productively to leaders who display certain competencies. But a key challenge in leadership talent development is knowing where to invest – and part of this challenge is people overestimating some of their capabilities and not being aware of others.

Lombardo and Robert (2009) rightly said that when leaders are not aware of the skills they possess or if they overrate themselves compared to their actual abilities, this can alter the nature of leadership and lead to leadership flaws. This is worst when the unrecognized abilities relate to the core skills or behaviours needed to complete a particular leadership task.

Blakeley (2007) describes a blind spot as that area on the retina which lacks receptors that respond to light. As a consequence, if an image falls on this area it will not be seen; it impairs the ability to see things properly. Van Hecke (2007) relates this to the potential danger which the blind spot in a driver's wing mirror can cause. It has the ability of swallowing up a passing car and causing severe harm if not properly managed. A driver must check that the blind spots are uncovered to ensure safety on the road. Images that may not be very visible to the driver may be very clear to someone else on the same road or perhaps even an adjacent road. This is an apt metaphor for leadership blind spots.

Blind spots can lead to leaders blaming others for the problems they contribute to; what Pienaar (2009) calls self-deception, a key reason for leadership ineffectiveness. Orr *et al* (2010) agree that leaders who do not recognize their hidden strength can spend time fixing what is not broken, focusing on less important areas and underutilizing core strengths. This can impair decision making and ultimately reduce performance.

Leaders' blind spots are usually noticed by the people working around them, and they can often provide a quick and accurate picture (Shelton, 2007). Being unaware of blind spots leaves the leader in a vulnerable position and open to being unsuccessful in performing to his or her potential. Blind spots and hidden strengths are not, in themselves, flaws but are areas that can be harnessed to increase effectiveness. It is only when they are ignored that they pose a threat to effective leadership (Blakeley, 2007).

Both underestimating and overestimating strengths increases the deficiency in leadership and reduces the leader's effectiveness (Van Hecke, 2007). As stated earlier, ignoring hidden strength and blind spots can cause a disconnect between the leader and the people they are leading, mainly because the leaders see differently and have a wrong impression of others' perceptions. In this sense, perception is reality or, quoting the Talmud (a central text of Judaism), 'We do not see things as they are; we see them as we are. We do not hear things as they are; we hear them as we are.'

The power of another's eye

Everyone has blind spots and hidden strengths but they have a greater impact in a leader because of their greater responsibility, their duty as a role model and their visibility to and influence on a great number of people. Blind spots and hidden strengths develop, change and emerge as we progress in our careers, handle different and greater responsibilities, and become familiar with various processes and cultures, etc. Many executives also hold leadership roles outside of the work environment, which may include involvement in community projects, clubs, mentoring family/relatives and so on. Through these activities, leaders build transferable leadership skills they may take for granted or may not even be aware of (Orr *et al*, 2010).

As such, a leader's peers, managers and other colleagues are usually better able to spot and identify specific leadership strengths that the leader may not have detected. In the same vein, some leaders overrate or overestimate their strength, perhaps because of previous experience in similar projects or their length of service. This is especially true in countries or organizational cultures where age and longevity of service are paramount when considering promotion or determining seniority and 'wisdom'.

Research into blind spots and hidden strengths

An effective way to uncover blind spots and hidden strength is to compare leaders' own self-assessment with those of their peers, their boss and the people they lead (Orr *et al*, 2010). This allows leaders to see themselves as other people they work with perceive them and to respond appropriately. This is the 360° feedback approach, which enables a calibration of perspectives from different angles, enabling the identification of specific areas that may require development (Bixler, 2011).

A total of 95 leaders from 21 different organizations were assessed using the LEIPA® leadership assessment tool (see Chapters 2 and 5 which describe LEIPA® in more detail). Each leader was rated against the 19 emotional intelligence (EI) capabilities listed in the previous chapter (Table 3.1), each defined by four granular behaviours. In addition to the leaders rating themselves, they were also rated by their bosses (one or two) and by at least three individuals from the following groups – 'peers', 'direct reports' and 'other'. The minimum of three raters in each group (except bosses) is to assure anonymity of the responses. The rating was based on the difference between observed and desired levels of behaviour (the 'difference index' – see Chapter 3). The data were then analysed to find the average score achieved by each leader for each of the EI competencies.

To find out the major blind spots and hidden strengths of each leader, the self-assessment was compared to the assessment of other raters for each particular leader. Capabilities where the leader assessed him or herself 'significantly' higher than other raters were identified as blind spots, and capabilities where other people rated the leader 'significantly' higher than the leader him or herself, were identified as hidden strengths. 'Significant' was defined in the difference index as greater than 0.5, using the scoring mechanism shown in Table 3.2 in Chapter 3.

For the LEIPA® process, each leader works with an accredited professional coach to interpret the detailed report and agree an action and development plan. The strategies and actions adopted are discussed in more detail in Chapters 5 (LEIPA® and 8ICOL® assessments), 6 (feedback/forward) and 7 (coaching).

Top three hidden strengths

To determine the most common hidden strengths among the leaders, each leader's hidden strengths were analysed and the most common were identified. The results of the analysis show that the most common were the EI capabilities of 'emotional self-control', 'building bonds' and 'organizational awareness'. As can be seen in Table 4.1, 31 per cent of the leaders in the study had emotional self-control as a hidden strength, 30 per cent had building bonds and 27 per cent organizational awareness.

TABLE 4.1 Most common hidden strength capabilities

Hidden strength capabilities	Percentage of leaders studied
Emotional self-control	31
Building bonds	30
Organizational awareness	27

1. Emotional self-control

Goleman *et al* (2002) define this capability as the ability to control disruptive emotions and impulses. The results show that the most commonly occurring hidden strength was a leader's competence in emotional self-control. Goleman (2004) affirms that this capability helps build leaders' confidence as they are able to keep any situation under control. The LEIPA® assessment tool identified four behaviours that make up this competency:

a Behaves calmly under stress.

b Does not act impulsively.

c Manages his or her emotions well.

d Does not take decisions on impulse.

This shows that many leaders are not aware of the perception other people have of their self-control. Our experience from facilitating leaders' understanding of LEIPA® reports is that they have often subconsciously learnt to give the impression of emotional self-control when in fact they do not feel this themselves at all. The leaders often feel that they are just hiding their emotions rather than controlling (or managing) them.

This shield of 'control' may give them an aura of self-control, but also create a negative perspective on other EI capabilities such as 'empathy', 'transparency' or 'inspirational leadership'. The fact that the leader learns that others believe he or she has emotional self-control can help towards building self-confidence and show how hiding emotions can create negative perceptions in other capabilities. This kind of learning can only be discovered in an environment where everyone can be encouraged to be truthful: the LEIPA® report is only being used as a development tool, not an appraisal of performance assessment, so it will not have a direct impact on promotion or remuneration.

Further analysis was carried out on the four behaviours listed above to determine the behaviour with the highest difference between the difference index of the leader and the other raters. The results show that the behaviour 'manages his or her emotions well' scored highest and 'does not act impulsively' was the second highest; see Table 4.2. This result allows us to narrow down the focus in terms of the most common granular hidden strength behaviour.

TABLE 4.2 Average difference indexes for behaviours in emotional self-control

Emotional self-control: specific EI behaviours	Average difference index		
	Self (A)	Others (B)	Difference (A-B)
Manages his or her emotions well	1.54	0.26	1.28
Does not act impulsively	1.04	0.08	0.96
Behaves calmly under stress	1.25	0.42	0.83
Does not take decisions on impulse	0.79	0.10	0.69

2. Building bonds

The research shows that building bonds was another common hidden strength among the leaders studied; 30 per cent had this capability as a hidden strength. Goleman *et al* (2002) describe this capability as the ability to cultivate and maintain a web of healthy relationships. This is different to team building, which focuses more on developing deep relationships to enable the effective performance of a small group. For Sharma (2010), building and maintaining successful relationships is crucial in determining leadership success, and as relationships grow deeper, leadership becomes better. Leaders engaging in social or sports activities with colleagues outside of the working environment is a form of building bonds and is closely connected to the affiliative leadership style. Although these activities may not be work-related, they can help leaders to build bonds between themselves and the people they work with (Brooks, 2009). However, building bonds is also about developing relationships outside of the company or organization the leader works in. It should include all stakeholders such as clients, suppliers, the community, etc, and the more authentic and transparent the relationship is, the better the overall leadership performance.

Experience tells us that extroverts tend to be better bond builders because they will reach out to people and quite often such leaders do not realize the value this brings to an organization. Often extroverts build bonds naturally whereas introverted leaders have to work harder and make a conscious effort to build bonds. The leadership assessment tool (LEIPA®) uses four behaviours that reflect this capability:

a Proactive in meeting new people and developing relationships with them.

b Continually developing and expanding his or her networks.

c Develops and builds strong relationships with colleagues.

d Utilizes relationships to achieve shared goals.

Further analysis was carried out to determine the behaviour with the highest difference between the assessment of the leader and other raters. The results show that the behaviour 'continually develops and expands his or her networks' had the highest difference index, followed by 'proactive in meeting new people and developing relationships with them'; see Table 4.3. Again this result identifies the granular behaviours that are the strongest hidden strength within this EI capability and will help leaders harness their hidden talent.

TABLE 4.3   Average difference indexes for behaviours in building bonds

Building bonds: specific EI behaviours	Average difference index		
	Self (A)	Others (B)	Difference (A-B)
Continually develops and expands his or her networks	1.59	0.30	1.29
Proactive in meeting new people and developing relationships with them	1.41	0.37	1.04
Utilizes relationships to accomplish shared goals	1.00	0.38	0.62
Develops and builds strong relationships with colleagues	1.00	0.42	0.58

The two highest hidden strength behaviours suggest the 'strength' is more about broadening relationships with a larger network than deepening them with colleagues. Many leaders are continually proactive in developing and expanding their networks in a way that their colleagues think is exemplary – or sometimes even 'over the top' (excessive) – while the leaders themselves believe they need to make more effort. It may be that non-leaders or lower level leaders do not always realize the importance of expanding their networks or maybe leaders do not need to focus as much as they believe on expanding networks.

The beauty of a 360° assessment that measures behaviours and is intended as a development tool is that with the support of the coach/facilitator, leaders can reach their own solutions to these quandaries, which perhaps warrant further specific discussions with their raters. It may even make leaders aware that perhaps the people around them need to increase their own expectation of expanding their networks.

3. Organizational awareness

The third most common hidden strength from the leaders studied was organizational awareness. This capability involves being socially aware, detecting crucial networks in organizations, and perceiving the power relationships and political state of the organization. It also involves reading a group's emotional currents, social networks, power structure and politics (Goleman *et al*, 2002). According to Brooks (2009), the political situation of an organization is always of interest to the majority of workers and leaders because of their desire to go higher up the organizational ladder and to be among the decision-making class.

This capability also encompasses the ability to recognize influencing and disruptive networks, being aware of group influences and managing them appropriately. The LEIPA® tool identifies four behaviours that reflect this capability:

a Understands how to get things done in the organization.

b Is politically astute.

c Does not let office politics get in the way of what needs to be achieved.

d Can work within the culture of the organization.

Further analysis was carried out to determine the behaviour with the highest difference between the leaders' ratings and the ratings of other participants. The results show that the behaviour 'is politically astute' had the highest difference index followed by, 'does not let office politics get in the way of what needs to be achieved'; see Table 4.4.

TABLE 4.4 Average difference indexes for behaviours in organizational awareness

Organizational awareness: specific EI behaviours	Average difference index		
	Self (A)	Others (B)	Difference (A-B)
Is politically astute	1.50	0.31	1.19
Does not let office politics get in the way of what needs to be achieved	1.20	0.28	0.92
Understands how to get things done in the organization	1.30	0.39	0.91
Can work within the culture of the organization	0.95	0.16	0.79

The specific behaviour of organizational awareness, especially being politically astute, is often perceived by raters to be a reason why a leader has been so successful or indeed how he or she got to that position in the first place. In our experience, executives with this hidden strength often assume everyone has this kind of 'savvyness' and therefore believe they need even more. It is not uncommon for leaders to be surprised that the people around them think they are so organizationally aware.

Summary of hidden strengths

Hidden strengths in emotional self-control, building bonds and organizational awareness probably mean that these capabilities were demonstrated without conscious attention to the related behaviours. The fact that these leaders were unaware of these particular leadership skills can actually reduce leadership effectiveness as the leaders are unable to leverage the perceived strengths (Orr *et al*, 2010).

Top three blind spots

The most common blind spots among the leaders studied were identified in the same way as the hidden strengths. The research showed that the most common blind spots were in the EI capabilities of change catalyst, emotional self-awareness and accurate self-assessment; see Table 4.5.

TABLE 4.5   Most common blind spots capabilities

Blind spots capabilities	Percentage of leaders studied
Change catalyst	33
Emotional self-awareness	33
Accurate self-assessment	30

1. Change catalyst

A significant majority of the leaders thought they were change catalysts and that they had the ability to champion and manage change. However, the people they work with thought otherwise. The leadership assessment tool (LEIPA®) identifies four behaviours that reflect this competency:

a Recognizes the need for change and proactively removes barriers.

b Challenges the status quo and the need for change.

c Champions change and enlists others in the pursuit.

d Demonstrates by actions the change expected by others.

Further analysis was carried out to determine the behaviour with the highest difference index between the leaders' ratings and the ratings of other participants. The results show that the behaviour 'challenges the status quo and the need for change' had the highest difference index, followed by 'champions change and enlists others in its pursuit'; see Table 4.6.

TABLE 4.6   Average difference indexes for behaviours in change catalyst

Change catalyst: specific EI behaviours	Average difference index		
	Self (A)	Others (B)	Difference (B-A)
Challenges the status quo to acknowledge the need for change	0.00	0.74	0.74
Champions change and enlists others in its pursuit	0.06	0.77	0.71
Recognizes the need for change and proactively removes barriers	0.33	0.96	0.63
Demonstrates by his or her actions the change expected of others	0.44	1.08	0.64

Leaders generally realize that it is important for them to be competent in the role of change catalyst. Change in organizations can sometimes be complex and difficult to deal with. Leaders are always at the heart of this with a prime responsibility of identifying new realities and leading the change process (Beerel, 2009; Gill, 2003). However, the reality is that many leaders are not good change agents, and as can be seen in Figure 3.1 (see Chapter 3) 'change catalyst' is the fourth most needed area of development among leaders.

Only a small percentage of leaders (and people in general) are natural change agents, with most being risk averse and preferring the status quo. The neuroscience of this is that our brains were designed for life in the Stone Age where change meant danger. Often followers can see the need for change sooner than leaders, partly because they are at the sharp end of business where things are changing, and partly because they do not take responsibility if the change goes wrong. (For leaders to overcome aversion to risk see the third Specific Action at the end of this chapter.) Being a change agent is at the core of leadership – and leaders know this – so it is not surprising that leaders rate their own difference index between observed and desired as very small.

2. Emotional self-awareness

Emotional self-awareness involves being aware of one's own emotions and the effect they have on a situation. This is one of the most important capabilities of EI (Goleman, 2004). The research shows that a third of the leaders in the study thought they were more aware of their emotions and their impact on others, but other participants thought otherwise. The four behaviours identified by LEIPA® that describe this capability are:

a Knows which emotions he or she is feeling and why.

b Realizes the links between feelings and what he or she thinks, says and does.

c Recognize how feelings affect performance.

d Takes time to understand his or her own feelings.

Further analysis was carried out to determine the behaviour with the highest difference index between the leaders' ratings and the ratings of other participants. The results show that the behaviour 'realizes the links between feelings and what he or she thinks, says and does' had the highest difference index. This was followed by 'knows which emotions he or she is feeling and why'; see Table 4.7.

In our experience, most leaders, in fact most people in general, feel they are more aware of their feelings and the effect of their feelings on their actions and performance than is perceived by the people around them. Quite often leaders are aware of their feelings but believe they can hide them behind a mask and keep them away from the people around them. This is often done subconsciously to avoid showing weakness. The reality is most people subconsciously read non-verbal signals and while they may not accurately assess what the feeling is, they will notice an emotional state.

TABLE 4.7 Average difference indexes for behaviours in emotional self-awareness

Emotional self-awareness: specific EI behaviours	Average difference index		
	Self (A)	Others (B)	Difference (B-A)
Realizes the links between feelings and what he or she thinks, says and does	0.06	0.93	0.87
Knows which emotions he or she is feeling and why	−0.22	0.60	0.82
Recognizes how feelings affect performance	0.11	0.91	0.80
Takes time to understand his or her own feelings	0.22	0.59	0.37

Because the perception is that leaders are not aware of their emotions and feelings, there will be the view that they are not aware of the *result* of the feeling. From our experience of coaching many leaders, it is apparent that leaders often do not realize how feelings affect the performance of themselves or others. A typical example is bosses who get angry and shout at their staff. Having let off steam they feel better and can get on with their work without realizing they have put their people in such a state that they cannot concentrate on their work at all – maybe for a long time.

3. Accurate self-assessment

The third capability where just under a third of the leaders studied overestimated their competence was 'accurately assessing themselves'. This involves accurately identifying and being aware of their strengths and limitations (Goleman *et al*, 2002). The LEIPA® tool identifies four behaviours that make up this capability:

  a Aware of own strengths and weaknesses.

  b Appreciates the value of reflection as a means of learning from experience.

c Open to candid feedback and new perspectives without getting defensive.

d Able to show a sense of humour and perspective about themselves.

This is perhaps the most crucial blind spot, as it is the essential source of all of the other hidden strengths and blinds spots. It is therefore important to pay attention to, and invest in. With regards to Goleman's classification of emotional intelligence competencies described in Chapter 3 (Table 3.1), 'emotional self-awareness' and 'accurate self-assessment' are grouped under the self-awareness EI competency, which is seen as one of the factors that distinguish high from low performing leaders (Goleman *et al*, 2002). This can be the 'motivational fuel' that helps leaders to accomplish their tasks and can also impede a leader's ability if ignored (Hughes *et al*, 2009: 243).

Again further analysis was carried out to determine the behaviour with the highest difference index between the leaders' ratings and the ratings of other participants. The results show that the behaviour 'aware of own strengths and weaknesses' had the highest difference index, followed by 'able to show a sense of humour and perspective about themselves' and 'open to candid feedback and new perspectives without getting defensive'; see Table 4.8.

TABLE 4.8   Average difference indexes for behaviours in accurate self-assessment

Accurate self-assessment	Average difference index		
	Self (A)	Others (B)	Difference (B-A)
Aware of own strengths and weaknesses	0.27	1.01	0.74
Able to show a sense of humour and perspective about themselves	−0.07	0.62	0.69
Open to candid feedback and new perspectives without getting defensive	0.47	1.13	0.66
Appreciates the value of reflection as a means of learning from experience	0.07	0.64	0.57

It is interesting to explore the data further. The scores from all of the 19 EI capabilities aggregated together were self-assessed as 0.80, and rated by raters at 0.61. The difference here is 0.19, which is actually very small. This suggests that the leaders generally have a good level of self-awareness. Yet, the difference between leaders and their raters in relation to the statement 'aware of own strengths and weaknesses' is 0.74. Alone, this suggests that leaders think they are demonstrating this awareness *more* than their raters perceive. Notice, however, this difference between the leader and rater scores (0.74) is much greater than the difference for all capabilities aggregated together (0.19). This suggests that although leaders were generally self-aware, specifically, leaders were not openly acknowledging their weaknesses to others and were perhaps also modest about their strengths.

While it is understandable that a leader may feel the need to do this, this lack of transparency serves limited purpose. This is because the people around them, who work with them on a daily basis, are generally aware of their strengths and weaknesses anyway – as indicated by the small 'difference' in the aggregate score of 0.19. So an important question to ask is, 'If you are more aware of your strengths and weaknesses than your raters think you are, what do you have to do differently so that their perception changes?' A more open, humble, vulnerable and transparent approach would perhaps gain the leader more respect and would be more likely to be seen as inspirational, and hence act as a role model. Orr *et al* (2010) assert that once leaders feel less sure of themselves by having their blind spots identified, it may actually be positive in the sense that they will seek change and continuous improvement.

Conclusion

Shelton (2007) rightly said that paying attention to blind spots and hidden strengths is a realistic approach to professional development. Where hidden strengths and blind spots are neglected, the situation is a liability, posing a risk to the organization in terms of the performance of its people and the achievement of its business goals. Like a car driver, leaders should be concerned about the invisible areas of their leadership competence and strive to continually improve. The good news is that increasing self-awareness to better understand blind spots and hidden strengths can help correct leadership derailment at any stage in a leader's career (Orr *et al*, 2010).

SPECIFIC ACTION POINTS

- Just contemplating blind spots and hidden strength can be a major step towards self-awareness and enhancing leadership effectiveness. Leaders should engage this tool and assess themselves through 'another's eyes'. This should be combined with support from qualified and trained facilitators who will guide them through the development process. Without professional support, identification of blind spots can be a major setback as it can lead to a lack of confidence when undertaking certain assignments and avoidance of new challenges. Therefore using best practice in the 360° assessment process is essential.

- There may well be a debatable disparity between the leaders' rating and that of other participants as we saw in the case of self-awareness where the data suggest that leaders were more self-aware than the people around them thought. In such cases it may be that the leader is more competent in specific areas but is not displaying or communicating it enough for the raters to see or perceive. An immediate action would be for leaders to think of such disparity in terms of what they need to do differently so it changes the perception of their raters. This approach should be taken in all capabilities where the leader feels the people do not have a correct or complete view of his or her abilities.

- Honesty when self-rating and acceptance of feedback are necessary to make the best of blind spots and hidden strengths. An easy but unhelpful route is to become defensive about feedback, but this would only lead to self-deception. Our Stone Age brain responds to challenge with fear (that we are not good enough or, in the extreme, might be fired) and one of the common results of fear is defensiveness or even denial. It is therefore a strong human instinct to be defensive about negative feedback and under those circumstances often difficult to show a sense of humour. Only the best leaders overcome these instincts and it requires a high level of inner self-confidence and emotional self-awareness.

- Hidden strengths have often been developed unknowingly outside the work environment through involvement in community projects, clubs, mentoring family/relatives, etc. Leaders should actively take a reflective view of life outside their specific job role and find out specific abilities that make them excel in other kinds of assignments. Most often these abilities, such as 'building bonds' (which was among the top three hidden strengths) are transferred unconsciously into the work environment. Leaders should also take a reflective view of previous successful assignments and projects and reflect on capabilities that they think made them successful. This reflective exercise will increase self-awareness and can build self-confidence.

FURTHER RESOURCES

Bixler (2011): in a systematic and clear way, Bixter shows how feedback can help reveal blind spots and how to work through them.

Blakeley (2007): is an easy to read and practical book about leadership blind spots and offers ideas about out what to do about them.

Canaday (2012): this book reveals more about perception gaps and how to deal with personal blind spots. It is a helpful book as it gives readers a clear understanding of how blind spots can influence personal and corporate life.

Molandro (2009): shows how blind spots derail good leaders. She presents strategies for overcoming blind spots and taking bold steps in leading an organization, team or department in the right direction.

References

Beerel, A (2009) *Leadership and Change Management*, Sage, London

Bixler, S (2011) *The Power of Feedback: A story of blind spots, insight, and breakthrough leadership*, Westchester Publishing, Danbury

Blakeley, K (2007) *Leadership Blind Spots and What to Do About Them*, John Wiley, Chichester

Brooks, I (2009) *Organizational Behaviour: Individuals, groups and organization*, 4th edn, Pearson Education, London

Canaday, S (2012) *You – According to Them: Uncovering the blind spots that impact your reputation and your career*, T&C Press, Austin, TX

Gill, R (2003) Change management or change leadership? *Journal of Change Management*, 3 (4), pp 307–18

Goleman, D (2004) What makes a leader? *Harvard Business Review*, 82 (1), pp 82–91

Goleman, D, Boyatzis, R and McKee, A (2002) *The New Leaders: Transforming the art of leadership into the science of results*, Time Warner, London

Hughes, R, Ginnett, R and Curphy, G (2009) *Leadership: Enhancing the lessons of experience*, 6th edn, McGraw-Hill Education, New York

Lombardo, M and Robert, W (2009) *For Your Improvement: A guide for development and coaching*, 5th edn, Korn/Ferry International, Minneapolis

Molandro, L (2009) *Fearless Leadership: How to overcome behavioral blind spots and transform your organization*, McGraw-Hill, New York

Orr, J, Swisher, V, Tang, K and Meuse, K (2010) *Illuminating Blind Spots and Hidden Strengths*, Korn/Ferry Institute, retrieved from http://www.lominger.com/pdf/insights_illuminating_blind_spots_and_hidden_strengths.pdf

Pienaar, C (2009) The role of self-deception in leadership ineffectiveness – a theoretical overview, *South African Journal of Psychology*, 39 (1), pp 133–41

Sharma, R (2010) *The Leader Who Had No Title*, Simon and Schuster, London

Shelton, C (2007) *Blind Spots: Achieve success by seeing what you can't see*, John Wiley, Chichester

Van Hecke, M (2007) *Blind Spots: Why smart people do dumb things*, Prometheus, New York

Transpersonal leadership journeys and assessment (LEIPA® and 8ICOL®)

05

JOHN KNIGHTS

EXECUTIVE SUMMARY

For the sustainable success of organizations in this ever-changing world we need leaders to be developed who put first the true stakeholders of their organizations (customers, employees, suppliers, the community, the planet, and yes, even the shareholders), rather than personal reward (usually money), personal power for control and personal prestige (including fame and celebrity status).

At the start of their transpersonal leadership development journey, leaders tend to be rational thinkers, ego-based, 'Stone Age default' leaders. At the intermediate stage of the journey they have developed to become robust, emotionally aware leaders and as advanced leaders they become radical, ethically authentic leaders. This journey has direction but no final destination – it is lifelong. One can and should always improve. Every one of us has our unique start point, and therefore need to spend more or less time at different steps in the journey, and revisit as necessary. The journey is holistic rather than linear.

Assessments form a very important part of the journey because it is the only way that progress can be measured effectively, to identify key strengths and development areas. The only way to truly measure the total leadership competence of leaders is by allowing all the groups they work closely with (bosses, peers, direct reports, and any other key group) to rate them – 360° assessment – for their behaviours, attitudes and mindsets (rather than the traditional business skills/competencies that measure 'management').

The LEIPA® tool described elsewhere in this book has been further developed, using many of the same best practices and measuring methods, beyond just emotional intelligence (EI) behaviours into an assessment tool that measures the eight integrated competencies of leadership (8ICOL®). This includes measurement of personal intellect and judgement, personal preferences, and values (split between those of personal conscience and self-determination) as well as emotional intelligence. 8ICOL® is the most complete and sophisticated assessment tool yet devised for measuring the development of leaders.

Transpersonal leadership

As the old Irish joke goes, when asked directions, the person answers, 'I wouldn't start from here'! Well, it is a bit like that with leadership development. The problem is organizations have not, 1) defined from the outset what kind of leaders they need for the future, 2) set about identifying the right kind of people, and then 3) developing them. What they have done is defined what business skills they want their managers to possess – and this has been the underpinning of the success of business schools around the world that produce managers rather than leaders. Of course this is not to be confused with the fact that a high proportion of organizational leaders have been to business school!

I have heard many times from executives and others that they admire their bosses for their strategic thinking, their razor-sharp analysis and their political savvy and yet they are not inspired by them, they don't trust them, they don't enjoy working with them, they don't enjoy their own work and they don't feel motivated or engaged. It is not the fact that they are intellectually 'smart' that is the problem, it is that they have not developed appropriate behaviours and don't have admirable values (or at least don't bring them to full consciousness and use them). Unfortunately, in most organizations people are not promoted because they can lead. It will be more likely because they have a lot of 'experience', have been around for a long time, are a safe pair of hands, are the most pushy, the loudest voice, politically astute, good connections; you name it! Whether these appointed leaders turn out to be any good seems to be worse than random. The reality is that the reason they got to be chosen as a top leader is likely to be precisely why they won't be a good leader when they are at the top.

So who is doing the choosing and what are their motivations? It will be either the board for a very senior position or their future boss for those lower down the ladder. They will have the support of Human Resources (HR) or external recruiters who will provide loads of data on competency skills but usually precious little on behaviours or values. The only way an organization will get the leaders it needs is to first define what it needs and then develop a plan to find and develop them – and it requires radical thinking and courage. We need transpersonal leaders, as described in Chapter 2.

This chapter describes the complete developmental journey and, most important, how to assess leaders' development to ensure they build on their strengths but also focus on the key areas of improvement that are barriers to their becoming excellent transpersonal leaders.

The transpersonal journey

The overview of the journey can be found in Figure 5.1. We have used the REAL mnemonic to help remember the three levels, described in detail in Knights (2012). Now think of the journey of a canoeist on a river that is generally slow moving but also requires travel through rapids and sometimes turning back up the river to collect something forgotten or lost.

At the start of their journey it is assumed that candidates have acquired their base business skills, maybe through an MBA or through in-house training and/or workplace experience. These are the task-oriented 'threshold' competencies everyone needs to have in order to function in an organization. In parallel to the leadership journey there will be a continued requirement to brush up management skills (though this will reduce as they move higher up the organization). The journey is launched at a level of REAL – Rational, Ego-based, As-usual Leaders, although each individual will be starting at his or her unique point.

Executives at this level have been educated and trained to think in a 'Rational' way. However, they often assume others think like them and will respond only to rational argument. They may have some level of emotional awareness and intuition but will not be fully aware of their capabilities and therefore not managing them effectively – so, for example, they might be

FIGURE 5.1 Overview of the journey

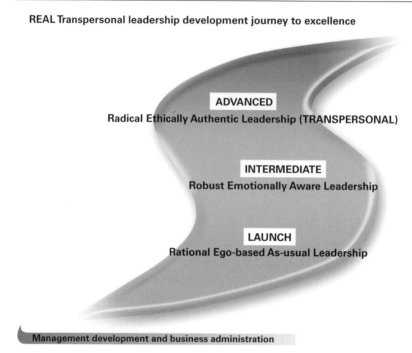

REAL Transpersonal leadership development journey to excellence

ADVANCED
Radical Ethically Authentic Leadership (TRANSPERSONAL)

INTERMEDIATE
Robust Emotionally Aware Leadership

LAUNCH
Rational Ego-based As-usual Leadership

Management development and business administration

bullying or unengaged at a personal level. They are also primarily 'Ego-based', seeking power, reward, prestige and/or recognition and one of these will be the prime driver for the leadership decisions they make. At this stage their ego is not in harmony with the needs of the organization and its stakeholders and therefore probably not focused on sustainability. Even if they are not ego-based, their minds will still need channelling to avoid them being used by others and being uncertain about the balance between, say, the organization and their family.

'As-usual' refers to the default behaviour we expect from leaders who have not been trained to manage their personalities. As described in Chapter 2, this often manifests itself as our genetic default of 'know everything and tell people what to do', a level at which many leaders operate most of the time; even the more developed leaders will get hijacked when stressed and revert to this kind of behaviour.

The steps of the journey to the intermediate stage, REAL – Robust Emotionally Aware Leadership is shown in Figure 2.1 and has been largely described in Chapter 2 in the section 'Developing emotional intelligence'. A brief description of all these steps can also be found in Table 5.1.

TABLE 5.1   The journey to Robust Emotionally Aware Leadership

This journey requires the development of 'seven essences of emotionally intelligent leadership':

1   *Understanding leadership* – a true understanding that effective leadership has changed dramatically in the last 10 to 15 years.

2   *Increasing self-awareness* – including basic neuroscience and understanding how to learn.

3   *Learn to manage own emotions* – understanding how to manage emotions to improve personal performance.

4   *Using different EI leadership styles* – developing competence in six leadership styles and when/how to use them.

5   *Creating a performance-enhancing culture* – learning how leaders can create the right climate and culture which in turn affects performance.

6   *Contract between follower and leader* – ensuring expectations are understood.

7   *Identifying strengths and key behavioural development needs* – a 360° assessment is unavoidable in achieving a complete assessment of oneself.

Arriving at the point of '*building on key strengths – develop new behaviours and habits*'. Building on key strengths involves looking for those granular behaviours that can help develop those competencies even further. Developing new behaviours to overcome perceived weaknesses is even more important. This is the hardest part and it requires time, practice in a safe environment and determination until the brain's neural wiring has formed new circuits and become hard wired – and becomes a new habit.

The part of the journey that has not been explained so far is number 5 in Figure 2.1, 'Create a performance-enhancing culture', which is of particular importance in that it provides for the identification of the current and ideal cultures of the organization and from that a determination of which leadership styles need to be developed and used by the leaders. It is a matter of experience from using the LOCS™ culture survey that we know that opinions vary throughout an organization as to what they think the actual culture is but generally agree across the board as to the ideal culture. This is a great beacon for the organization to head towards!

At this intermediate stage, 'Robust' signifies that individuals have reached a level of inner self-confidence where they will say what they think when they need to, are willing to take risks and communicate unambiguously. They can also take criticism impersonally, make hard decisions and be transparent with people. While this is admirable, without also being 'Emotionally Aware' this leader would neither engage people nor attract followers. So it is also important to be conscious of and sensitive to people's feelings (empathy), to understand how their behaviour affects the mindset and behaviour of others, and to act accordingly. Finally, reaching this level enables the leader to deal in facts and perceptions while avoiding bias and eliminating discrimination.

The final stage of the journey to the advanced REAL – Radically, Ethically Authentic Leader – is a new way of developing leaders in an organized and planned way. This part of the journey is usually travelled through random experience and serendipity combining with the nature of the person's personality. The best that organizations usually do is to provide a path of experiences of increasing seniority. In very rare cases this has resulted in amazing leaders but our goal, as leadership facilitators, is to provide a path that helps support all those people who have the potential to become amazing leaders to reach this zenith as a transpersonal leader – beyond their ego! In developing this advanced part of the journey we have referred to the work of a number of experts in the field including Block (1993), Fry (2003), Greenleaf (1970), Grof (1988), Maslow (1964) and Zohar and Marshall (2000).

Transpersonal leaders need to be Radical because we need a new breed that does not follow the herd. They need to be independent of thought, courageous and fearless. They also need to be Ethical, which means more than just integrity but also a social conscience and willingness to follow the rules (or get them changed if that is required). It means working for the greater good.

Finally, they need to be Authentic, to act as they truly are and transparently. Not only must they be honest with themselves and others but also be the same person in all circumstances. Perhaps most important, their values must act at full consciousness – always in the mind, not buried in the unconscious or left at the door of the office. To enable this, the budding transpersonal leader needs the foundation of EI to provide the inner self-confidence, emotional awareness and empathy so as to be open and fearless in operating in an authentic way. The nine transpersonal steps to develop from the intermediate to the advanced level are shown in Figure 5.2 and described further in Table 5.2.

TABLE 5.2   The journey to Radical Ethical Authentic Leadership

The journey from Robust Emotionally Aware Leadership to **R**adical **E**thically **A**uthentic **L**eadership involves 'the nine steps to transpersonal leadership':

1   *The Eight Integrated Competencies of Leadership (8ICOL®)* The 8ICOL Model has been developed to provide a complete competency framework that supports the transpersonal journey towards leadership excellence. It is a model that integrates rational intelligence (IQ), emotional intelligence (EI) and spiritual intelligence (SI) – the 3Is – together with personal preferences (PP). The model contains eight prime competencies:

   a) personal intellect, logic and intuition

   b) personal preferences

   c) self-awareness

   d) self-management

   e) social awareness

   f) relationship management

   g) self-determination, and

   h) personal conscience.

2   *Neuroscience stage 2* – bringing recent neuro-scientific knowledge into the areas of leadership development.

3   *Intuition, instinct and insights* – understanding the 3Is is critical to decision making and judgement.

4   *Ethical philosophy* – making sense of the three key ethical drivers, which further steer our own decision making and judgement.

5   *Personal conscience* – who I am – uncovered.

6   *Self-determination* – this is all about movement and direction. How do I release myself to get to where I want to be?

7   *Develop transpersonal leadership characteristics* – while transpersonal leadership characteristics are impacted by their context they are altogether more holistic in nature.

8   *Choice* – maybe unique to the human species, we have the ultimate power to choose between right and wrong.

9   *For the greater good – beyond the ego* – once the fundamental choice is made it is a question of making decisions that benefit all stakeholders in the right priority.

And then:
Continue development of behaviours and transpersonal attitudes and mindsets – continually improving leadership skills – Behaviours, Attitudes and Mindsets (BAM) – is a life's work.

FIGURE 5.2   The nine transpersonal steps to develop from the intermediate to the advanced level

REAL Transpersonal leadership development journey to excellence

The development of 8ICOL®

This project was started in 2006 to attempt to incorporate all the competences needed for excellent leadership from the realms of the rational, the emotional and the transpersonal (values and beyond the ego) as well as personal preferences. While EI has proved to be powerful and important in the improvement of leadership development, EI alone is only one step in the development of leadership excellence. We have proven empirically from the implementation of successful leadership programmes and the LEIPA® assessment tool (see Chapters 2, 3 and 4) that the EI approach when well implemented can lead to improved behaviours and leadership competence. However, it does not directly address the value-based and transpersonal aspects of leadership that are critical to attaining leadership excellence.

Considerable investigation into cognitive, emotional, intuitive and ethical concepts and competencies, together with reference to recent research in neuroscience (Harris, 2010) has led to the development of eight broad

FIGURE 5.3   8ICOL® components

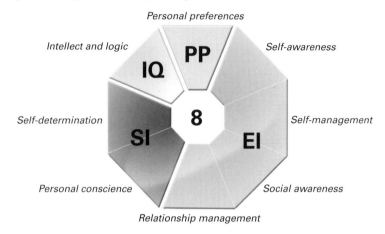

8 Integrated Competencies Of Leadership (8ICOL)®

Rational intelligence	Personality and preferences	Emotional intelligence	Spiritual intelligence
Technical and skills competence	Personal preferences	Self and interpersonal effectiveness	Drives and values

integrated competencies that encompass the full requirements of leadership excellence (Figure 5.3).

Perhaps most important is to split values into 'personal conscience' and 'self-determination'. Personal conscience can be described as 'who I am', whereas self-determination is 'what I am going to do with who I am' – and this is truly the leadership aspect of values. An often raised issue here is that if a leader is only looking to become transpersonal in order to benefit him or herself (or the organization aspires only to profit for the shareholders/ owners without regard to other stakeholders), this is an egocentric and 'non-transpersonal' approach. The reality is that this is often a natural starting point and it is very human to initially seek to become a transpersonal leader for selfish reasons. So even though the transpersonal path is not ultimately about enlightened self-interest, most individuals and organizations begin the journey in that mindset.

However, as individuals and organizations travel on the transpersonal path they eventually reach a different place. They learn that the transpersonal journey is about their own personal transformation, rather than the material or personal gain that comes from it. The reality is that once the focus is about personal transformation, and the leader and organization use the competencies of personal conscience and self-determination for altruistic reasons and become genuinely authentic, the individual and organization become more robust, sustainable and successful. Like other development and journeys, the 'forming, storming, norming, performing' syndrome is common in following a transpersonal path, perhaps with even greater highs and lows.

As discussed earlier in Chapters 2, 3 and 4 leaders can be best assessed using a 360° format. However, some of the more spiritual aspects of transpersonal leadership cannot be assessed by others in the normal way. There are certain aspects such as meaning and beliefs that cannot and should not be assessed by others as they are very individual and beyond the right of another human to question. However, to become a truly transpersonal leader there should be non-judgemental discussion and openness about an individual's understanding of meaning and belief. Regardless, transpersonal leadership has to demonstrate itself in authentic, virtuous behaviours and we see no reason why these aspects cannot be assessed and measured between 'observed' and 'desired' in a 360° format, so that the individual leader can become more aware of his or her transpersonal performance as perceived by others and be able to identify the key areas of development. We would suggest that this feedback is indeed necessary to enable any leader to reach towards the pinnacle of leadership excellence.

The purpose of 8ICOL®

There are three main purposes. The first is to measure all the competences needed for excellent leadership at a granular level. There is a series of statements for each competency and sub-capability that if all were answered 'always' or 'fully competent', then that individual would indeed be an excellent, perhaps even perfect leader. This can be something to aspire to although in practice, of course, unreachable.

The second main purpose is to place these statements in a series of different assessments to be used as appropriate at different steps in the individual's journey of development to leadership excellence. The competencies/ capabilities are separated out into three 360° assessments – one each for IQ (rational intelligence), EI (emotional intelligence) and SI (spiritual intelligence).

The third and last main purpose, and perhaps most important, is to be able to use this competency structure as a foundation for measuring development through a complete set of leadership programmes. A separate module (or multi- or part module) is provided for each sub-capability such that when in an assessment the response to any statement is less than perfect (by the self or other raters), there is a 'how to' module to enable the individual to develop that specific capability.

It should be noted that one of the broad competencies, 'personal preferences', can best be measured by one or more of the well-known self-assessment psychometrics such as Myers Briggs MBTI Step II (**http://www.myersbriggs.org/**), FIRO B and/or Learning Styles questionnaires. Various Myers Briggs publications demonstrate the connection between personality preferences and EI and how the use of coaching (and other interventions) can enable individuals to focus on developing the natural weaknesses of a particular profile. There is also an important input from MBTI Step II into the whole concept of intuition.

The integrated competencies and sub-capabilities

The 8 Integrated Competencies of Leadership (8ICOL®) are as follows and shown in Figure 5.4:

Personal intellect, intuition and logic	IQ/cognitive intelligence
Personal preferences	as in MBTI Step II
Self-awareness	part of EI and SI
Self-management	part of EI and SI
Social awareness	part of EI and SI
Relationship management	part of EI and SI
Self-determination	part of SI
Personal conscience	part of SI

FIGURE 5.4   8ICOL®

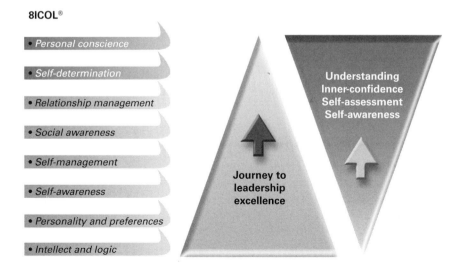

TABLE 5.3   8ICOL® competencies and subsets

8ICOL® COMPETENCIES & SUB_COMPETENCIES

Personal Intellect, Logic & Judgement:
- Problem Analysis
- Verbal Reasoning
- Numerical Analysis
- Creativity
- Analytical/Logic Analysis
- Intuitive Judgement
- Practical Learning
- Strategic Thinking/Planning
- Collecting External Knowledge
- Awareness of the Word Around Us

Personal Preference:
(From MBTI Step II)
- Extroversion vs introversion
- Sensing vs Intuition
- Thinking vs Feeling
- Judging vs Perceiving

Self-awareness:
- Emotional Self-awareness (as per LEIPA®)
- Spiritual Self-awareness
- Accurate Self-assessment (as per LEIPA®)
- Self Confidence (as per LEIPA®)

Self-management:
- Achievement Orientation (as per LEIPA®)
- Optimism (as per LEIPA®)
- Emotional Self-control (as per LEIPA®)
- Transparency (as per LEIPA®)
- Adaptability (as per LEIPA®)
- Initiative (as per LEIPA®)
- Tenacity
- Decisiveness
- Vulnerability
- Spiritual Self-Management

Social Awareness:
- Empathy (as per LEIPA®)
- Organizational Awareness (as per LEIPA®)
- Service Orientation (as per LEIPA®)
- Compassion
- Universal Awareness

Relationship Management:
- Developing Others (as per LEIPA®)
- Inspirational Leadership (as per LEIPA®)
- Influence (as per LEIPA®)
- Change Catalyst (as per LEIPA®)
- Conflict Management (as per LEIPA®)
- Building Bonds (as per LEIPA®)
- Teamwork & Collaboration (as per LEIPA®)
- Communications (as per LEIPA®)
- Delegation
- Empowerment
- Flexibility
- *Spiritual Relationship Mastery*

Self-determination:
- Purpose
- Motivation
- Drive (Intense Will)
- Power
- Energy
- Courage
- Resilience
- Aspirations
- Continuous Development – CPD

TABLE 5.3 *continued*

Personal Conscience:
- Meaning
- Beliefs
- Morals
- Ethical Behaviour
- Values
  - Fairness
  - Trustworthiness
  - Conscientiousness
  - Humility
  - Patience
  - Truth & Honesty
  - Excellence
  - Integrity
  - Forgiveness
  - Altruistic Love

- Principles (Transpersonal Practices)
  - Value led vision
  - Positive use of adversity
  - Holistic Approach
  - Engagement with Diversity
  - Though Independence
  - Asks fundamental Questions
  - Objective Reframing
  - Spontaneity
  - Reflection
  - Sense of Vocation
  - Enjoyment
  - Respect for & Appreciation of Others

As can be seen in Figure 5.4, these eight integral competencies have a natural order for focus as the leader develops towards excellence. These competencies can be broken down into subsets, as listed in Table 5.3. Each subset contains a specific list of statements, some of which are shown in the Tools section later in this chapter.

Developing leadership journeys and appropriate assessments

First of all there are five factors that need to be taken into account.

1 In general, leadership development programmes require the same kind of interventions that are already included in EI leadership development such as coaching, peer group facilitation, action learning, workplace practice, experiential learning and reflection. However, as we move into the more transpersonal and intuitive learning programmes, we also use other interventions such as mindfulness (aka full consciousness), meditation, relaxation exercises, etc.

2 Not all statements in 8ICOL® can be 'rated' by third parties. For example, who can accurately judge, 'Makes career choices based on

a desire to do something worthwhile' other than the individual? Therefore it is has been necessary to carefully decide for each statement whether it can be part of a 360° assessment or not. There is no reason that a single assessment cannot contain a mixture of self-assessment and multi-rater statements. (See the Tool at the end of this chapter for examples of granular statements to be measured.)

3 The measurement of the level of competence and the development required is obtained by asking all raters (the candidate only in the case of self-assessment) to score observed ('How often do I observe this?') and desired ('How often I would like to observe this') as follows:

TABLE 5.4

Numerical value	absolute level of 'observed' and 'desired'
1	Never or almost never
2	Occasionally
3	Quite often
4	Usually
5	Always

Based on our experience with LEIPA® we can identify the following broad categories of how the gap analysis refers to development needs, as provided in the table below. However, what is most important in this context is to identify those few behaviours or attitudes where the gap between 'observed' and 'desired' is greatest. Working on these will have the greatest impact on improving leadership competence:

TABLE 5.5

Performing beyond expectation	less than 0
Performing at expectation	0
Performing close to expectation	less than 0.5
May need improvement	between 0.5 and 1.0
Indicates need for change	between 1.0 and 1.5
May indicate significant shortfall	greater than 1.5

We know that LEIPA® works best where the raters know the candidate well or have a relationship that is interdependent. It is the same or to an even greater extent for behaviours related to transpersonal leadership.

It is important to note that this is not a psychometric assessment and we are less interested in the absolute measurements than in the difference between observed and desired; the larger the difference, the greater the need for development.

4 We have discovered there is a natural order for leadership development. The reason is that most people will not be able to address certain advanced aspects of leadership until they have developed a good sense of inner self-confidence and self-awareness and have become open-minded about trying less familiar approaches – in other words, until they have developed a high level of emotional intelligence! Most managers and leaders will only be comfortable initially with addressing rational/logical development areas because that is primarily what their development has been about at home, at school, at university and even (perhaps especially) at business school.

There is good reason and evidence to believe that LeaderShape's Foundation EI Leadership Programme is a good introduction for leaders who wish to develop beyond 'management'. Through working with Eugene Sadler-Smith at Surrey University on the subject of intuition (Sadler-Smith, 2007; 2009) we have discovered that the understanding and development of 'intuition' is a very good 'connector' between emotional and spiritual development and forms an integral part of the transpersonal journey, together with understanding the role of insights and instincts in our decision making.

5 To make a leadership development programme cost-effective with high value-add for an organization, it is recommended that candidates 'graduate' from the EI 'school' before moving on to the more advanced transpersonal programmes.

With all this in mind, a complete leadership programme might be organized as follows.

Phase 1: Emotional intelligence – towards robust emotionally-aware leadership

1 Foundation EI programme – 3 modules: a) Leadership in the 21st century; b) EI and leadership styles; c) Shaping culture.

2 LEIPA® 360° assessment.

3 Development of EI competencies requiring attention (group or one-to-one depending on needs).

4 Experiential and work-based projects to test the EI development and learning.

5 Re-evaluate further EI learning and repeat mini-LEIPA.

6 The formation of a peer group to encourage continued learning and building of awareness.

Phase 2: Transpersonal – towards Radical Ethically Authentic Leadership

1 Foundation transpersonal programme – 3 modules: a) Moving beyond the ego; b) Transpersonal decision making; c) Choice for the greater good.

2 8ICOL® assessments.

3 Development of transpersonal competencies requiring attention (group or one-to-one depending on needs).

4 Experiential and work-based projects to test transpersonal development/learning.

5 Re-evaluate further transpersonal learning and repeat assessments.

6 The continuation of a peer group to encourage lifelong learning and building of awareness.

Such leadership development programmes are available from organizations such as LeaderShape, either as in-house programmes or in cooperation with the University of Chester, as a series of accredited Postgraduate programmes (from Postgraduate Certificate up to Master's degree).

From 'know' to 'do' – life's journey to excellence

In summary, becoming a REAL transpersonal leader requires:

- Increasing self-awareness and developing emotionally intelligent competencies.
- Developing a range of leadership styles and using them in the right context.
- Learning to create the right climate to enable the right culture.
- Moving beyond the ego for the benefit of all stakeholders.
- Developing an enhanced level of judgement through better use of intuition, insights and instincts.
- Developing ethical authenticity.
- Developing personal conscience and self-determination to full consciousness.
- Understanding choice and working for the greater good.

It is not a simple linear experience. It is iterative, circular and holistic. Self-awareness increases continually at different levels. Behaviours can continue to develop and improve with effort, determination, focus, practice and time. Increased self-awareness and changed behaviours will positively impact attitudes and mindsets.

Developing into a transpersonal leader of the highest level requires intense development over a considerable period of time and it requires hard work. But most leaders have already shown they are determined, hard-working and committed in what they do, so if they decide they want to develop into a transpersonal leader they can probably do it (Syed, 2010)!

SPECIFIC ACTION POINTS

This chapter provides further evidence to Chapter 2 that there is a need for fresh thinking in leadership development. However, for leadership programmes and assessments to be successful it is necessary that the vision and strategy of the organization set clear goals or at least a direction towards sustainability, relationships with stakeholders, corporate responsibility, and development of its people. The Catch 22 is that these things are unlikely to be incorporated in a serious and authentic way unless the organization has transpersonal leaders, but an organization is unlikely to focus on developing transpersonal leaders unless the above mentioned aspects of vision and strategy are actually in place.

In reality there is more chance that the top leaders can be persuaded to invest in the development of the next generation of leaders as 'transpersonal leaders' (either organizational insiders or outsiders) compared to convincing the top leaders that they need (want?) to change and develop more fully their own transpersonal leadership characteristics.

Ideally, the journey towards transpersonal leadership should be embarked on in some way by everyone in the organization, and maybe some time in the future this can happen. But we need to start somewhere, so let us concentrate here on how best to identify and develop the next generation of top leaders. The following is a series of suggested steps to achieve this:

1 Establish a framework of the key characteristics required to be a truly transpersonal leader in your organization. This can be achieved with the following steps:

   - Identify the ideal culture that the leaders and employees in the organizations would like to have. This can be done using the LeaderShape LOCS process. Our experience is that leaders and all staff usually have a similar view about the ideal culture.

   - From this the priority leadership styles to develop the ideal culture can be determined.

   - Once the leadership styles are known, the key EI capabilities can be identified.

- Combine this with the desired core values of the organization, the most important personality traits, and the key intellectual competencies, and a broad framework can be established.

2 Through questionnaires and workshops with current leaders and senior HR executives it is then possible to hone down the core requirements of the next generation of leader.

3 This can be used both to identify candidates for senior leadership positions (internal or external candidates) and as a guide in the design of leadership development programmes.

4 One of the processes to choose suitable candidates is a behavioural interview whereby the core requirements can be checked against previous performance. This is particularly useful to select external candidates who will not be so well known for their behaviours, attitudes and mindsets as internal people.

Of course none of the chosen candidates will meet all the criteria perfectly, so this is an ideal opportunity to make an agreement, a 'contract of expectation and commitment', that to be chosen for development as a potential next generation of senior leader, the candidate has to commit to work on developing those areas where performance has been or is in the future identified as needing improvement. This is a particularly powerful mechanism when employing future leader candidates from outside the organization – they have some idea from the results of the behavioural interviews of what they need to develop in advance of joining the organization.

Once the potential next generation of leaders has been identified they should participate in a programme similar to those outlined in this chapter.

FURTHER RESOURCES

www.leadershape.biz: provides a broad and open resource to leadership development. In particular for this chapter see **http://www.leadershape.biz/emotional-intelligence** and **http://www.leadershape.biz/transpersonal-leadership.**

Stanislav Grof's official website: **http://www.holotropic.com/.**

Sam Harris's official website: **www.samharris.org.**

The Greenleaf Center for Servant Leadership: available at: **http://www.greenleaf.org/whatissl/**, accessed May 2012.

http://dzohar.com/: provides numerous references and information on spiritual intelligence including extending the principles of quantum physics into human consciousness.

http://sqi.co/: a website dedicated to spiritual intelligence.

References

Block, P (1993) *Stewardship: Choosing service over self-interest*, Berret-Koehler, San Francisco, CA

Fry, L W (2003) Toward a theory of spiritual leadership, *The Leadership Quarterly*, **14**, pp 693–727

Greenleaf, R (1970) *Servant Leadership: A journey into the nature of legitimate power and greatness*, Paulist Press, New Jersey

Grof, S (1988) *The Adventures of Self-Discovery: Dimensions of consciousness and new perspectives in psychotherapy and inner exploration*, State University of New York Press, Albany, NY

Harris, S (2010) *The Moral Landscape: How science can determine human values*, Transworld Publishers, London

Knights, J (2012) *The Invisible Elephant and The Pyramid Treasure*, Tomorrows Company, London; a free PDF is available at http://www.leadershape.biz/ielaunch where a hard copy can also be purchased

Maslow, A (1964) *Religions, Values and Peak-Experiences*, Ohio State University Press, Ohio

Sadler-Smith, E (2007) *Inside Intuition*, Routledge, London

Sadler-Smith, E (2009) *The Intuitive Mind: Profiting from the power of your sixth sense*, John Wiley, Chichester

Syed, M (2010) *Bounce: The myth of talent and power or practice*, Fourth Estate, London

Zohar, D and Marshall, I (2000) *Spiritual Intelligence: The ultimate intelligence*, Bloomsbury, London

CASE STUDY   West Midlands Pension Fund

Nadine Perrins,
Head of Pensions Services and Administration,
West Midlands Pension Fund

(Nadine's role includes responsibility at senior management team level for people development as well as the administration of one of the UK's largest local government pension schemes.)

West Midlands Pension Fund (WMPF) is one of the largest funds in the UK primarily serving local government. It has over 257,000 members and 300 scheme employers. The assets of the fund of approximately £9 billion are primarily managed in-house by a team of investment professionals. WMPF is facing unprecedented change because of reforms to the UK pension industry and because of the declining and increasingly competitive core market that is providing members with more pension provider options. Nadine Perrins was recruited to manage the restructure of the organization and the performance and development of the people to meet these changing needs alongside the introduction of a new national pension scheme in 2014.

One goal was to develop the management (leaders) of the future so that the organization could be more flexible and better utilize its human resource capital to improve performance and meet the changing demands of the pensions market. LeaderShape was appointed to provide a transpersonal leadership development programme that included advanced 8ICOL® and LEIPA® self- and 360° assessments, which enabled each candidate to identify key individual and group areas for development as well as individual leadership potential.

Having increased their awareness of self and the effects of their personality preferences, their behaviours and use of values, these assessments, particularly the 360° assessments, helped candidates to identify the specific granular behaviours that would have the greatest impact on their leadership performance.

How does WMPF use assessments for developing leadership talent?

Ground rules

First of all we adopted some key ground rules on assessments for development. Even though WMPF arranged and funded the programme, and allowed the participants the time to prepare and attend, it is primarily the responsibility of the individual to manage his or her own journey of change and development. Therefore, the assessments are owned by the individual and can be considered his or her own development manual for ongoing reference and regular updating. The reasons for this are:

- The assessments are not intended to 'measure' performance to evaluate remuneration but to help the candidate to develop and improve performance. This needs to be done with an external coach who is an expert in the assessment tool.

- Once the raters know that the response is not going to be used by HR or senior managers to 'measure' performance, there is no incentive to give anything other than honest feedback. This significantly increases the value of the exercise compared to standard 360° assessments.

- The candidate will be much more likely to be open to accepting and understanding both negative and positive feedback if it is carried out with the help of an external independent party whose only role is to assist someone to develop to become a better leader.

In summary, the process allows for raters to provide their feedback anonymously (except from the candidate's direct line manager) and for the candidate to keep the data confidential. Individuals are encouraged to share as much information as possible to aid their self-knowledge. They must commit to informing their raters of the key areas of development they have identified and seek their raters' ideas on individual improvement. This involves peers and direct reports in the development of the individual as well as his or her manager, and identified development areas can then be included in the ongoing appraisal system so that the improvement of these behaviours can be observed and reported.

An integrated programme

In this project, WMPF identified around 30 individuals who required development in leadership and three cohorts of nine were run in series (an ideal number for one facilitator to handle alone while providing for mini-groups and sufficient individual airtime). At the time of writing this case study, two cohorts have completed the programme.

Throughout the programme there are various self-assessments on learning styles, leadership styles, EI behaviours and preferred culture styles. However, the main assessment after three Master Classes is to assess the EI behaviours and the competence in different leadership styles and compare this to the importance of each leadership style in the current roles. We established that any one person can only work on improving a couple of behaviours at a time so we used LeaderShape's LEIPA® tool to enable the participants to identify the few behaviours that will have the greatest impact on their leadership performance. They work with their coach to identify how best they can practise the new behaviours and embed new habits.

After the individual LEIPA® exercise, the cohort meets again to discuss the 'team' LEIPA®, which is produced by consolidating the data of all the individual LEIPA®s without disclosing the data of any individual. This allows the cohort to then identify which development areas are common across the group and are therefore useful to work on as a team, and which areas individuals need to develop on their own. Teamwork is both a lower cost per person and more effective overall – they can learn from each other, and it is helpful in creating a more open, supportive culture.

The following Master Classes focus on transpersonal leadership (see definition and description in Chapter 2) where individuals work on how to balance doing the best for themselves with serving all of the organization's stakeholders. During this, the candidates carry out enlightened self-assessments on values relating to both their personal conscience and self-determination. This helps them identify which values and related behaviours they need to bring to generate greater consciousness when taking decisions and in their interactions with other people.

What benefits have been gained?

Most of the participants have been surprised by the results of the LEIPA® assessments as they have identified valuable new behaviours that can become new habits through focus and practice. This is probably because in the previous regime and style of leadership they were not encouraged to create change or show initiative, so never had an opportunity to reach their potential or develop their self-esteem.

The biggest single factor in the development of these new leaders is that most of them have increased their self-confidence and hence self-belief. The online questionnaire also requires raters to answer open questions, for example about individual responsibility and personal opinion. A minority have discovered in an enlightening, and non-blame culture way, that their best career opportunities may lie elsewhere (eg, one person who is excellent technically is perhaps more suited to training than leading). Some who are near to retirement or have specific personal obligations decided that they did not want to make the effort to change even if they agreed with it intellectually. That kind of conscious realization is really important for both the individual and the organization and provides a real transparency for succession planning.

As a group of leaders (though not the same for every individual) we realized our strength was in visionary leadership but that we needed to develop coaching, affiliative and democratic styles and behaviours. This is of course totally in keeping with the need to develop a more inclusive and supportive culture that also improves achievements. We also identified that as a group, each cohort had become a cross-silo team that could be used to make the organization more effective. We also realized that as a group of leaders we needed to focus primarily on developing 'empathy', 'conflict management' and 'developing others' by working on the granular behaviours that had been identified as the key barriers. We were confident we could do that as we were also identified to be 'achievement and service orientated', and 'adaptable'.

The outcome of this is that the large majority of the participants are performing at a higher level, improving the effectiveness of their teams, are more active in leadership across the organization, and have the confidence to respond to the continuous rate of change in the pensions industry.

Learning points

We have found that a process where the reports are confidential to the individual and the input from raters is anonymous, increased the value and validity of the feedback. The fact that the report feedback and subsequent action plan were facilitated by an accredited coach ensured that there was not only real learning about what needed to be developed but that the participants were guided to convert those identified behaviours into new habits.

Often, we find that 360° assessments are done in large numbers without an adequate understanding of the purpose, process or science by either the participants or the raters. The output from the feedback report is often too broad to act on, there is no one to get advice from on 'how' to improve, and often the output is about management competencies rather than leadership behaviours. The process used here overcame all those weaknesses, producing a positive outcome.

The participants were amazed how, with the guidance of their coach, they were able to identify a few granular behaviours that could make a fundamental difference to performance in a leadership style that had been identified to be important for their current job role. For example, one individual identified that increased 'transparency' would improve their visionary style of leadership, the most important style for the role. It is difficult to understand how to improve 'transparency' but when broken down into granular behaviours, it was found that the most important behaviour to improve in this area was supported by the statement 'Does what s/he says s/he will do'. This is a feasible area of improvement.

The key lessons learnt are to follow a process that demonstrates 'best practice' and choose a 360° assessment tool that identifies the granular behaviours that have the greatest impact on leadership performance, which results in value for money!

CASE STUDY   Oxford University Hospitals NHS Trust

Greg Young

In 2010, the appointment of a new chief executive for the Oxford Radcliffe Hospitals NHS Trust, a renowned teaching and research group of hospitals within the UK's National Health Service, saw the implementation of a restructure towards a clinically led organization. In a rigorous selection process, 21 senior clinicians were appointed to lead the operations of the Trust through a structure that comprised six divisions that were envisaged as operating along the lines of business units. By 2012 the Trust had been renamed the Oxford University Hospitals NHS Trust (OUH) acknowledging its relationship with the University as a teaching hospital and reflecting their combined ambition to become recognized as an Academic Health Science Network. OUH is one of the best known research and teaching hospitals in Europe and has a world class reputation in many fields. Today, OUH's key statements of intent are:

> We aim to be at the core of a world leading, innovative academic health science system, working in partnership locally, nationally and internationally to deliver excellence in compassionate healthcare, education and research [and] We plan to do this by means of clinical leadership; staff engagement, wellbeing and development; good governance and assurance; and continuing work to improve outcomes for our patients and value for money for taxpayers and those who commission our services.

This case study is about the leadership development of the 21 newly appointed clinicians. LeaderShape was appointed in 2010 to deliver a programme for the five divisional directors and 15 clinical directors. Influence, behaviour, confidence, technical skills and knowledge – these were the touchstones and concerns that emerged, as discussions began about how to turn these diverse and very experienced individuals into a coherent team of organizational leaders.

The leadership development programme and use of assessments

The clinician leaders and their needs

The participants in the programme covered a broad range of levels and types of leadership experience. A few were highly experienced with significant management experience and heading towards their professional retirement, whereas for some individuals, this was their first significant leadership post beyond management responsibilities within their specific clinical areas.

LeaderShape recognized that it needed a customized approach for this clinical audience. In particular it was anticipated that senior and experienced doctors, many of whom were global figures in their fields, both clinically and academically, would require a programme that was fast paced, appropriately pitched intellectually, and immediately relevant. We found that:

- Doctors need to see an early value in activities they undertake.

- Concepts were grasped quickly so material needed to be presented with style and pace.

- Some participants were not natural reflectors and needed strong directive facilitation to participate; once they did so, the vast majority appreciated the value of learning from each other and hearing all voices.

- Most participants were initially sceptical about the value of assessments used, namely MBTI Step II (Myers Briggs Type Indicator) and LEIPA 360° but enjoyed the process and found it gave them great insights into themselves and others.

- Some were not initially comfortable with being coached but most did enjoy the opportunity to reflect on challenges they were facing. By the end of the coaching programme most acknowledged it to be of real value.

At the same time the Trust was developing strategic planning processes and establishing new governance structures to increase effectiveness, avoid duplication and support organizational change. So these and other technical and business areas, such as quality control, patient care, finance and marketing also needed to be covered in the programme.

Running the programme

Once the programme had been established, an early issue arose regarding specific concerns common to almost all these clinicians in their new roles. These included: tackling difficult conversations, dealing with colleagues' behaviour or resistance to change, addressing colleagues' performance, challenges regarding job planning and appraisal, managing an avalanche of e-mails, prioritizing demands because of too little time, and personal confidence in areas outside their professional comfort zone.

LeaderShape adopted a flexible 'action learning' approach to the programme, to facilitate a team orientation and allow group work to find solutions. These were often quite informal (sometimes working over lunch). The overwhelming majority of the participants appreciated these so-called 'Hot Topic' sessions and generally commented that they provided an opportunity for all voices to be heard and avoided discussions being dominated by one or two individuals with strong opinions.

Once solutions had been discovered, many of the clinical leaders found benefit in being able to discuss during the coaching sessions 'how' they could implement the solutions. Often this required learning new behaviours to handle situations and people in different ways. They realized that as organizational leaders with many stakeholders to serve they needed to operate differently than as masters (or mistresses) of their expert domain (eg an operating theatre). This is where the LEIPA 360° assessment tool added value as it helped them identify their 'best' and 'need for development' behaviours according to different groups of raters – their peers might have one perspective and the people who reported to them another. It emphasized the fact that they needed to learn to use different leadership styles than the ones they were used to, especially the coaching style, which would over time allow them to delegate more responsibility and allow them to focus on top priorities.

Programme details

The programme consisted of the following main strands:

- Completion of a Myers Briggs (Step II) Type Indicator questionnaire (as an extended self-awareness exercise) and a one-hour facilitated feedback session.

- An introductory workshop – two days for divisional directors and one day for clinical directors.

- Four one-to-one coaching sessions spread over six months, which included completing LeaderShape's proprietary LEIPA® 360° leadership assessment.

- Seven full day workshops: these generally included 40 per cent on behavioural leadership, 40 per cent on strategy and operational knowledge, and the remainder on Hot Topics and reviews of the day.

- Supporting materials including reading lists, workshop hand-outs, preparatory exercises, workbooks and follow-up reference materials.

The workshops consisted primarily of facilitated discussions, team coaching and group work to promote learning and development through personal and shared insights. There was limited formal teaching on EI, shaping cultures and change management. Knowledge was primarily acquired through the preparatory reading and exercises, allowing the maximum time for the group to learn together. Corporate directors and other senior managers of OUH were involved in preparing, presenting and leading discussions in all the technical workshops, facilitated by LeaderShape faculty.

The MBTI Step II was completed prior to the introductory workshop and coaching sessions spread across the programme. The LEIPA® 360° assessment was conducted towards the end of the programme once the participants had a better understanding of their role and the key issues. This provided an action plan for ongoing development.

What benefits have been gained?

The clinician leaders who participated in the programme have benefited in the following ways:

- Obtained a working vision and understanding of shared values.

- Individuals who previously did not know each other are now used to supporting and challenging one another, coming to a consensus and taking initiative jointly.

- The beginnings of greater trust and understanding between corporate and clinical leaders.
- Realization of the scope and scale of clinical leadership roles.
- Exploration of key issues such as job planning and appraisal of medical staff.
- Acquisition of coaching skills.

In addition:

94 per cent of participants at the end of the programme agreed or strongly agreed they were confident they had the leadership skills to perform well;

80 per cent felt that participation in the programme had increased their self-awareness and nearly 95 per cent that it had extended their range of leadership styles;

88 per cent felt that it had helped them to change their own behaviour;

70 per cent felt it had improved their ability to influence others and helped them tackle difficult conversations;

88 per cent felt it had deepened their understanding of the leader's role;

82 per cent believed it had increased their effectiveness;

95 per cent felt it had helped them to think more about the development needs of their own team.

Learning points

One of the key learning points is that although all leaders needed to learn to adopt the method used to create the insights that initiate a change in behaviours, the approach depends on the participants and the context and therefore needs to be customized. A group of clinician leaders is very different to a team of leaders from a firm of accountants, or from a university, or from a recruitment firm. But what we have also learnt is that the key EI development areas are fairly common to all leadership groups. These are: empathy, change catalyst, developing others, conflict management, and inspirational leadership.

Another important learning point from this project was the confirmation of the value of integrating behavioural leadership and operational management into the same day where this is practical and part of the remit. Limiting the amount of time on one subject allows for better absorption and retention of the facts and a greater chance that the participants will put learning into action.

Leaders who have learnt through their professional experience and roles, as well as their own inclination, to be directive and authoritative are willing and able to move to more collaborative and participate styles of leadership if they understand the benefit of doing so. The skill is in providing the right environment and stimulus for participants to gain their own insights.

TOOL   Values self-assessment questionnaire

John Knights

What it is and when to use it

This is a self-assessment tool that is used as one of the learning exercises to create greater self-awareness in the journey to the advanced level of transpersonal leadership development. It measures those values that have been shown to be the most often desired in employee surveys and references (eg Collins, 2001) and are split between values of personal conscience and those that are special to leadership (self-determination).

Figure 5.5 shows the programme that takes leaders through the development of the nine steps of transpersonal leadership towards the advanced level of Radical Ethical Authentic Leadership. More details can be found early in this chapter and in Knights (2012).

Although there is no substitute for a complete 360° assessment, during step 1 of the advanced transpersonal leadership development journey, where participants discuss the 8ICOL®, they are provided with a self-assessment taster so they begin to understand what will be required to develop their values and bring them to full consciousness in everything they do.

FIGURE 5.5   The nine steps of transpersonal leadership

© LeaderShape 2012. All rights reserved

Using the values self-assessment questionnaire

The process is to ask participants to complete the questionnaire shown in Figure 5.6, giving them the following instructions.

Instructions

Against each statement score yourself from 1 to 5 according the listing below as to how often you perform/achieve the behaviours described in the questionnaire:

1   Never or almost never

2   Occasionally

3   Quite often

4   Usually

5   Always

To get the full value from this exercise try to be honest and objective. The completed forms will be retained by you, and you only share the information you wish to.

Complete the sub-totals and totals for each section as marked.

Now complete the blank rows as follows:

X = Values – Personal conscience

A = Trustworthiness

B = Truth and honesty

C = Integrity

D = Humility

Y = Values – Self-determination

E = Motivation

F = Drive (intense will)

G = Courage

You now have a complete picture of your own assessment of your competence in seven values, four of which are key values of personal conscience, and three of which are important values of self-determination.

You can rate your competence in personal conscience as follows:

The maximum score is 95.

If you have 76 or above, you have a highly developed level of personal conscience but may still need to work on bringing some specific aspects to full consciousness.

If you have 57–76, you have a good level of personal conscience but may need some further development.

If you score 38–57, some improvement is probably needed to be a transpersonal leader.

If you scored less than 38, a significant improvement is needed.

You can also rate your competence in self-determination as follows:

The maximum score is 60.

If you have 48 or above, you have a highly developed level of self-determination but may still need to work on bringing some specific aspects to full consciousness.

If you have 36–48, you have a good level of self-determination but may need some further development.

If you score 24–36, some improvement is probably needed to be a transpersonal leader.

If you scored less than 24, a significant improvement is needed.

(Note: Most leaders in our experience will have a higher rating, eg, 'natural', 'good', 'some improvement', 'significant improvement', in self-determination than in personal conscience.)

Finally, take a look at the granular behaviours where you scored lowest compared to your other scores. What would it take for you to improve these scores? Choose one, two or three granular behaviours to work on to improve your transpersonal leadership.

Most will agree that it is much easier to work on improving a specific granular behaviour such as 'Does not make commitments unless s/he strongly believes it will happen' rather than something as broad as 'integrity' where most would just assume they have high integrity without questioning their granular behaviour.

Depending on the situation and how open your organization is, candidates can discuss the results with colleagues, with their mentor, or perhaps best of all with their coach. Our experience is that this exercise creates real insights even though candidates are assessing themselves. One should of course make the point that the result of the questionnaire is only their view – what would the people they work with say?

This is an area where some leaders will be reluctant to do a full 360° assessment even though the information will be confidential to them. This is almost always based on fear (Rossiter, 2006), the most insidious emotion and most difficult to overcome, but critical to becoming a transpersonal leader.

FIGURE 5.6 Values self-assessment

8ICOL® – VALUES SELF-ASSESSMENT			
X			
A			
1	Treats people with respect and dignity		
2	Trusts others to do a good job		
3	Can be trusted to keep a confidence		
4	Cares about the people in the organization		
5	Has high moral standards and can be trusted to be ethical		
6	Can be trusted to do a good job for the company		Sub-Total
B			
7	What he/she says is believed		
8	Encourages others to give timely and honest feedback		
9	Discusses with people in advance of decisions that will affect them		
10	Communications to all stakeholders give a true and complete account		Sub-Total
C			
11	Acts in a way that is consistent with stated values		
12	Does not make commitments unless s/he strongly believes it will happen		
13	Does what s/he says s/he will do when s/he says s/he will do it		
14	Provides early full communication if a commitment cannot be kept		Sub-Total
D			
15	Acknowledges own limitations		
16	Accepts and appreciates negative feedback from others		
17	When he/she makes a mistake, accepts it gracefully, proactively and learns from it		
18	Happy to recognise he/she is only one of the players in the group/team		
19	Believes own importance/success comes from luck and timing as well as own capabilities		Sub-Total
		Total	A – D
Y			
E			
20	Believes in carrying out duties as well as possible		
21	Feels there is value and worth in his/her role		
22	His/her role gives real satisfaction and enjoyment		
23	Actively provides environment to motivate others		Sub-Total
F			
24	Has determination to strive for goals that have been accepted		
25	Encourages and supports others to reach agreed goals		
26	Actively takes on barriers and hurdles to reach goals		
27	Usually finds a win:win way around obstacles		Sub-Total
G			
28	Applies resources in creative ways when faced with overwhelming odds		
29	Confronts situations with the confidence to ultimately succeed		
30	Has the ability to confront without fear of the consequences		
31	Follows own ethical standards regardless of the result		Sub-Total
		Total	E – G

References

Collins, J (2001) *Good to Great: Why some companies make the leap... and others don't*, Harper Business, London

Knights, J (2012) *The Invisible Elephant and The Pyramid Treasure*, Tomorrows Company, London

Rossiter, A (2006) *Developing Spiritual Intelligence: The power of you*, O Books, New Alresford

TOOL   The Mindfulness Triangle

Tony Wall

What it is and when to use

A simple way of thinking about mindfulness is as an outcome – a mental (and physical) state of peacefulness in the mind, which has significant effects for being able to deal with situations that might be challenging. A route to this outcome is through continuous practice, or through a process of mindfulness. Carefully paying attention through mindfulness can be applied to almost any activity, as long as it does not jeopardize a person's own health and safety, or that of others.

Shapiro and Carlson (2009) provide a more thorough resource on mindfulness and a very useful way of thinking about the subject. I think of their three characteristics of mindfulness as the Mindfulness Triangle: a way to mindfully pay attention to a particular situation. The three aspects, which can be seen as a simple process to engage in, are described below (see also Figure 5.7). Another way of looking at is 'bringing everything to full consciousness'. Purpose and judgement are always there, playing behind the scenes in our subconscious or unconscious mind. Mindfulness is about bringing these sub-, non- and un-conscious thoughts into full consciousness – and paying attention to them.

On purpose, with purpose – paying attention, on purpose, with a purpose; being clear about a particular outcome that you want. An example might be becoming more self-aware of our reactions or responses to things, in a much more attuned way, where we can sense the start of a particular trigger and an associated, unproductive behaviour. Another outcome might be to explore why we feel in a particular way in order to become attuned to our unconscious and create an intimate knowing or self-awareness.

Paying attention – paying attention to the physical sensations in and outside of us, and becoming intimately attuned to what is happening in our body and around it. When we are focused on the immediacy of these things, one thing at a time, we are not focused on other things, like the past (which is in the past and therefore cannot be changed) or the future (which might never happen).

In paying attention to breathing, for example, we can pay attention to our nostrils, to the temperature of the air that enters our nostrils and leaves our nostrils, to the lifting and the lowering of our chests. There is a real richness to the sense we can pay attention to.

A key mantra here is to accept that our mind will be distracted, allow it to happen and 'let go' of any idea that it should be any other way. Allow it, accept it and let go of the distraction. Let it peacefully move along, without frustration. This means it is crucial to

FIGURE 5.7   The Mindfulness Triangle

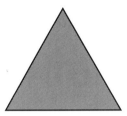

On purpose, with purpose

What outcome do I want?

Paying attention

What can I feel right now?
See right now? Hear right now?
Sense right now?

Without judgement

Look, see, feel, sense.

No judgement,
interpretation, or evaluation

know *how* we pay attention – without judgement. Paying attention is a particular technique that enables us to be calm while energizing our brain.

Without judgement – without judgement, interpretation or evaluation. This takes practice, but over time it is possible to make sense of things from a different perspective. This new perspective becomes more sensitive to the additional psychological filters and processing we develop over time to deal with events. And in doing so, we are able to sense more of a situation without these filters, and gain more access to information from our unconscious. From such a place, we can make less emotionally attached decisions, which can lead to more productive responses and behaviours.

Using the Mindfulness Triangle

This might appear a simple process – it is. There is a large variety of mindfulness processes to choose from, but these are useful principles to remember and apply in everyday tasks. The scientific results are generally impressive for such simple processes (see Shapiro and Carlson, 2009, as a starting point).

You can use the Mindfulness Triangle yourself, or share it with people who may want to explore their responses to situations. The starting point might be the top of the triangle – figuring out what they want from their mindfulness practice; this becomes the mantra before a mindfulness practice. Then, it is about spotting times and occasions to pay attention – without judgement.

Reference

Shapiro, S and Carlson, L E (2009) *The Art and Science of Mindfulness: Integrating mindfulness into psychology and the helping professions*, American Psychological Association, Washington, DC

06

Feeding (back and) forwards for talent development

TONY WALL and DANIELLE GRANT

EXECUTIVE SUMMARY

We have all received feedback about some aspect of our performance, about a particular behaviour, a talent, or maybe something a lot more personal. When it is done badly, it can create not just a demotivated workforce with low morale, but it can also impact the bottom line – increased staff turnover, absence and even litigation. When it is done with the intention to authentically help people learn and grow – or move forward in some way – it can significantly and positively contribute to the creation of a highly motivated, creative and innovative environment. This is an environment where people feel free to share ideas and commit to their organization's goals.

This chapter identifies some key principles and practices for giving feedback in a way to 'feed forward' to develop talents and performance. It draws on research from brain science (see, for example, Rock and Schwartz, 2006), which tells us that there are five key areas to consider when giving feedback. Each can contribute to an optimal psychological state to be able to receive and action the feedback being offered – or, conversely, close down and stifle any talent development and ongoing relations. Rock's (2008) SCARF model helps shape what and how feedback is offered. The five areas are: status, certainty, autonomy, relatedness and fairness. Key questions in relation to each of these are:

- How might *what is said* affect a person's sense of SCARF?
- How might the *way it is said* affect a person's sense of SCARF?
- How might *where feedback is offered* affect a person's sense of SCARF?
- How might *who offers the feedback* affect a person's sense of SCARF?
- How might *how feedback is offered* affect a person's sense of SCARF?

Making feedback feed forward through to enhanced performance

The importance of feedback

Can you remember one of the best bits of news you got from someone, which was about you? Now can you remember one of the worst bits of news from someone? A key theme emerging from brain science over the last decade or so is the overarching organizing principle of maximizing reward and minimizing threat (Gordon, 2000); in other words, we work *towards* things (pleasure) or *away* from other things (pain). We also now know that there is another response – paralysis – where we keep still until we are out of the situation that caused it. The organizing principle is a major influence on how we make decisions or behave (Dixon *et al*, 2010).

What is fascinating about the towards-away responses is that they can apply to all areas of life – driving a car, being in a conflict situation at work, having to deal with decisions in relationships. And it is particularly relevant to the context of going through a rigorous leadership assessment process (as in any feedback process) – from the perspective of the person being assessed, there is a large opportunity for pain. That is, social pain, but this is irrelevant to the brain – from the brain's perspective, the potential physical pain of breaking an arm or burning a hand on an iron, can be processed in the same way as the potential of perceived, social pain received through feedback.

Drawing on this brain science research, Rock (2008) developed the SCARF model. Each of the letters refers to a 'domain of human experience', which can activate towards-away responses, and therefore is a useful way to think about feeding back. The focus, or goal, of the feedback is an approach to keep the person in more of a *towards* state, which is a state that can more readily accept, deal with and act on the feedback that is being offered. In other words, it enables the feedback to feed-forward into future practice. In this way it is a conscious strategy to maximize the value from the leadership assessment, or indeed any other situations of giving feedback. The SCARF model is:

Status	one's sense of importance in relation to others.
Certainty	one's sense of being able to predict the future.
Autonomy	one's sensed ability to control events.
Relatedness	one's sense of safety with others, or a feeling that an interaction is with more of a friend than a foe.
Fairness	one's sense of being treated fairly in any exchanges (communication, decision making, etc).

The next section outlines some key strategies that are specifically designed to establish and maintain a *towards* state, to enable feedback to be taken forward with motivation and commitment. Examples are given for each strategy, but it is important that those who feed back practise and hone their skills in each. Dixon *et al* (2010) also provide other strategies.

Status

Key strategies for being sensitive to Status include framing and the development sandwich, which focuses on behaviours rather than the person.

Framing refers to the angle on which we look at something: is the glass half full or half empty? Was the team member almost late or did they actually achieve the deadline? Within feed back, to focus on the lack can jolt motivation, commitment and relationships – and to acknowledge achievement can establish or maintain a *towards* state to receive the messages within the feedback. This approach might be difficult to maintain when the person giving feedback strongly believes in a particular way of looking at something – but it is important to be clear about the intention of feedback: within our experience, to authentically hold the *intention* of helping the person to grow their talents is crucial. The person giving feedback might feel an element of their own SCARF has been attacked in some way, but they need to be aware of this before giving feedback.

Example of framing

After undertaking a leadership assessment process, Jack decided to develop his ability to regulate his emotions during meetings. Jenny is Jack's manager, and notices he can still have outbursts in manager meetings. Using an achievement frame, she says:

> *Thanks for that sales report, Jack. It's really clear. By the way, thank you for letting me sit in on one of your sales team meetings last week – your new style seems to work well with the team. I see you brought out Jim's ideas skilfully. And you also contributed really good ideas in the manager meeting this morning; what do you think?*

This provides an opportunity for Jack to share his thoughts in a supported space. The last question points to the manager meetings, subtly guiding Jack's attention to that topic.

The 'development sandwich' is a tried-and-tested strategy that focuses on giving praise, followed by the development area, followed by praise again. It is a useful strategy to encourage people into a *towards* state, through praise and appreciation. This works on the psychological ideas of the primacy effect (the first thing you hear sticks) and the recency effect (the last thing you hear sticks). In the middle, the sandwich filling, is a development area of behaviour or action, rather than personal things or things the individual cannot change. Have you ever heard of someone being asked to be less jolly? Or be criticized for being too tall or small? It happens – such stories hit the newspapers.

Example of the development sandwich

Combining framing and the development sandwich, Jenny might have said:

> *Thanks for that sales report, Jack. It's really clear. Thanks for letting me sit in on one of your sales team meetings – I like how your new approach seems to work well with the team – especially with Jim. You really enabled him to contribute his ideas. I also really liked your idea in the manager meeting this morning. How do you feel it went?*

This is the praise, plus opportunity to raise a development area in a *towards* state. Jack replies with some ideas, but did not mention the outburst. Jenny might reply:

> *Yes, I think they are useful ideas. And I think you handled John's comments very calmly, which was great because it was a controversial idea. Were there any points where you think you could have responded differently to suggestions from others?*

Again, praise and opportunity to raise a development area. Another opportunity for Jack to respond in a *towards* state, but more pointed. If Jack does not raise it, Jenny might reply:

> *Yes, I like how you responded to John's ideas. I wonder what the outcome would have been if you responded in the same way to the new sales idea at the end?*

Praise and opportunity to consider alternative options – a subtle and positively framed way to direct attention to a development area. Jack might suggest ideas, and Jenny may then close the feedback with the praise:

> *Well, I think they are really useful ideas. I think you are making great progress – like I say, the way you are conducting your sales meetings, and the way you responded to John are a real credit to you, well done.*

A SCARF-unfriendly version might be to say: 'Jack you are still losing control of yourself in manager meetings. It makes you look stupid. Stop it, now!' Perhaps you could imagine your own natural reaction to this? This is a much quicker and direct response, but re-read the version above, imagining you are Jack.

Certainty

Key strategies for being sensitive to certainty include setting well-formed outcomes and modelling/exemplifying behaviours – all helping the person know what is in the future through clarity and precision in thinking. 'Well-formed outcomes' refers to setting goals in a way that is clear and measurable. Being SMART is another similar concept (Specific, Measurable, Achievable, Realistic and Time-bound). There are different versions of well-formed outcomes, but Dilts and DeLozier's (2000) version highlights five key conditions:

1 Be stated in positive terms – so that the focus of attention is on the thing that is desired (a *towards* state) rather than an issue (an *away* state).

2 Be defined and evaluated in terms of perceivable evidence – so that the person developing his or her talents, and the facilitator guiding him or her, can establish growth towards the goal.

3   Be contextualized (ie consider specifically when, where and who with) – so that it is clear which outcome is wanted, and where the behaviour is useful. For example, it might be useful to shout assertively in some situations, such as when a fire breaks out and it is important to get people out of danger.

4   Be initiated and maintained by the person that desires the goal – so that he or she can feel a sense of ownership, and is motivated *towards* it.

5   Preserve any positive by-products of the current situation (ie consider what might be lost and whether it is worth it) – so that there are no unintended negative consequences of the new state or behaviour. Behaviours can have benefits that might be unknown or unconscious, and replacing them could lead to new, destructive behaviours.

Example of a well formed outcome

Jack might have discussed the following outcome with his facilitator:

I want to stop having outbursts all the time.

Positive? No! An alternative might be: *I want to stay calm.*

Perceivable evidence? No! An alternative might be: *I want to say the positives and the areas to develop when people offer ideas.*

Appropriately contextualized? No! How about: *Specifically, in monthly sales manager meetings when responding to others' ideas.*

Initiated and maintained by Jack? Yes! Jack expressed it.

Preserve any positive by-products of the present situation (what will be lost and is it worth it?) After exploring this, Jack explains that he feels that the 'outbursts' give him a sense of status in the meetings. So Jack needs to find a way to still achieve that sense of status using a different behaviour – otherwise it might reappear in more aggressive attempts.

A SCARF-unfriendly version of an outcome might be: to stop having outbursts all the time. The lack of clarity makes it difficult to know exactly what it is and to measure any progress towards it – but places the attention on the behaviour to be avoided. This is an unhelpful *away* state.

Modelling or exemplifying is about showing the person about a desired state or behaviour, rather than telling them. Imagine telling a person to 'be calmer' or 'be more enthusiastic'! Showing gives the person a lot more sensory data (visual, auditory, kinaesthetic), with their subtle nuances, than telling, which focuses primarily on words and sounds. This is particularly helpful to show nuances or to share the specific desired behaviours with people who have not personally experienced that behaviour.

Example of modelling or exemplifying

In modelling the behaviour, Jenny may ask Jack to observe her, or someone else in the manager meetings, and ask him to focus on:

- The visual cues – what does the person do, specifically? What are the expressions on their face during the meeting? Where does the person put their hands? How do they sit in the chair?

- The auditory cues – what does the person say, and how? What tones are used? How fast do they talk? What words are used? What frames are used (see above)? How do they use silence?

- The kinaesthetic cues – what are you feeling in your body as you observe the meeting?

- The outcomes – what are other people's reactions to the above during the meeting?

Autonomy

Key strategies for being sensitive to autonomy include allowing for a range of priorities or approaches, such that people feel that it is their choice if and how to proceed and they have ownership and accountability. This requires the facilitator not to have a preconceived 'fix'; to be genuinely open to different ways of undertaking the task and cognisant that what may seem obvious and easy to him or her could be entirely out of character for the client.

Consider how you react to being 'told' what and how to do something. The risk of being prescriptive in the feedback process is that the message is disregarded because the client feels the solution is being imposed and, consequently, throws the 'baby out with the bath water'. In a situation where people feel that the entire process has been forced on them by their organization, they may well come to the feedback predisposed to resist.

Key points here echo those in the previous section, given that the way the person chooses actions to take forward is a key part of creating areas of certainty. Using a framework whereby coachees choose something they want to move towards (positive), that can be measured or identified (perceivable), that is relevant to them in their world (contextualized) and that can be practised or an example can be identified (exemplified) is key to providing ownership and responsibility for action.

Example of a discussion providing autonomy

Jack might have discussed the priority areas pinpointed by the LEIPA® 360° with his facilitator. The facilitator might have a clear view on what he or she feels the key point is, but the skill is to remain sensitive to the autonomy of the individual, so the conversation might be:

'So, Jack, of the development areas in this report, which do you feel would be most valuable to prioritize?' *This allows Jack to choose an area – it may be appropriate to challenge this if the facilitator has a strong sense that the 'easiest path' is being chosen without addressing other areas where the message from the data was stronger.*

A challenge that threatens autonomy might be 'But you are ignoring the evidence that developing your team scores higher in your report than developing your initiative' *An alternative might be:* 'What did you make of the comments about initiative?' *then, depending on where that leads, perhaps following up with:* 'How do you feel about the feedback about developing your team?'

This approach allows Jack to identify any shortfall in his own thinking, and leaves him with the decision. The next stage is to ask Jack to break his actions into specific, defined stages. This part of the process reinforces the desired outcomes Jack is working *toward* (positively desired), measures of success (perceivable evidence), a defined situation where the new behaviour will be practised (context) and, if appropriate, providing a safe space for 'rehearsal' with the facilitator (exemplified).

Sometimes there are consequences contingent upon a particular choice made by the client. For example, if undertaking some independent research or additional work would enrich the choices or improve the outcomes potentially open to the individual, the facilitator might legitimately outline that option but allow the client the autonomy to choose freely whether to 'go the extra mile' in the knowledge of the benefits and limitations of that choice. This is a particularly difficult challenge for a line manager who may have a vested interest in directing towards a particular output or outcome that, in his or her view is beneficial.

The issue of autonomy is supported by ideas from psychological models such as organizational transactional analysis (Phillips, 2005). The aspect that is relevant here is that of 'ego states', which states that each of us carries an internal 'parent', 'adult' and 'child'. These 'ego states' each have distinct characteristics, both negative and positive. The parent is an amalgamation of our experiences from our own parent-figures and can be 'nurturing' (praise and recognition as a positive aspect or smothering and over-protective as a negative) or can be 'critical' which, as the name suggests, offers negative feedback and criticism or, in a positive mode, provides structure. The adult is a moderating, analytical element that is unemotional and manages logical interactions (so it does not have a positive or negative aspect). The 'child' can be an 'adaptive' child, which in its negative aspect is rebellious or recalcitrant, or in positive mode can be cooperative and compliant. The 'natural child' can provide energy, enthusiasm and imagination in its positive aspect, or can be rowdy or over-emotional in its negative aspect. In the context of autonomy the interaction can be seen to be about using an adult-adult approach to the process of developing people. The more directive pathway is likely to evoke a critical parent-adaptive child response – hardly surprising if it leads to resentment or rebellion!

Ultimately, I am reminded of the old adage of 'you can lead a horse to the water but you can't make it drink'. Attending to the SCARF implications of feedback by allowing autonomy sets up the conditions where the 'horse' will decide to drink!

Relatedness

Key strategies for being sensitive to relatedness include ensuring that the client feels confident with the facilitator; the client needs to be able to trust that the facilitator is 'on my side' and supportive. We all know what it feels like to be the last person chosen for the football or netball teams in the playground – it's not nice, is it? Relatedness is about creating a place of safety and support so that challenges are seen as appropriate and not as judgemental. Relatedness is about making that human connection, being fallible and transparent as a facilitator and framing questions in a way that is warm rather than harsh.

There is a fine balance to this because it is not about being a 'pal' and unconditionally, uncritically supportive (which is collusive). Some of this is about finding common ground and building rapport in a natural way. It is more challenging to do this if the first time the client and facilitator meet is at the feedback session, because the client may be apprehensive going in and therefore less open to establishing trust and confidence.

Nevertheless, while it is very valuable to have met the client prior to the feedback session, with skill relatedness can still be established. Simply put, it starts with body language: making eye contact, a comfortably firm handshake, smiling and perhaps sharing appropriate humour or discovering shared interests. This activity generates oxytocin in both parties, which is a bonding hormone and has been hailed as the 'empathy gene' (see Paul Zak PhD, **http://youtube/gZualGYWQFk**).

Example of a discussion providing relatedness

A good way to start off the discussion following building that initial connection is to use 'clean language' (see Grove, **http://www.businessballs.com/clean_language.htm**) so asking a question such as 'So what would you like to happen today?' as a precursor to speaking about the feedback gives the client a sense that the facilitator is there to help achieve that outcome (therefore is 'on my side').

An example of how to *not* create a sense of relatedness would be: 'So, Jack, as you can see from the data you are really deficient in empathy – you need to think about how others feel.' This makes Jack feel judged and failing relative to others. A better way to tackle the issue in a way that supports relatedness might be to say: 'Jack, what do you think these scorings around empathy are telling you?' Then, drawing attention to the key points, follow up with a question such as: 'What is the specific focus within the empathy area where an improvement would most impact your performance?' It is important to make him understand his scores are not unusual by saying, 'This is very typical of high performing executives, because our accumulated data shows that a majority of LEIPA® respondents have empathy within their top few development areas. How do you see that playing out for you? How can I best support you in taking that forwards?'

This makes a huge difference to relatedness in that Jack feels his results are normalized vs others in similar positions and he has an explicit offer of support. Maintaining a warm persona, good eye contact (not excessive, staring down or challenging) and smiling are all-important ingredients in sustaining relatedness and the *towards* state it helps engender.

Fairness

Key strategies in ensuring fairness include establishing clear and mutual understanding of the process and 'ground rules' at the start. In coaching terms this is about 'contracting'. To paraphrase what Rock (2008) states:

> unfair exchanges generate a strong threat response [that] sometimes includes activation of the insular, a part of the brain involved in intense emotions such as disgust... People who perceive others as unfair don't feel empathy for their pain, and in some instances, will feel rewarded when others who are seen as being unfair are punished.

This explains why we feel such satisfaction when somebody we perceive to be unfair receives their 'comeuppance'. In normal circumstances most of us would find no pleasure in the discomfort of another but the feelings of hostility aroused by a perception of unfairness are some of the most powerful we experience. This can be illustrated by the low level of disapproval for the wronged spouse who has cut up the clothing of a cheating ex, frequently arousing an observer's smile rather than a frown!

In the context of this chapter, this should start with the initial commitment to the assessment and feedback development process between the organization and the individual. The purpose and aims of the programme need to be articulated and understood and an opportunity given for questions or challenges to be openly dealt with. The process itself should also adhere to good practice, so that confidentiality is paramount and nobody involved in either the rating (if it is a 360° assessment) or as a candidate has any doubt about how the information will be dealt with and disseminated. This means having sufficient raters providing feedback to aggregate their responses so that no individual scores may be singled out (other than the boss's); clearly this principle follows through to the entire process of analysis, feedback and development planning. In the LEIPA® 360° process, the fairness is further underpinned through the individual feedback with a facilitator who can be questioned about information and its relative importance, rather than having a computer-generated analysis that can leave individuals feeling 'judged' with no voice of their own.

In addition, there is the framework that supports candidates in discussing their chosen development priorities with their raters, gaining clarification on any points directly, and requesting further and ongoing feedback on the action plan. This is fair because it is framed in the initial process agreement, it underpins the value of the raters' input (fair to the raters and invests them in the development process), and fundamentally is fair to the candidates in being able to gain all the understanding they feel they need of what lies beneath the data.

An example of a discussion that provides a framework of fairness

So, Jack, the LEIPA® feedback process was explained to you at the outset, by your line manager and during the briefing session. As we go through the report, I will help you pull out key themes that emerge for you. Please stop me at any point you feel important so we can dig into the data and clarify an understanding. Questions so far?

A less fair way to deal with the situation would be either a printed report with no explanation or discussion to provide a judgement on the person, or something along these lines:

Right Jack, I don't know what you know about this process, but now I'm going to give you the heads-up on what your colleagues really make of you. You have scored OK on most things, but you've certainly rubbed a couple of people up the wrong way!

I hope nobody reading this chapter would dream of offering feedback in such a patently one-sided and unfair way (what does 'OK' really mean in this context, anyway?) This will automatically make Jack feel he's been left in the dark, defensive and judged, with no opportunity to put his case or understand the underlying issues.

Fairness is fundamental to us from our earliest years; one only has to walk down any supermarket aisle to hear young voices wailing: 'Aww! Mum, you *promised*. IT ISN'T FAIR!'

SPECIFIC ACTION POINTS

● After assessments, feeding back in a way to feed forward into future action is crucial – invest in making sure it is done in ways to create *towards* rather than *away* states. The SCARF model is a useful tool to think about the way feedback is given and to avoid harmful feedback, which could stifle talent development.

- *Status* is about being sensitive to a person's sense of importance in relation to others. Key strategies here are framing and the development sandwich. They can be used together to point attention to development areas in ways that enable people to retain or even bolster their sense of status.

- *Certainty* is about helping people receiving feedback predict their future by being clear and precise. Key strategies here are well-formed outcomes and modelling/exemplifying. In addition to providing clarity about the talent development area, they also try to minimize any harmful side-effects of new behaviours learnt.

- *Autonomy* is about the person's sensed ability to control events. Key strategies here are to allow for different approaches or priorities – even a small amount of perceived autonomy supports certainty and enables the individual to withstand stress. It is also about maintaining an adult-to-adult interaction that dignifies individuals' right to make their own choices and challenges them in a way that is appropriate, not critically judgemental.

- *Relatedness* is about the person's sense of safety with others, or a feeling that an interaction is with more of a friend than a foe. Key strategies here are to make a connection with the person, ideally before the feedback session. Do this by smiling, being alert and interested, developing rapport and making eye contact, thereby enabling the generation of oxytocin. This enables our brains to view the other person as 'friend'.

- *Fairness* is about a person's sense of being treated fairly in any exchanges (communication, decision making, etc). Key strategies here are to frame a clear understanding of the process from the outset, to allow for challenges and questions to be dealt with in full, and to use the facilitated feedback to reinforce the agreed process. It means using a meaningful and anonymous sample and taking the time to deal with the feedback and any areas where the information is unclear. It also includes sticking to the agreed process.

FURTHER RESOURCES

David Rock Net: **http://www.davidrock.net**. The 'Resources' area is a major source of easily accessible neuroscience information, including the SCARF model. It includes academic and industry journal articles; particularly interesting articles include 'SCARF: a brain-based model for collaborating with and influencing others', 'Turn the 360 around', 'Learning that lasts through ages', and 'Managing with the brain in mind'.

Encyclopaedia of Systemic NLP and New Coding: **http://nlpuniversitypress.com/**. A major free resource online (enables up to 25 pages per day without payment). Particularly useful entries are for 'Well-formedness conditions for outcomes' (pp 1548–50), 'Senses' (pp 1199–200), 'Sensory acuity' (p 1201), 'Sensory experience' (p 1201), 'Visual' (pp 1538–9), 'Auditory' (pp 68–9), 'Auditory submodalities' (pp 69–70), 'Kinaesthetic' (pp 573–5) and 'Kinaesthetic submodalities' (p 576).

Harvard Business Review blog: **http://blogs.hbr.org**. A useful, credible source for interesting articles about feedback, including 'Feedback that works', 'How to give your boss feedback', 'How to get feedback when you're the boss' and 'How to give feedback to a perfectionist'.

Wikipedia entries: **http://en.wikipedia.org/**. Has a number of useful entries related to 'Feedback', 'Feedforward, behavioral and cognitive science', 'Methods of neuro-linguistic programming', 'Representational systems (NLP)' as well as for transactional analysis.

YouTube entries: **http://www.youtube.com/**. Has a number of useful entries for feedback, feedback sandwich, development sandwich, and modelling – and how *not* to give feedback. It is helpful to see examples of alternative strategies for giving feedback, but more important, through this medium, the visual, auditory and kinaesthetic subtleties of giving feedback.

Institute of Development Transactional Analysis: is an organization that specializes in TA within organizations and education rather than in a clinical setting – an overview and further information may be found here: **http://www.instdta.org**.

http://mountain-associates.co.uk/ego_states.html provides a simple, effective explanation and detail on ego states (parent, adult and child).

References

Dilts, R and DeLozier, J (2000) *Encyclopaedia of Systemic NLP and New Coding*, NLP University Press, Scotts Valley, CA

Dixon, P, Rock, D and Ochsner, K (2010) Turn the 360 around, *NeuroLeadership Journal*, 3

Gordon, E (2000) *Integrative Neuroscience: Bringing together biological, psychological and clinical models of the human brain*, Harwood Academic, Singapore

Phillips, K (2005) *Transactional Analysis in Organizations*, Keri Phillips Associates, Handforth, Cheshire

Rock, D and Schwartz, J (2006) The neuroscience of leadership, *Strategy and Business*, 43

Rock, D (2008) SCARF: A brain-based model for collaborating with and influencing others, *NeuroLeadership Journal*, 1

CASE STUDY   Indirect feeding-forward for entrepreneurial growth

Tony Wall

This case reports examples of feedback that were used by a newly appointed leader (named Jason here) during a strategic change and development initiative within an entrepreneurial educational organization. The organization had a turnover of over US$60 million, and was investing in ways to increase the flexibility of its staff and systems to respond more rapidly to client needs – and to increase profit. Global competition for educational qualifications had increased significantly, and this greater agility was seen as key.

As part of this investment, the organization had undertaken multiple restructures and had invested in new leadership talent. The newly appointed leader, Jason, inherited widely different teams and there was a consolidation of the teams in to one new department, decided by a wider leadership team. The new department included teams that previously identified themselves as primarily administrative, project-delivery, project-leadership, technology-development, training and development, new product development and academic teaching.

Jason had experienced a variety of emotions from the new staff including excitement about what the future could become. However, other staff did not see the same future and focused on the problems of such a transition. Yet these people also displayed high levels of expertise and other leadership talents that were seen as key to the entrepreneurial growth of the new department, and the organization. Ways of sharing feedback with these individuals in a constructive and positive way are discussed below.

Indirect feeding forward through team activity

Jason, experienced in leadership development, was aware of some of the key stages in the leadership journey explored in this book, and had undertaken a variety of assessments with the team. The key one was a MBTI (Myers-Briggs Type Inventory) with each member of the team – a psychometric questionnaire that suggests particular preferences for particular behaviours including decision making. Though the profiling was undertaken and fed back individually by a qualified MBTI profiler, there was a wider team-profile sharing activity, within a team exercise.

The primary intention of profiling in this way was to encourage greater empathy in the newly formed department, rather than for any selection activity. In addition, over time, the leader had developed close relationships with each member of the team to identify leadership potential, particularly in terms of drive, commitment and enthusiasm.

The first team member identified as having potential was Lisa, but she was experiencing the transition negatively and most interactions with Jason were met with resistance. Yet Jason saw the high levels of drive and commitment to a high quality experience for the customer when engaging with Lisa's team, and she was highly respected and very influential within the team and their client networks. The bottom line was that Lisa was part of the highest performing team in terms of profit generation.

The MBTI profiling exercise identified Lisa as a person who prefers to have a clear decision and plan agreed that is logical and consistent. So, rather than addressing the resistance behaviour directly, Jason decided to hold a visioning exercise with the team (rather than the individual) where agreement was established on general values and principles of operation. In this way, various SCARF (Rock, 2008) elements were directly addressed:

- An external facilitator helped deliver the visioning exercise, dealing (to an extent) with different power relations in the team, so the experienced *status* of each team member was considered. This also meant Jason was able to communicate with Lisa indirectly through the team exercise, rather than individually, about the sorts of collaborative working they were seeking to encourage. This also nullified the need for direct feedback statements about being so resistant to Jason's presence; rather, it was modelled.

- There was a greater *certainty* about what the new department was and how it would operate – it had been agreed. It was, however, emphasized that *how* it did its business might change.

- The team had *autonomy* in how to create themselves and their future within the department – they had agreed it.

- The meeting had been facilitated to make connections amongst the disparate teams, so there was a sense of *relatedness* among the participants – the common values and operating principles had been agreed.

- Each member of the team had had an opportunity to express their views, so there was a sense of *fairness*.

The change in behaviour after this exercise was significant and many of the team's members had noticed a major shift in the connectedness of Lisa to all new parts of the team from which they had previously been disconnected. New social activities started and a new team positivity emerged within weeks.

The interpersonal relationships developed between Jason and Lisa until a formal professional review needed to be done (an annual process of the organization). A key message of the feedback was about Lisa using more of her expertise and abilities to grow her team. Jason asked an open question to encourage an autonomous response: 'What do you feel would be your next step, professionally?' The response was that Lisa was very happy with the status quo, designing and delivering projects with the team. She wanted this to continue. Jason was convinced that Lisa had the ability to influence others towards their team values and goals.

Jason encouraged a more direct line: 'What are your thoughts about managing more projects?' And it was this question that revealed one of Lisa's very interesting beliefs – she did not want to become 'management'. She felt that to do so was against her own personal values as management had treated her so badly in the past. Jason provided the space for Lisa to talk, and eventually realized that a reframing of his original question was in order – the powerful belief was creating a barrier to enabling leadership talent development, and it was not a belief that was going to be changed suddenly within the formal professional review.

Jason replied, 'OK, so you don't want to be management. What could we do to enable you to deliver even more projects that you want to do?' The response was positive, and Lisa said she would like to consider ways with the wider team. Jason was very happy with this response, as it was actually displaying a participative and collaborative style of leadership that was very important to the area Lisa was working in. This was also particularly important to Lisa, with her MBTI profile. This process in itself demonstrated, through observable behaviour, that Lisa could experience leadership in a different way to management.

After discussing this with the team, a new job description and title were agreed that did not use the word 'management', and rather, used the word 'lead'. This was identified collaboratively with Lisa and her new team as useful and acceptable to the values they wanted to portray. Through this non-directive, facilitative approach, the potential leader became a stronger leader, creating greater value with and through the wider team. Again, this demonstrated a different style and approach to leadership through involvement rather than direct management, which Lisa had been so resistant to.

What benefits have been gained?

Feeding forward in a *towards* state (rather than an *away* state) built positive relationships in this case. It also contributed to enabling organizational change in a time of structural turmoil, and developing a more dynamic culture that was much more positively focused on achieving values and operating principles than specific and rigid procedures.

The bottom line was that the sales and profit of the team continued to increase, along with the number of projects that created new income streams. Creativity also increased; a good example was when a member of staff left through progression. The team decided to adopt another use for the associated salary budget that had been allocated for the member of staff who had left. The team decided to divert it in a new way to fund even more projects, all of which addressed their key values and operating principles. In turn, these projects created a greater brand image for the team, which expanded their client networks nationally, and created a virtuous cycle of profitability for them.

Learning points

Jason entered in a time of turmoil, and it was generally a stressful time for many people, though taking a particular approach of feeding back to the wider team was much more indirect and vision-building – rather than directive. That is not always appropriate, but it did put the new team into a *towards* motivational state, rather than an *away* state. Key learning points from this experience were:

- There are circumstances where a leader may have to face the consequences of a situation and its history, which can make it very difficult to give feedback directly to individuals. There are ways to give feedback that are not directed at an individual, but can communicate a key message to him or her – thereby maintaining a sense of status. This encourages the likelihood of reaching a *towards* state of motivation.

- Assessment tools can help a leader understand particular preferences of team members and help them decide how to package the form and content of feedback.

The SCARF model can help identify key aspects to address – in this case, there was a need for certainty.

- Participatory and collaborative vision building is a way of creating a direction through a sense of autonomy – it forms a key form of indirect feedback if the leader is part of this process, agreeing and shaping it in line with the values and operating principles of others in the team, but also modelling the types of behaviour he or she wants to support.

Reference

Rock, D (2008) SCARF: A brain-based model for collaborating with and influencing others, *NeuroLeadership Journal*, **1**

TOOL   SCARF check tool

Tony Wall

What it is and when to use it

This tool provides a simple memory aid of the things to consider in giving feedback after leadership assessments.

The grid has two axes, creating a matrix. Each box within the matrix contains an area to consider in giving feedback, or designing a more formal feedback strategy. On the first axis is Rock's (2008) SCARF model, usefully reminding us of the areas to consider in establishing or maintaining a motivational and productive *towards* state: status, certainty, autonomy, relatedness and fairness. The SCARF axis, used alone, is a simple but powerful tool for giving feedback.

The second axis identifies different dimensions to consider within each SCARF element – what and how feedback is given, where and when it is given, and who is giving the feedback. The last of these, 'who is giving feedback', may have one person specified, but may also raise who else might need to be involved, or special conditions, to achieve a higher level of that SCARF element.

The resulting matrix can be used to consciously consider the subtleties of a feedback strategy – particularly in difficult or sensitive situations, or in situations where the consequences of giving the feedback are of high impact or importance. Though the matrix may be used for detailed consideration of feedback strategies, its use may become in-built and natural over a period of time.

Doing a SCARF check – example

When giving feedback in a way to feed forward in to practice, do a quick check with the SCARF tool. Table 6.1 is an example of how it can be used to give feedback with a member of staff (Jack) after a leadership assessment exercise; Table 6.2 provides the template. Only the key boxes for your situation need to be completed.

TABLE 6.1   SCARF check – example

	What and *how* feedback is given	*Where* and *when* feedback is given	*Who* is giving the feedback
Status: sense of importance in relation to others	a Use development sandwich (see Chapter 6) on total assessment and areas Jack wants to focus on. b Ensure that the positives are highlighted and understood. c Ensure that Jack feels his results are similar/typical to others.	Jack and facilitator only, in HR executive room	Facilitator, with security of confidentiality
Certainty: sense of being able to predict the future	a Ensure that feedback is fully understood and what the benefit/ outcome of making changes will be. b Agree well-formed outcomes at the end of meeting.	Agree date, time, location, aims of feedback and who with	Facilitator, with clarity of communication channels
Autonomy: sensed ability to control events	a Ask Jack where he wants to focus and how to develop. b Ask him about any support he may wish to have.	When/how he feels he wants to next review progress	Facilitator

TABLE 6.1 *continued*

	What and *how* feedback is given	*Where* and *when* feedback is given	*Who* is giving the feedback
Relatedness: sense of safety with others	a Emphasize the confidentiality of the process and the facilitator's role in supporting Jack to enable the feedback to be of greatest use to him. b Ensure he sees the value of consulting with raters and having their ongoing support	On company premises	Facilitator, with opportunity to go back to source (colleague) feedback and to talk to line manager
Fairness: sense of being treated fairly in any exchanges	a Ensure clear ground rules are agreed at the start of the process. b Ask Jack to highlight the areas he wants to develop.	At time/place Jack can make	Facilitator, with security of confidentiality

TABLE 6.2   SCARF check – template

	What and *how* feedback is given	*Where* and *when* feedback is given	*Who* is giving the feedback
Status: sense of importance in relation to others			
Certainty: sense of being able to predict the future			
Autonomy: sensed ability to control events			
Relatedness: sense of safety with others			
Fairness: sense of being treated fairly in any exchanges			

References

Rock, D (2008) SCARF: A brain-based model for collaborating with and influencing others, *NeuroLeadership Journal*, **1**

Rock, D and Schwartz, J (2006) The neuroscience of leadership, *Strategy and Business*, **43**

Coaching for talent development

07

DANIELLE GRANT

EXECUTIVE SUMMARY

Coaching is becoming more common, however very often it is carried out because it seems like a good idea, without a clear purpose or defined outcome. Sometimes, even when the intent is developmental, the coachee wonders if it's really remedial! Coaches are not a homogeneous bunch with a defined background, set of processes and standardized qualifications, unlike, for example, solicitors or accountants, so the tools and techniques they bring may not always address, align with or make any attempt to track or measure progress against real development needs.

Starting a development programme with an understanding of the need for self-awareness and concepts on Emotional Intelligence (EI) forms an important plank to precede a leadership assessment, such as Leadership and Emotional Intelligence Profile Assessment (LEIPA®) 360°. This gives the participant clarity of which leadership behaviour needs to be enhanced and embedded. A core part of this is a clear action plan, designed to be easily digested and turned into realistic steps, meaning the impact can be tracked and measured over time. Integrating the 360° feedback with coaching sessions opens up opportunities to encourage experimenting with different behaviours to help achieve better outcomes. Trying out a new behaviour then reflecting and feeding back what happened, like a 'live laboratory', allows insights and positive new habits to be formed. Recent neuroscientific research (Rock and Schwartz, 2006) offers a biological explanation of how to enable new and more productive behaviour to replace unhelpful habits.

This chapter looks at best practice, summarized in these four principles:

1 Identifying the focus for the coaching programme from a leadership assessment (such as a 360° assessment).

2 How to create a 'live laboratory experiment'.

3 Coaching to solutions not problems.

4 Coaching to embed positive new behaviour.

Drawing together practical experience and established learning theories, with a neuroscience perspective, creates an approach that a) enables insights (Kolb and Fry, 1975; Race, 2001; Rock and Schwartz, 2006), b) supports reflection on the behaviour, and c) supports experimenting with the behaviour, which provides the key to changing habits for the long term and thus freeing up real potential.

Setting it up clearly

I have had a number of large corporate clients engage me to coach high-potential talent, who, typically, were just at or aspiring to a board appointment. In one memorable case, it took as many as three of the coaching sessions to finally persuade the person receiving the coaching that the programme was not covertly about 'fixing' him in some way! The messages he had received from his HR director and line manager on the main board were consistently about developing his potential. The three-way objective-setting meetings also underlined this as the purpose. Reflecting on this over time has enabled me to appreciate that the underlying issue was that he did not have a clear baseline to understand precisely what behaviour needed to change. The conversation in the three-way meeting and captured as objectives in the Sponsor Programme Evaluation Report (SPER)* was about coaching the person to enable him to develop the 'gravitas', 'focus' and 'broader perspective' that were being aimed for, to justify his next promotion. Translating these objectives into granular behaviours was a matter of interpretation, trial and error and guesswork on the part of the client to enable a sense of progress to be identified. (*SPER – this is a form that is integrated into our coaching practice, based upon the Kirkpatrick level 4 Evaluation model (1994) to capture objectives and progress towards those at the midpoint and end of a coaching programme, with the input of the coachee and sponsor.)

Each of the first three coaching sessions with this individual started by following what became a repetitive pattern of the client asking me where the organization thought he needed to improve or change and if the HR director had confided any dissatisfaction with his performance. Each time we ran through the rationale of why the company (against a backdrop of being owned by venture capitalists, who are renowned for taking a relatively short-term view of their investee companies) would be prepared to make the level of investment to hire an experienced and qualified external executive coach to work with him, if all it was trying to do was fix or move him out, given there were capable internal coaches within the HR team.

Even where the individual does not have such self-doubt the importance of identifying measures of improvement is vital. In one case an international divisional MD of a global entertainment company was my client. Here, he identified his own developmental goals, which were ratified in a subsequent conversation held with his California-based boss. We looked at how progress towards a given goal might be measured. One example was to have his European team be seen as integral to the division's strategic direction by their US counterparts and to be consulted. This was broken down by questions such as, 'What will tell you that this is happening?' 'What is the current reality of your interactions?' 'What will be different?' 'How can you quantify this?' 'What is the first step to moving in that direction?'

Almost to his own surprise, this client was able to clearly describe how often contact was being initiated on strategic matters by the United States, how often he would like it to happen, what needed to change to shift habits, and clearly articulate how he and his European team would behave to start the process. The success of this can be seen in the quote from the sponsoring HR director: 'a straight talking, business focused approach to executive coaching has provided great results for us. It's a pleasure to work with such a professional who is as keen on evaluating her own results equally as much as the client'.

So, you might ask, if it's that straightforward why go to the trouble of a 360° feedback process? As you will have gathered from the two brief examples I have already described and from the earlier chapters, people (even successful senior executives), are not universally self-aware or have accurate views of what is holding them back from achieving their potential. Often, we do not see ourselves as others do or perceive the impact of our habitual behaviour and responses on those around us. Experience suggests that most people in senior roles consider how to relate to their team and the person to whom they report (at best). To become an excellent leader means balancing the needs of all the stakeholders, not just one or two groups, which requires an understanding of how one is perceived by key stakeholder groups.

Starting with a leadership assessment

Since we are in the business of shaping the best transpersonal leaders the journey is initiated with a robust way of determining both the start point and the direction of travel – and this is where leadership assessment contributes. One of the most objective ways of doing this is through a LEIPA®. The process has been explained in earlier chapters, but the value of this in creating an action plan that provides a coaching focus cannot be underestimated.

Another example, of a chief operating officer 'in waiting', from a finance background, operating in a business-to-business service industry environment shows how the information in the LEIPA® enables reflection and understanding of the perspective of other stakeholders. Here is an extract from the LEIPA® action plan.

Overall aspirations for improvement and development

I will endeavour to:

- Balance a focus on task with attention to relationships particularly with my direct reports. Understand why direct reports feel I only occasionally support the decision of the team.

- Work with my direct reports to identify opportunities and stimulate them to achieve their full potential.

- Explore why there is such a difference of priority on coaching between my boss and everyone else and who/how/when I can use this style to develop others.

The resulting actions in this individual's LEIPA® action plan can be seen to directly relate to the development needs identified through the 360°:

Specific behavioural statement identified for development: Identifies opportunities and stimulates individuals to develop to their full potential:

- I plan to discuss with my direct reports their long-term career plans and aspirations.

- As part of the above process we should consider setting longer-term aspirations and objectives with direct reports rather than completion of narrow recurring tasks.

- Explore 'Do more of' comments that link into this objective.

- Discuss with Peer Group and Other Group why they ranked coaching as their number one priority. Who to? How?

- Identify in conjunction with above, opportunities (perhaps on projects outside my team) for my direct reports to add value and achieve potential.

As another divisional managing director of a listed company says: 'The LEIPA® process and feedback was invaluable... (as a result of the Action Plan identified)... I am spending more time on one-to-ones with direct reports, establishing a more communicative, empathetic and empowering relationship with them'. In the return on investment feedback report they estimate this will add 30 per cent to their own effectiveness, defined as increases in productivity, employee satisfaction, customer satisfaction and business income. The 'headlines' they quote are that 'more people owning more responsibility... managing challenges and achieving results more effectively'. Quite an impact in a multi-million pound service business!

Using a leadership assessment process such as the LEIPA 360° makes it easy to identify the focus for the coaching programme. The sheer clarity with which the key messages coalesce from the mass of data means that the individual is more likely to accept the validity. From there it is a short step to helping the person accept that how others experience him or her is their reality. And, if that is not the way he or she sees themself or wants to be seen, the detail and granularity of the behavioural statements pinpoint where changes will have the most positive impact. It is not as easy to identify how to change if the feedback is 'you need to develop your people' whereas a precise indicator such as needing to 'offer useful feedback to help people improve', indicates exactly what needs attention, providing some real precision for the coach to work with. The skill and experience in the feedback process and the involvement of raters are key to ensuring that the actions really address the changes and that the coaching objectives are aligned.

The 'live laboratory'

Leaders (obviously) need to change their habits at work to see how this impacts their performance and that of their organizations. The workplace is the practical 'laboratory' to try out and reflect on what works and how to tweak it to work even better. Reflection is, in the majority of cases, one thing that most leaders spend too little time on. Most are so busy 'doing' or 'telling' others what to do, or else thinking that people in their organization are not behaving in the way that will yield results. This means that they often tend to (using an equestrian metaphor), 'get the horse to jump the fence first and, only then, consider how to approach it'. (I fear this is too late, as the fence might have already been knocked over!) The coaching process allows reflection time and space and a way to work through options, anticipate obstacles and how to overcome them, before moving to action – in other words, not just 'steadying the horse for the approach' before 'jumping the fence', but checking the right training, practice, direction and equipment are in place before mounting, taking hold of the reins and encouraging the horse around the course.

Various academics have established effective ways of working and learning, including Kolb and Fry (1975) and Honey and Mumford (1982). These describe learning as a cycle with each person having preferred learning styles that correlate to one phase of the learning cycle (see Figure 7.1). The process of considering (ie reflecting on and making sense of) how to go about making the behaviour changes identified, then testing it out and doing it, follows as a cycle, so all stages and ways of learning are employed.

FIGURE 7.1   The learning cycle

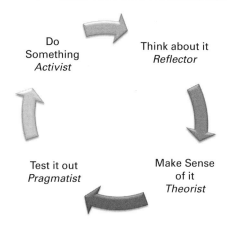

Do
Something
Activist

Think about it
Reflector

Test it out
Pragmatist

Make Sense
of it
Theorist

© LeaderShape 2012, Adapted from Kolb, Honey & Mumford

Another learning theory, Race's Ripples Theory (see Figure 7.2), identifies the absence of emotional connection and motivation in the 'traditional' learning cycle theories – in other words, if people don't start by wanting or seeing a need to learn (and/or change) then no amount of reflection will make them do so!

More recent neuroscientific evidence develops this concept with greater applicability in coaching. Rock and Schwartz (2006) describe the ARIA model® (Attention, Reflection, Insight and Action). This model identifies the need to pay 'Attention' – a vital step, as shown in research using functional magnetic resonance imaging (fMRI) scans, which has demonstrated that the quality and focus of attention physically changes the wiring in the brain

FIGURE 7.2 Race's Ripples Theory

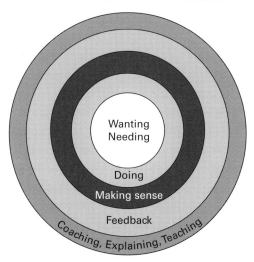

Wanting
Needing

Doing
Making sense
Feedback
Coaching, Explaining, Teaching

Race (2012)

to create new habits. 'Reflection' follows on from paying close attention to the issue. The reflective process allows refinement of thinking, connection to feelings and leaps of understanding to be made. These come together to enable an 'aha!' moment when the person has a realization, which can often be visible to an observer in a shift in posture as well as a sense of excitement. This is the physical sign that ownership and energy for change have shifted in the person. This is the moment of 'Insight' which provides the energy to fuel 'Action'. Therefore, it is not enough to take a person around a learning cycle if the quality of attention is not present to generate the desire and insight that are necessary to overcome the natural discomfort of change.

Making the live laboratory work

Getting an 'experiment' going is simply a matter of asking questions that allow the individual to spot the next opportunity he or she will have to 'try out' the new way of working. For example, with one person ('Alan') who had recently been promoted to a board role in the UK division of a global retailer, it was clear from the differences in rater group feedback that his direct reports were substantially more positive about how he approached teamwork and collaboration than were his peers. A simple question: 'Who do you consider your team to be?' elicited a response that gave a critical insight into the feedback of the different groups. His reply showed that he still viewed his direct reports as his team. This allowed a realization for him that, while the promotion had happened the needed shift in awareness that his 'team' now encompassed the other board members as well as direct reports had not taken place.

Following this question with one on how he dealt with and communicated to his direct reports compared to his new peer group allowed him to see ways his behaviour was different. From there it became very clear to him that he needed to change his approach to engage better with his peers. We looked at what their priorities and concerns were and how he could support those through his department. This was a way of working on his empathy and his teamwork and collaboration at the same time. This was just the starting point, as the conversation then turned to the preferred communication styles of key individuals, so we could work through or even rehearse how he might approach them to feel confident this would have the intended effect. This dramatically increased his awareness of how to approach the 'difficult conversation'.

The knock-on effect of this shift in awareness was that he was not only seen as more collaborative and supportive but he began to be seen as more strategic and having more gravitas. This was because he was demonstrating a more holistic appreciation of business issues rather than a 'local' perspective. This does not happen overnight; it takes trial, open reflection on what is making a difference and what more needs to happen to create the improved relationships. So in scientific terms, it is experimenting with one variable, then tweaking it or changing another in response to the results.

Looking at this example through the lens of Rock's ARIA model demonstrates how we paid close *Attention* to the issue both in the coaching session and during the interactions with others, where change was needed. *Reflection* time was devoted to the response and outcomes both as an individual as well as with the coach, noticing and capturing those moments of *Insight* that inform further *Action*. Often during these coaching sessions, because he or she is standing outside the relationships, the coach can spot a pattern of behaviour between people that brings to mind models such as the Transactional Analysis approach (TA) of parent, adult, child (where behaviour habits learnt in childhood may inappropriately be brought into the workplace) or stroking patterns (human recognition patterns) (Hay, 2009). Sharing these models explicitly is a way of offering a different lens through which to view relationship challenges that has often made a positive contribution to the strength of the client's insight and willingness to 'experiment'.

Coaching to solutions, not problems

Building on these ideas, it is important to enable the client to keep focused on solutions rather than problems. Taking forward the brain science principles, the questions you ask focus attention. As Schwartz, in his interview in 'Coaching the Brain' says: 'Where you focus your attention, you make connections' (Rock and Schwartz, 2006). Focus your attention on something new, and you make new connections. This has shown to be true through studies of neuroplasticity, where focused attention plays a critical role in creating physical changes in the brain.

By extension therefore, if we ask questions that focus on the problem then the problem is all we see. If we focus on solutions, however improbable, that puts the mind in a state of making new connections and that is when the insight and solution start to crystallize. One interesting process to use with coachees is to ask them to imagine they had a magic wand to overcome the sense of blockage. There is an old proverb that speaks to this: there are no obstacles, merely challenges to find ways to overcome.

It is interesting to note that when President Kennedy committed to putting a man on the moon by the end of the decade in 1960, NASA's response was to start from the end point and look at what was required to achieve that goal. It did not start from their point of origin and look for problems. The remarkable achievement of the moon landing in 1969 is testament to the power of solutions focus. Neuroscience, over 40 years later, now allows us to understand the phenomenon.

One client, 'Janet', the UK MD of an international biotech company felt she had an intractable relationship problem with a direct report (let's call her Suzanne). Suzanne frequently paid her boss compliments, whether about dress sense, hair style or other personal matters not connected with work. This made Janet very uncomfortable and she felt uncertain as to how she might interpret this behaviour, how to deal with it or whether there was anything potentially unprofessional in the attention. Knowing that Janet prided herself on being very professional allowed me to see that she felt mired in a situation where she was being drawn into what, to her, was far from a business-like interaction.

I asked her what she felt the reason was for this continuing and perhaps inappropriate attention and what affect her discomfort was having on the way she worked with Suzanne. This did not elicit much enlightenment! The focus was on the problem. I then had an insight of my own and shared the TA 'stroking pattern' model with her ('stroking' is the TA term that represents the recognition of one human being by another). My questions moved to ask her to focus on what Suzanne was (covertly) telling her about her own needs for recognition. This enabled the 'insight' moment for Janet that there was a need in Suzanne for greater recognition than she was currently experiencing and, having recognized the opportunity for a solution, the conversation then moved swiftly towards ways in which it would be appropriate and comfortable for her to provide recognition for Suzanne. From the start point of being 'stuck', the solution focus provided the insight and energy to act that ultimately transformed their working relationship. More than this, because there was a need to keep her attention on the solution over the time it took to change the dynamics, it provided a connection, making her more aware of clues to solutions 'hidden' in the behaviour of others.

Coaching to embed positive new behaviour

The key to transformational development is embedding new behaviour into habit. To do that one has to let go of unhelpful old behaviours. There is a concept called 'free won't' (coined again by Schwartz), which builds on the principle discovered by Libet *et al* (1983). Libet says that when we have an urge to do something, that thought is initiated three-tenths of a second before we are consciously aware of it. We then have a further two-tenths of a second to decide *not* to act on that thought. That is the brevity of the thinking space for 'self-awareness and self-control'. It is this space, where we choose to focus attention, that makes all the difference between default behaviour and more helpful responses.

Interestingly, not only do we create new connections in the brain (through neuroplasticity) when we have an insight, we cause these pathways to become stable (a habit) by continuing the ARIA principle. A helpful aspect is that if, in that brief pause for self-awareness, we keep using these new 'habits', the connections that kept us behaving in old habitual ways start to break down, so they become less automatic, helping the positive new way of behaving to become increasingly natural.

So, as coaches, how can we help clients embed those positive new habits? A good way is by asking clients to feed back or (ideally) to capture brief written reflections on how behaving differently is impacting their work, relationships, stress levels, productivity and their general sense of things being positive. This maintains the *Attention* and *Reflection*, which, in turn, will fuel deeper *Insights* that energizes them to take *Action*; creating a virtuous circle. Sometimes it is justified to 'hold' clients to their commitment by e-mailing or calling for a brief conversation to check in with them to offer a reminder and support to help them continue with their behavioural changes. We are all so overloaded with the speed of response needed at work today that, even with the best of intentions, it is possible to be overwhelmed. I can live with being 'Jiminy Cricket' as the voice of conscience, holding the client to his or her desired path, in the short term, as the virtuous circle becomes established. (This metaphor is from the classic story of *Pinocchio* where Jiminy Cricket sat on Pinocchio's shoulder to remind him to hold to the right path.)

One client, 'Rachel' a newly appointed senior executive in a public private partnership building new health centres, was taking over responsibility for chairing meetings with senior figures from PCTs (Primary Care Trusts, which were until April 2013 UK commissioning and management bodies for local health care facilities), local councils and key directors of major project contractors. She dreaded these meetings and worried about them throughout the week leading up to them. When we reflected on how these meetings were set up and run, it was clear that Rachel felt that she needed to follow the format and process that she inherited from her predecessor.

Her leadership assessment (LEIPA®, in this case) feedback included comments that she needed to step up to lead more. This was also reflected in other parts of the feedback on conflict management and dealing with difficult people. Her key insight, when we paid attention to the solution to all these seemingly disparate bits of feedback, was that she had to do things 'her way' and that this would provide greater confidence and make her feel better prepared. She identified that preparing in her own way would give her a greater sense of authority over the meetings. Solutions that she implemented included changing the agenda of the meeting to make it work better for her. When this way of working proved its value, it enabled her to really accept that it was 'OK' to work differently than her predecessor by approaching this mission-critical meeting in a different way.

Reflecting with her, both in e-mail exchanges and in subsequent sessions, on how these changes had impacted her feelings and the progress made during the meetings, helped her see the links to dealing with conflict in the meeting. She identified strategies including speaking to individuals to understand their priorities and positions as well as building better relationships prior to the meeting and preparing better. This included ensuring she had all the data and had considered how to structure the meeting beforehand. She also started thinking through what her responses needed to be, ahead of time, and when necessary took advice from others. This enabled her to deal with any conflicts. Her own words on what has enabled her to make a long-term change in her approach and 'default behaviour' are telling: 'I have also learnt the importance of reflecting on the week's work, which helps me better understand what things need changing and improving.'

SPECIFIC ACTION POINTS

So, what are the actions that an organization should take to maximize the learning and development from a coaching programme?

First, identify a 360° feedback tool that provides a detailed and actionable framework for the development programme (we refer to the LEIPA® process here). Ensure that this is robust and adheres to good practice. Doing so enables the resulting information to be accepted as valid by the candidate/leader undergoing the process.

Secondly, ensure that the feedback and action plan align the individual and organizational needs and benefits. The development points need to be broken down into clear and actionable steps with specific measures of progress. To do this most effectively requires a professionally trained and experienced coach who is familiar with brain-friendly methods such as those described in Chapter 6, on feeding back and forward.

Thirdly, ensure the coach and client identify opportunities to try out the behaviour in the workplace and to reflect on outcomes, using the ARIA principles. A great way for the coach to be alert to how effectively he or she is enabling insights is to watch the client's body language to spot the four Faces of Insight©, described in the model in Figure 7.3 – each 'face' relates to a stage in the ARIA model.

FIGURE 7.3   Four Faces of Insight©

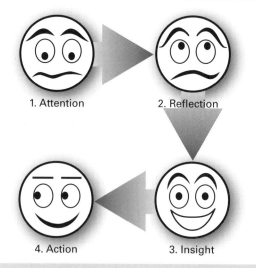

1. Attention   2. Reflection

4. Action   3. Insight

Adapted from Rock, 2006

1 When first becoming aware of a dilemma, the face looks a little unhappy, frowning or perplexed. The eyes might be squinting slightly. *(Attention)*

2 When reflecting on an issue, the face changes. Most people look up or slightly up and across and get a dazed look on their face. The mouth might tense up as they think more deeply. Nearly everyone goes silent for a moment. The coach should try not to rush the client through this phase. *(Reflection)*

3 When an insight occurs there is a shift of energy, eyes widen and pupils may dilate: this is the 'aha!' moment and the energy from this needs to be captured while motivation is high. *(Insight)*

4 When people have just had an insight, their eyes are racing ahead, ready to take action; this needs to be acted on with the coach enabling them to write down their insight and/or commit to a specific action to take the insight forwards as soon as possible. *(Action)*

The coach needs to help prepare clients to ensure that the conversation they feel they need to have (very frequently the first Action) with others in the organization 'lands well'. Achieving this involves the coach asking questions to elicit, in some detail, what the other person's personality, preferences, style, perspective and priorities are. This enables the client to 'walk a mile in their shoes', which is an interesting definition of empathy. After trying out the actions in the workplace to embed and deepen the new habits, the coach should help the client pay further attention and reflect on how the changes are making him or her feel and how others are responding to them.

Finally, to help clients gain more 'will' to take action it can be valuable to help them become powerfully aware of the two-tenths of a second opportunity to decide what to do! One way is to ask them to try to be aware of the bodily warning signs in themselves that signal that their default knee-jerk reaction is likely to be triggered. This may be a knot in the stomach or tension in the shoulders, clammy palms or something else, unique to them. Once they are aware of the 'early warning' signs they can choose 'free won't'. It's possible to offer techniques such as taking a thoughtful moment or perhaps bringing a memory to mind or some artefact that they associate with calmness,

ing order

to help self-management. One example is that of a client who was a runner, who had a pebble he had picked up out on a run; touching or grasping it was his 'anchor' to enable that self-awareness and control in the moment. These steps repeated in an iterative fashion will enable long-term habits to be established that are positive for the organization and the individual, with measurable results.

FURTHER RESOURCES

Daniel Goleman, a leading authority in EI (and whose work inspired the LEIPA 360° feedback process) has written a new book, *The Brain and Emotional Intelligence: New insights*, available digitally via Kindle. The 'Creative brain' section shows how insights can be promoted and what happens in the brain. The chapter on 'Self-mastery', helps with managing impulses where we need 'free won't'. The publication also speaks to mindfulness in managing stressful moments and motivation as well as the role of coaching (in the chapter on EI). Goleman also speaks on You Tube about the moment of insight – **http://youtube/fZmTY8d9Jy4** – 'Daniel Goleman on the "aha" moment'.

David Rock addresses coaching through the moments of insight and building commitment to act on the insight by being 'Jiminy Cricket' (in my words): **http://youtube/47SL7YhNcZE** – 'David Rock – Moments of Insight' (You Tube).

Brain-friendly principles: your own curiosity may take you in a number of directions from this start point, whether down the route of developing greater understanding of neuroscience and how we rewire our brains or wanting to deepen your knowledge in other areas. The first publication that got me hooked on the whole idea of brain-friendly principles is by developmental molecular biologist, Dr John Medina – hilariously funny at times and very insightful, it makes sense and is highly recommended; see **www.brainrules.net** Medina, J (2008) *Brain Rules: 12 principles for surviving and thriving at work, home & school*, Pear Press, Seattle.

Open source videos including a number of videos on You Tube – TED talks and RSA Animate are informative, so do browse. For 'neuroplasticity', which is the most important concept in changing habits, you might want to look at these: **http://youtube/iAzmyB9PFt4** 'Neuroplasticity' Liz Reynolds Losin, and **http://youtube/TSu9HGnIMV0** – 'Brain Plasticity – Discovery Channel' this You Tube clip shows, in a most dramatic way, how extensive re-wiring can be.

Phil Race's Ripple Theory: further information can be found here: **http://www2.le.ac.uk/departments/gradschool/training/resources/ teaching/theories/race**, which states 'Taken from **How to be an e-tutor** by Dr Richard Mobbs. Used with permission.'

References

Hay, J (2009) *Working it Out at Work – Understanding attitudes and building relationships*, Sherwood Publishing, Hertford

Honey, P and Mumford, A (1982) *Manual of Learning Styles*, Peter Honey, London

Kirkpatrick, D (1994) *Evaluating Training Programs: The four levels*, Berret-Koehler, San Francisco, CA

Kolb, D A and Fry, R (1975) Toward an applied theory of experiential learning, in (ed) C Cooper, *Theories of Group Process*, John Wiley, Chichester

Libet, B, Gleason, C A, Wright, E W and Pearl, D K (1983) Time of conscious intention to act in relation to onset of cerebral activity (readiness-potential): the unconscious initiation of a freely voluntary act, *Brain*, 106, pp 623–42

Race, P (2001) *Using Feedback to Help Students Learn*, The Higher Education Academy, York

Rock, D and Schwartz, J (2006) The neuroscience of leadership, *Strategy and Business*, **43**

Rock, D and Schwartz, D (2006) A brain-based approach to coaching, *International Journal of Coaching in Organizations*, 4 (2), pp 32–43

CASE STUDY   Coaching to support alignment to corporate objectives

Danielle Grant

This case study describes the developmental assessment and coaching of a high potential Disney Commercial vice president (VP) recently appointed to a pan-European role with broad ranging responsibilities and new upward reporting lines into a California-based US senior vice president (SVP). He was offered 12 months' coaching, underpinned by a LEIPA 360° assessment (described in detail in Chapter 5) to refine and support the development needs identified. These were aligned to a clear set of objectives and outcomes that were initially agreed in three-way conversations with HR and his line manager. During the period of the engagement individual situations were discussed in detail and a range of options to deal with them were explored. These scenarios were looked at in terms of how they would best be implemented in the identified priority leadership styles and how the requirements to increase certain EI behaviours such as developing others, balancing task and relationships or having a range of influencing strategies could be utilized and practised to achieve the objectives. The shift in awareness and behaviour because of the clarity of the process was evident to the coachee and the organization as a whole. The tangible results could be seen in terms of achieving business objectives as well as a sense of personal growth.

Background

The client had recently been appointed to the position of Commercial Vice President at Disney Consumer Products working with toys and electronics in Europe. He had been promoted from being Category Director for the Electronics category only. The new role encompassed Games, Toys & Electronics where he became responsible for the entire category management team, some of these were UK-based and some in-country. Additionally, his responsibility extended to the seven country directors across Europe and thereby, the performance of their business units. He reported into a United States-based SVP. This was a relatively new relationship, as he had (in his previous role) reported into a United Kingdom-based SVP who had hired him into Disney originally.

Disney culture is highly achievement-oriented and a challenge for the client was to rapidly establish a productive and effective relationship with the SVP (where trust was built and greater delegation made possible). The underlying aim was to demonstrate real leadership value to the European business unit (measured in terms of business growth against targets and recognition of his role in developing the team members to deliver this). A programme of one-to-one executive coaching over 12 months supported by a LEIPA 360° process was agreed. The objectives for the programme included the importance of developing the relationship with the SVP and being perceived as taking the lead with country directors. To pinpoint needs and provide a really clear focus for his leadership development, the LEIPA® process was key. Tangible results were recorded as a result. As the client says in his own words:

[My coach] is an excellent coach and mentor. Her insights, straight talking and determination to do what's best for her clients have been a huge help to me over the last 12 months. Not only have I exceeded the career goals which we set, I feel as though I have matured as a person and now have the confidence to over-achieve in whatever I do.

The engagement

Disney has always engaged executive coaches for senior executives to foster their development and position them for promotion through the organization. The organization runs regular talent assessment meetings to identify those who have potential for development and individual programmes to suit. These would take the form of annual collaborative conversations between business unit heads and HR managers responsible for talent development, where the progress and potential of individuals in the business units would be assessed against projected business needs.

These meetings would identify and match these individuals with one or more of a range of interventions such as formal training, coaching, matching with a suitable internal mentor, secondment or a stretch project. Disney has a strategic approach to high performance that is demonstrated through formally setting clear objectives for development of individuals and tracking these through the engagement using an internal form to capture these at the start of the programme and regularly evaluating progress. This dovetails strongly with the process used in this situation.

The LEIPA® assessment was carried out within the first three months of engagement. Given that this was not part of a full leadership development programme for a cohort, but an individual one, the usual preparatory workshops described in Chapter 2 were not appropriate, so the topics were covered by means of individual discussion with the coach and independent reading on the key EI leadership topics. The coachee's self-assessment and information from briefings with HR and his boss were compared for common themes and any discrepancies with the LEIPA® data to provide the primary focus for the remainder of the coaching programme.

The key learning and actions from the LEIPA® were that the coachee could rely more on his 'gut feel' – he self-reported being highly analytical and not trusting intuition, which was borne out by verbatim comments and the response to a specific question in the LEIPA about making decisions based on both logic and intuition. The value here from the coaching was to enable him to reframe 'gut feel' as being the result of 'accumulated experience'. He had previously never really considered 'gut feel' as anything other than an emotional response that he felt was therefore not cognitively valid. He agreed (as did others in his feedback), that he tended to over-analyse situations and 'shield' team members by assuming they would find certain issues difficult and dealing with them himself through pre-judging a situation.

Learning to be more confident and trusting would enable more energized proactive behaviour and support the development of his team members by facilitating him to provide opportunities for them to take more initiative. It was perceived that he would then be able to give them broader guidelines and looser but very clear reporting frameworks in which to operate according to their own best judgement, rather than either very close direction or the opposite.

The performance challenges in the country teams were reviewed between the coachee and coach. The perspective used was to assess if these could be addressed through increasing the VP's EI capabilities identified for development. This process helped support the value of giving priority to EI capabilities of initiative, teamwork, collaboration and change catalyst. The most important leadership styles that were prioritized for development were the pacesetting style (very typically Disney – setting high objectives and milestones to reach challenging goals) and the visionary (moving people towards a shared vision and goals) and coaching styles. The coachee's most observed leadership style at the time of the LEIPA® assessment was affiliative (described in the LEIPA® process as creating harmony by connecting people, good for team building, and to strengthen connections).

The coaching took the client through a series of 'live' examples of situations, which were explored in the light of the action plan priorities. One of the priorities was to develop a more 'pacesetting' style whilst ensuring this was done in a positive manner through using a 'coaching' approach. Here, the client identified an opportunity to challenge country directors to work to a master template for reporting and presenting their analysis of their businesses to the SVP in regular update visits he made to Europe. This required them to undertake a more thorough assessment of their business and competitive environment and to recommend actions to maximize the opportunities they identified. This stretched their thinking and ambitions for their country's potential achievement. This was a critical process to enable the SVP to agree and, importantly, be fully committed to deliver against proposed targets and budgets. He enabled the country directors to create their business planning presentations such that they considered what their 'audience' needed to know as the key emphasis.

He established specially convened meetings, attended by the SVP and colleagues from across EMEA for these presentations to take place. This, in turn, provided greater positive exposure for the country directors and enhanced understanding as well as their own and his reputation in the wider organization. The result of this was to provide a clear profile for his own leadership role that carved out a purpose and value recognized by the United States and overall organizational HR. This had been one of the original coaching objectives that was given real direction and impetus through coaching to the LEIPA® feedback that had identified the exact behavioural changes needed.

What benefits have been gained?

The benefits of coaching to the 360° action plan were to enable the coachee to achieve his development objectives in a timely and focused manner that responded to both his own identified needs and the organizational objectives. This translated into clear outcomes from the granular behaviour identified in the LEIPA® which, in broad terms, were to establish a stronger relationship with the SVP, create real value in his new role and be seen as an effective leader for the EMEA business group. This process of having a framework of theory combined with the practical application and trial in the workplace supported his learning to embed the new behaviour into habit in a way that was relevant, enjoyable and effective. This was later evidenced by his own testimonial and feedback from his senior vice president and organizational HR.

Learning points

The learning points from this project to ensure effectiveness of coaching to support assessment for talent development are:

- The impact of assessment feedback when carried out effectively and supported with coaching is far more powerful in creating real development and ownership of change in coachees.

- The importance of the coach taking the assessment feedback and working with the coachee to identify how the key development points identified can be translated into a real-world context, thereby creating a 'live laboratory'.

- To support coachees to anticipate and decide how to behave differently in the situation they are facing.

- To enable coachees to bring their 'live laboratory' experiences back into the coaching to reflect upon and further enhance and refine their learning.

- To provide support (but not judgement) if there is any slippage back into 'old' undesirable behaviour along the way.

- To identify and help coachees value their own progress.

TOOL   Structure of a problem

Danielle Grant

What it is and when to use it

This is a practical tool to enable an individual (coachee) to identify the sources of blockage to movement and the first steps towards action. The purpose of using this tool is not necessarily to generate a solution but, more important, to help coachees move from a 'problem state of mind' to a 'solution focus state of mind' where they are empowered and motivated.

This tool can often be useful when the topic for the coaching session is a problem that may be difficult to resolve because of a negative mindset or where the client feels stuck and unable to see how to 'untangle' a number of issues surrounding the problem area. It is a very valuable tool to use to create clarity and a visual/kinaesthetic representation of the issue.

How to use it

The tool gives a structure to a problem – all problems are made up of the following elements: a person or persons who want something to be better or different than it currently is, and perceives they are prevented or inhibited from having it changed. Containing the elements on simple sticky notes or index cards makes sense of what seems like a complex or difficult situation to work through.

Each element of the problem situation should be written in a few clear words on individual index cards or sticky notes and arranged in the pattern indicated in Figure 7.4. This provides a visual/tactile representation of each of the perceived 'obstacles' between the 'reality' and 'desired state', which means each element can be removed, or repositioned so the perception of a fixed state is changed to one where the coachee has the ability to move and reposition the blockages.

Step-by-step process for resolving problems (with typical question to ask):

Agree the topic (issue to be tackled) for the session.

Q: So what is the situation you would like to resolve?

Agree the goals/desired outcome for the session.

Q: What would be a good place to be at the end of the session?

Establish a clear picture of the desired future state.

Q: How could you capture a sense of the way you want things to be in just a few words?

Establish a clear picture of the current state.

Q: What is really going on right now?

FIGURE 7.4   Setting out the problem

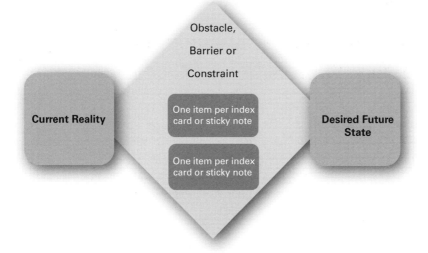

Identify each of the barriers to achieving the desired future state:

Capture each element, by writing a short summary of it on a single index card or sticky note, eg:

- Not enough information to make a decision.

- Boss doesn't understand the situation.

- There is no budget until xxx for implementation.

Group the obstacles in their locations by physically moving the index cards/sticky notes to suit the location of the barriers that must be identified as lying in one of three domains:

1 *In the coachee* (not enough information – only the coachee can find a way to begin to remedy this.)

2 *In another (named individual)* (boss doesn't understand – how can coachee help this to change to a better understanding?)

3 *In the environment* (there is no budget until xxx – how or what can the coachee prepare meanwhile or how else might that be overcome?)

As the groups of obstacles are moved around, the sources of the obstacles and patterns or linkages between them will become apparent.

A first step to a solution will also become clearer. Most commonly this will provide the insight that often the first 'shift' possible is in the group of obstacles that lie within the control of the client. In the example above, the coachee might identify that doing some more research (for example), which is in his or her own control might provide information that helps his or her boss to understand the situation differently. From this he or she might find he or she has an ally in the boss to secure the budget earlier.

Benefits

Enables the identification of one step, however small, to overcome at least one obstacle and set the client on the path to creating a cascade of solutions.

Workplace projects for talent development

08

TONY WALL and DENISE MEAKIN

EXECUTIVE SUMMARY

How many times have you sent staff on, or have been sent on, training courses? How many times did the learning last beyond the initial 'enthusiastic implementation' period – and make a direct contribution back in to the workplace? Experience tells us that this is hugely variable and that training remains a big part of training budgets globally. Yet there are real alternatives that can deepen learning insights for long-lasting behaviours – and that can make an immediate and direct impact in the workplace.

This chapter is about how to design real workplace projects for learning purposes, as a serious addition or even alternative to structured training interventions. It focuses on the practical steps facilitators and managers can take to enable authentic, deep talent development, which also directly contributes to the business – precisely because it is based on real work activity that cannot be replicated in a training environment.

The chapter also offers two key ways to embed a commitment to learning from doing projects, in terms of projects designed primarily for learning, and other projects primarily designed for business outcomes. The first is to find ways to continually salvage learning from projects, whether or not they have achieved the desired quality, budgetary or timeline requirements. Such strategies can be used to enable the development of sustainable projects and project talents to enhance future project outcomes. The second is to reward and further strengthen commitment to learning and deep learning through designing projects in ways that can also attract university credit. Accrediting work-based learning projects is powerful in recognizing new expertise as part of a globally recognized university qualification such as a degree or Master's. This benefits the learner (recognition and reward), the manager (clarity of learning and impact), and the business (business outcomes).

Learning through real workplace projects

Projects as a high-value, high-impact learning strategy

Leadership assessments can provide detailed information about the areas of strength and development for professionals, and it is a powerful strategy to designate a facilitator to help negotiate which specific areas to focus on – we saw in Chapter 6 how powerful a coaching approach to this particular stage is for gaining commitment and enthusiasm for particular talent development goals. This is also true in using projects as a learning strategy. Using real work-based projects as a learning strategy means clearly outlining a focus of learning, creating a plan for that learning using best or innovative practices or ideas, and then enacting it. Sounds simple. The value of the strategy lies in its reality and relevance to the individual and his or her workplace:

- it is real in the sense that it is based on real work activity that needs to be done, and/or is part of an activity that has an impact on business operations or outcomes;
- it is real in the sense of being experienced first-hand, or experientially;
- it is real in the sense of being framed and constrained by the pressures and interruptions of real work.

In these ways, learning-through-doing cannot be matched by other learning and development interventions for the authenticity of the learning, and hence it can potentially have high and deep impact for the learner, with immediate and direct impact on business operations and outcomes. For example, developing empathy behaviours in the context of sales contexts could involve a work-based project on:

- the learner becoming much more aware of his or her approach;
- planning a new approach;
- planning how to measure the changes as a result of that new approach; and
- measuring what happens.

Although this in itself can be a major source of insight, it is also the richness of the reality of the situation that can provide prompts for discovery through reflection and critique on what happened – what Schön (1992) refers to as reflecting *in* action (during the project), and *on* action (after the project). We will discuss this in more depth in the next section, but it is important to know why this works so well, from a neurological perspective. Davachi *et al* (2010) say that the AGES model, which is based on neuroscience, tells us the factors that create an optimal environment for learning (and also, by implication, what can create a sub-optimal environment). These are outlined in Table 8.1, in the context of work-based projects for the purposes of talent development.

TABLE 8.1   The factors that create an optimal environment for learning – AGES

A: Attention	**Workplace projects encourage learners to get and keep a clear focus on the learning outcomes of a project, which makes it easier to learn.**
	Neurologically, we find it more challenging to learn something quickly and well if we are unclear about what we should be doing, or if we focus on multiple things. We used to say that the conscious brain can handle 5 +/– 2 bits of information at one time; now we understand it is more like one piece of information at one time. This is the key focus of the project.

TABLE 8.1   *continued*

G: Generation of ownership	**Workplace projects encourage learners to reflect on their experience and learning from a project, which can make it easier to learn and make it last longer.**
	Neurologically, if we have to make sense of something complex, for example reflecting on what is happening during the project, or reflecting on the outcomes after the project, it is processed in more and deeper parts of the brain. This means it is more likely to be kept by the brain (and body) – similar to the central idea of the Chinese proverb: 'Tell me and I'll forget; show me and I may remember; let me do, and I'll understand.'
E: Emotions	**Workplace projects live in the tensions of real emotions and politics – this is a valuable benefit to direct what is realistic in practice, but it is also something to be managed by a skilled facilitator.**
	Neurologically, emotional 'content' grabs the attention of the learner and helps focus the learning on the importance of something. Work-based learning projects for developing leadership behaviours are 'lived out' in the reality of a situation, including all of the tensions of a modern workplace – politics, competition, collaboration and so on. Learning that integrates this is highly valuable – but it is also important to ensure there is a positive facilitator to help guide the learner into positive emotional states throughout the project.
S: Spacing	**Workplace projects can be spaced to the actual pace of work tasks, which can make the learning stick better and longer – rather than short, intensive blocks of learning.**
	Neurologically, creating space between learning interventions enables better memory and retention of learning, compared to short, intensive blocks of learning. As real workplace projects can be spaced to requirements, it enables the learner's brain to more easily absorb the key points of their reflections and learning.

How to design projects for learning

There are many ways in which work-based projects can be designed, developed and implemented: the key is to be clear about what it is you want to achieve and who will benefit from it. Before discussing the 'how to', it is crucial to emphasize how important the role of a project learning facilitator is. There is no doubt that facilitators influence learners and the learning process by their presence, style and manner. In any learning project, facilitators need to build and maintain a connectedness with learners, keeping in step and maintaining rhythm. Hogan (2003) poetically describes this process as an 'artful dance' between the facilitator and the learner. The role of the project learning facilitator will be discussed as we progress through this chapter.

It is difficult to quantify the learning that will take place through conducting a work-based project, but we know that learning will always be driven by hands-on experience in the workplace. As such, learners are encouraged to reflect on experience and whether or not their chosen project is relevant to them and/or their organization. Facilitators need to be mindful that the projects that learners negotiate should, whenever possible, contribute to a recognized strategic development within the organization and thus enhance working practices. Projects that are not aligned to a recognized strategic development may be, and be seen to be, wasted effort and hence negatively affect the motivation for all those involved.

For example, this could be learning about leadership strategies for innovation and creativity as an important development area in the business. Using relevant best practice and academic models and theories (wherever possible), this can frame the learners' thinking about an area before wide-ranging practical engagement in the field at work, and then also help them to validate, verify and reflect on practice within the organization. The idea is not necessarily to agree with these published sources, but to use them, and alongside our experiences, evaluate how useful they have been for the purposes, thereby creating both focus and new insight. Rather than wide-ranging practical engagement, it could also be the case that the learner is actively involved in a very specific area of project work which involves him or her in current and future strategic development (University of Chester, 2012).

So how do we design a project which creates such positive outcomes? Davachi *et al*'s (2010) AGES model, mentioned earlier, identifies some key principles. For facilitators, this means:

- Attention – Focus attention on the first steps of defining the project: a particular issue or problem within the learner's leadership assessment (or broader area of work) needs to be identified.

- Generation of ownership – The learner needs to discuss and negotiate the focus of the project with the facilitator and/or other people involved in the project so it is clear who 'owns' it and who is responsible for it. The learner should also be encouraged to reflect, and discuss his or her progress, evaluation and learning generated by the project.

- Emotion – The facilitator and learner need to work in collaboration to create a positive environment. The facilitator needs to provide positive feedback and support so that the learner has clarity in his or her objectives (see feeding back/forward in Chapter 6).

- Spacing – The facilitator and learner need to create space and time for reflection in order to make sense of the project stages, development, impact, etc.

We might intuitively think that equal consideration or weighting is given to each stage of a project. However, arguably, the biggest chunk of any project comes in the time we need to plan, in terms of thinking energy. Note the time ratio between planning/thinking and acting in Turner's (1993, 2008) project cycle in Figure 8.1.

FIGURE 8.1   The project cycle

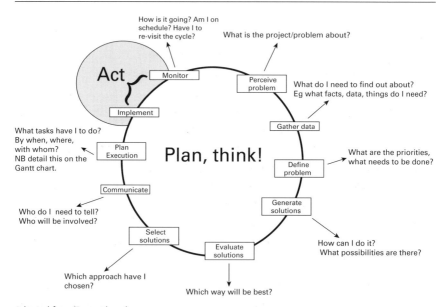

Adapted from Turner (1993)

Facilitators need to have the skills to ask the right questions and encourage the learner to ask the right questions before, during and after the project (Heron, 2005). In other words, the ability to reflect (for both the facilitator and the learner) is integral to conducting any project. But, what do we mean by 'reflection'?

Have you ever stopped to ask yourself what you mean when you use the word 'experience' or, indeed, if this meaning is shared by others? If experience is something that is valued, then it is important to have some insight into what is actually being valued. When educationists refer to 'learning from experience' in relation to personal growth and development, they are usually referring to a learning process in which the learner is actively involved. This view encourages learners to reflect on their experience; in other words, to look back at what they have learnt from the experience.

Reflection (as opposed to critical reflection) is sometimes characterized as largely instrumental in purpose (Moon, 2004). Simply looking back is not enough. Surely, the purpose of reflection is to look back with a view to learning from what has happened during or after the experience? In this way, consideration of past experiences can often be an invaluable guide to any future action that one may take. For example, if a learner has had a negative experience in developing his or her leadership skills in the past, this can surely affect his or her confidence, approach, and/or willingness to engage in future development projects. The skill of the facilitator is invaluable here. Facilitators are in a privileged position and need to understand the learner's perspective from the outset.

Reflection in the context of learning is a general term in which individuals engage to explore and analyse their experiences in order to lead to new understanding. In other words, reflection is learning from doing, and about looking back and forward in an analytical way. This process is known as 'critical reflection', and there are various models that can help learners frame their thinking. For the work-based learner involved in project management, Schön's model is a good introduction. Schön (1992) advocates two types of reflection: 1) *reflection in action* – where the learners reflect on a situation while performing it, so they are able to change the direction of the situation accordingly (a great skill in project management when things do not go according to initial plans and they need to change); and 2) *reflection on action* – where the learners look back and critically analyse the situation after the event, with a view to doing things differently in future scenarios, whether they are similar or not. It is also useful to remember that reflection does not have to have negative connotations. There are usually many positive things that come out of project learning and the facilitator needs to be able to offer positive feedback in line with the 'emotion' and 'spacing' elements of Davachi's AGES model above.

So how might critical reflection be encouraged in designing work-based projects? It is important that project facilitators understand that the learner is in charge and should be encouraged to negotiate whenever possible. Typical steps in the process of designing a project underpinned with critical reflection include:

- Negotiate and identify a particular issue or problem to be investigated. The learner will negotiate with the facilitator a feasible project title and whether the project is realistic.

- Devise a way of analysing the problem or approaching the new initiative. The learner will negotiate with the facilitator how to explore the possible options for resolving any problems. Burke (2003) suggests that each option should be examined in turn.

- Identify any barriers to effective implementation.

- Negotiate and set out specific objectives and timeframes; Gardiner (2005) encourages the use of Gantt or project management charts.

- State actions to be taken to ensure the success of the project.

- Determine how to communicate the problem, proposed solutions and implementation plans of proposal, to colleagues/managers.

- Negotiate and select how the project will be assessed and how the learning will be measured in terms of the objectives (see the next section of this chapter). Heron (1999) suggests many ways in which the facilitator can work with the learner so that the learner becomes more empowered to make choices for his or her own benefit.

- Agree the way in which the learner will critically reflect on the whole process from the planning to the implementation and evaluation stages. There are many models of reflection that the learner may use to help frame his or her reflective thinking (for example, Boud *et al*, 1985; Ghaye and Lillyman, 1997; Gibbs, 1998; Rock, 2007; Schön, 1992).

Salvaging learning from projects

As already mentioned, we should not underestimate the learning that happens before, during and after projects – and it is possible to tap in to and build on that learning over time to increase the sustainability of projects and project talents to enhance future project outcomes. Whether or not the learner has achieved the desired quality, budgetary or timeline requirements, the learning project facilitator should consider how he or she might encourage learners to salvage the inevitably rich and authentic learning from their projects. Developed over many years, the Meakin Salvage Strategy, shown in Table 8.2, was specifically developed to do this positively with project learners.

TABLE 8.2   The Meakin SALVAGE Strategy

S: Setting the scene	Here, we encourage free discussion where learners simply talk about their ideas, reflecting on their experiences and how these might impact on their future projects.
A: Allow to happen	The facilitator should use a laissez-faire approach ('allow to happen'). Let the learners drive the pace and decide on the approach for themselves.
L: Live it	Live all experiences and learn from them. Learners should be encouraged to use all experiences as learning opportunities, even if they see them as negative.
V: Verify it	Learners should be encouraged to back up their assumptions with relevant evidence from their experience, and/or published sources (whenever possible).
A: Accept and Action	Learners should be encouraged to accept the project stages and put their plan/s into action. This also means that they should act on the 'findings' of the project.
G: Grow	We encourage the learners to grow and learn from the project as a whole. Be confident that new learning has taken place and that limiting beliefs have dissolved, or actions are set to start that process.
E: Evaluate	Learners should see evaluation as a dynamic process during and following each stage of the project and not just on its completion.

Rewarding project learning through academic credit

An increasingly popular way to reward and recognize the learning achieved through projects is by awarding academic credit for that learning. This is where the learning and the evidence from the workplace project is assessed as part of a first or Master's degree. This gives an independent stamp of approval to the quality and significance of that learning, one which is internationally recognized. When accredited in this way, the individual can have a greater sense of commitment to the project, and in doing it with a higher level of rigour and challenge: it can lead to something even bigger. A discussion of how work-based learning projects can impact organizations is discussed by the UK's Higher Education Academy (HEA, 2008). An example of such accreditation is the LeaderShape-approved Postgraduate Certificate, Diploma and Master's degree in Transpersonal Leadership.

The key added aspect is assessment or measurement of the learning against the international standards of higher education. The United Kingdom and the United States, like many other countries, have declared national standards, and in Europe there is a regional framework that has currency beyond borders, which usually specify what is expected from a particular qualification such as degrees. Getting credit for work-based projects against these international standards is most easily achieved through negotiated work-based learning programmes. These programmes are specifically designed for this – the learners decide the focus of their studies (sometimes with their employer), they decide when to study, they decide how to study and, importantly in the context of learning through workplace projects, they decide specifically what they will learn and how their learning will be assessed. One of the leading centres of its kind for negotiated work-based learning is the University of Chester's Centre of Work Related Studies (see **http://www.chester.ac.uk/cwrs**).

These ideas directly mirror and align to the processes discussed in this chapter so far, and build a significant level of ownership, commitment and enthusiasm for the learner's project and learning. Working with a university that offers the flexibility of a negotiated work-based learning degree means a key decision is on the form of assessment, or measurement of the learning that will be accredited as part of a degree. There are many different ways in which learning may be assessed, and examples that are more applicable to the workplace include:

- *Reports* – these are perhaps the most popular choice, whereby an authentic workplace report is used as part of the assessment, for example, a sales-impact report of developing a particular leadership skill or behaviour. The quality of the report it judged on its purpose within the context. *Reflective reports* are a variant; they include the personal reflections of the individual. Although reflective reports enable much more of a personal exploration of individual learning, they may not be appropriate in some business contexts.

- *Professional discussions* – these are discussions between an assessor and the learner, where the emphasis is on exploring and judging the learning together. An example might be a discussion on a particular leadership skill, and may include a demonstration of the new skill within the session. A variant is a *Professional interview*, which is where an assessor asks specific questions of the learner and judges the responses. The interview approach is much less collegiate in making collective judgements on areas of strength and development.

- *Presentations and posters* – having to design a persuasive presentation or poster to colleagues can be a challenging task, but provides an ideal opportunity for learners to express and share their learning enthusiastically through visuals and interactivity. Visuals or movies of new skills are a powerful way to demonstrate the subtleties of behaviours.

- *Reflective journals or reviews* – these are reflective 'pieces' in various forms, such as journals, diaries, essays or short reports, which primarily aim to help the learner reflect in action and on action. They help learners in exploring alternative ways to look at things in their project, thereby enabling and encouraging greater insights into what is happening, and what might be done as a result.

- *Workplace artefacts* – new products, sales scripts, websites, promotional campaign briefs, team structure design, customer feedback, process diagrams – these are the readily available, tangible objects that learners might produce throughout their workplace project. It is important that the artefacts chosen are used as prompts to question both what went well and what else might have been done.

- *Portfolios of learning evidence* are a mix of the above.

So there are many different ways to assess the learning, and key guiding questions in designing assessment strategies are:

- Does the assessment strategy actually measure the intended focus and outcomes? Or does it measure more or something else? For example, in developing empathy-related behaviours, would a poster actually assess it – or would artefacts such as customer ratings and feedback be more reliable?

- Does the assessment strategy actually encourage more, deeper learning? Or is it assessing for some other purpose such as promotion? For example, in developing abilities to regulate one's own emotions, would uninitiated feedback from a colleague assess it – or would personal reflections in a diary encourage a more sensitive exploration?

- Could the assessment be simpler, to encourage more of the above? The more complex the assessment, the more the assessment can become inauthentic and unmotivational. Remember the 'attention' aspect of the AGES model – clarity of focus supports learners in developing their talents.

SPECIFIC ACTION POINTS

This chapter has focused on the value of real, workplace projects for learning purposes, as a serious addition or even alternative to structured training interventions. It outlined the practical steps facilitators and managers can take to design workplace projects, and how they can develop commitment through continually salvaging learning from projects and rewarding it through university credit. The key action points from this chapter are:

- Consider workplace projects as serious options for talent development – they can significantly build commitment and motivation, and can have a direct and immediate impact in businesses.

- Establish who is best placed to negotiate the focus and detail of the project, and who can facilitate the learners as they progress through the project – this may be a formal or informal mentoring or coaching relationship.

- This facilitator needs to be someone who can negotiate a focus with the learner, negotiate involvement of others who need to be involved in the project, create a positive environment for learning (see Chapter 7 on coaching), and who can help the learner create space and time for reflection.

- Encourage project planning – planning workplace projects is a rich source of initial learning, especially if it involves collecting intelligence from inside or outside the organization on how other people have undertaken similar projects.

- Encourage reflection – reflection is a rich source of learning through the project (reflecting *in* action), and after the project (reflecting *on* action), and critical reflection creates a more rigorous form of learning based on analysing and exploring alternatives and evidence.

- Salvage learning from all projects – this will help a virtuous cycle of learning from projects for different talent development goals (SALVAGE = Setting the scene, Allowing it to happen, Living it, Verifying it, Accepting and Acting, Growing, Evaluating).

- Consider university accreditation to add another layer of commitment and motivation, because it is widely recognized and valued – it is important to choose a flexible university that operates a negotiated work-based learning programme.

- Identify which forms of assessment are the most important for measuring what they should be, for encouraging deeper learning, and doing this in the simplest way possible.

FURTHER RESOURCES

Business Balls Online – **http://www.businessballs.com** – has many free resources on assessing and evaluating the outcomes of learning, training and development activity. References related to 'evaluation', 'Kirkpatrick' models of evaluation and 'Return on investment' are interesting and tried-and-tested approaches. It has a useful list of different evaluation models/frameworks for learning and development activity that can be identified through Google searches (**http://google.co.uk**).

Chartered Institute of Personnel and Development (UK) – **http://www.cipd.co.uk** – this professional body has a number of resources online related to learning and development assessment and evaluation strategies.

David Rock Net – **http://www.davidrock.net** – the 'Resources' area is a major source of easily accessible and informative neuroscience material, including the AGES model. Includes academic and industry journal articles. Particularly interesting articles include 'Learning that lasts through AGES', 'SCARF: a brain-based model for collaborating with and influencing others', and 'Managing with the brain in mind'.

Encyclopaedia of Informal Education – **http://www.infed.org/** – a useful resource of theorists that contribute to learning through experience (experiential learning). Key entries include David A Kolb, Donald Schön, John Dewey, Chris Argyris, experiential learning, learning theory, reflection, but there are many others.

Mind Tools Project Management Resources – **http://www.mindtools.com/** – a useful set of techniques for managing and monitoring projects. Areas include: project management phases and processes (including stakeholder analysis, business cases, project initiation documents, scheduling, sequencing and Gantt charts), structuring the project, planning cycles, implementation tools (such as prioritization, testing and benefits management), and programme management (multiple projects).

UK Funding Council Report – **http://hdl.handle.net/10034/116736** – report on facilitating employer engagement through negotiated work-based learning sent to all UK universities including Oxford and Cambridge, about how to facilitate negotiated work-based learning, including through work-based projects.

Wikipedia Reflective Practice – **http://en.wikipedia.org/wiki/Reflective_practice** – this has a useful review of many classic models for reflection, including Argyris and Schön, Kolb, Gibbs, Johns, and Rolfe.

References

Boud, D, Keogh, R and Walker, D (eds) (1985) *Reflection: Turning experience into learning*, Kogan Page, London

Burke, R (2003) *Project Management*, 4th edn, John Wiley, Chichester

Davachi, L, Kiefer, T, Rock, D and Rock, L (2010) Learning that lasts through AGES, *NeuroLeadership Journal*, 3, pp 1–11

Gardiner, P (2005) *Project Management: A strategic planning approach*, Palgrave, Basingstoke

Ghaye, T and Lillyman, S (1997) *Learning Journals and Critical Incidents*, Quay, Dinton

Gibbs, G (1998) *Learning by Doing: A guide to teaching and learning methods*, Oxford Further Education Unit, Oxford

Heron, J (1999) *The Complete Facilitators Handbook*, Kogan Page, London

Heron, J (2005) *Helping the Client: A creative practical guide*, 5th edn, Sage, London

Higher Education Academy (HEA) (2008) *Work-based Learning Impact Study*, HEA, York

Hogan, C (2003) *Practical Facilitation*, Kogan Page, London

Moon, J (2004) *A Handbook of Reflective and Experiential Learning: Theory and practice*, Routledge Falmer, London

Rock, D (2007) *Quiet Leadership: Six steps to transforming performance at work*, HarperCollins, New York

Schön, D (1992) *The Reflective Practitioner*, 2nd edn, Jossey-Bass, San Francisco, CA

Turner, J R (1993) *Handbook of Project Management*, McGraw Hill, London

Turner, J R (2008) *Handbook of Project Management*, McGraw Hill, London

University of Chester (2012) *Negotiated Experiential Learning Module Handbook*, University of Chester, Chester

CASE STUDY   Workplace project for empathetic behaviours

Tony Wall

This case study reports a workplace project designed to address the specific development needs of a senior leader (named 'Naseem' here) within a division of the largest retail bank in the United Kingdom. The banking group had an annual turnover of over £18 billion (US$30 billion) and had experienced a number of changes within the last five years, including acquisitions. Remaining strong during the economic downturn, it nevertheless continued to invest in its leadership.

Within this new context, a number of leaders were identified within the group to undertake a leadership development journey that encouraged them to identify their own development agenda. For one senior leader, this meant focusing on developing empathetic leadership (a key development area for leaders according to the research presented in Chapter 3). According to a leadership assessment tool (LEIPA®), this meant designing a project that would develop behaviours in the following areas:

1   Listening attentively to what people say.

2   Demonstrating an awareness of how people are feeling.

3   Accurately identifying the underlying causes of the other person's perspective.

4   Expresses an understanding of the other person's perspective.

This case example reports some of the key actions that were taken as part of the project, including reflective practices, and some of the key impacts that resulted, such as a change in personal perspective, confidence and job satisfaction.

A project for empathetic behaviours

How does an organization use assessments for developing leadership talent? For this particular project, the senior leaders involved in the leadership development programme were given autonomy to choose areas of their leadership practice they wanted to develop. The leaders used feedback from colleagues and customers as stimuli to consider which elements of their behaviours they wanted to develop – mainly 'reflecting on action' that had already happened. The leaders worked in groups of similar leaders from within the banking group to positively and constructively question each other to identify key issues of both personal and strategic importance for the banking group. An independent, external facilitator (see Chapter 9 on director peer groups) supported the group meetings.

Each leader worked with the external facilitator to design actions that would develop the leadership behaviours he or she desired. Together, these actions *were* the workplace project that the senior leaders would implement, evaluate, reflect on, and then identify further actions to continue development in these areas; in other words, a cycle of development. The role of the facilitator in both the group and one-to-one intervention was to encourage attention and generation of ownership on the positive outcomes that the workplace projects should *aim* to achieve – as per the AGES model.

Naseem was questioned by the members of the group about his ability to demonstrate empathetic leadership behaviours, and he found great insight in continuing this line of thinking. Naseem decided he needed to invest time and energy in developing this side of his leadership practice. For him it was about becoming more connected to the other person whether a customer or colleague, with whom he could better communicate.

According to the LEIPA® assessment tool, Naseem needed to develop the four sub-behaviours listed above. He agreed the focus of the project would be to develop empathetic leadership behaviours and, more specifically, aim to demonstrate these sub-behaviours according to the perceptions of others. Hence, the project was entitled 'Learning new and effective empathetic leadership behaviours with colleagues'.

Naseem then identified and analysed the different ways of achieving the behaviours. For example, he researched the 'perceptual positions' technique used within neurolinguistic programming, whereby a person intentionally adopts different positions within a situation (Dilts and DeLozier, 2000). The aim of the tool is to generate different insights into what might be occurring from different angles. In Naseem's case, this included his own position, the position of a colleague he talks to in the same organizational division, and an independent, objective observer. The idea was that stepping in to the other person's or an objective observer's position would encourage a distancing from the situation to see new perspectives – and thereby opening up new ways to react and respond in a specific context.

It was also agreed how Naseem would critically reflect during the project, and on the whole process, from the planning to the evaluation stages. Schön's (1992) concept of reflecting in and on action was used, with additional reflective questions from Boud *et al* (1985), such as, 'What might be happening here?', 'So what might explain this?' and, 'Now what might I do?'

Alternative ideas were analysed in depth and the limitations of each approach were acknowledged to encourage Naseem to be aware of what can (and cannot) be legitimately concluded from the project learning experiences. The total composite of actions was agreed with the facilitator. An example of an approach with a leader is:

- Apply a *mindful listening* technique – specifically to address the attentive listening behaviour, involving paying close attention to the colleague's body language.

- Apply *perceptual positions* technique (see above).

- Ask for open feedback on key interactions.

- Reflect on own applications in action.

- Reflect on own applications on action.

Next, any barriers to effective implementation of the approach were identified. In particular, potential conflict situations were identified by Naseem as blocks to being able to effectively apply the perceptual positions technique. Here, an intense high-conflict state could prevent the flexibility to appreciate the other's perspective (an unproductive 'away state'; see Chapter 6). In addition to the above approach a further aspect was included: Apply a *breathing technique* before responses – to mitigate the negative emotional states that would prevent using the perceptual positions technique.

Naseem then set out specific targets and time frames using a Gantt chart, which included:

Weeks 1–5: practise techniques and getting 'naturally occurring feedback' from colleagues (discussed below).

By week 6: have reflected on three applications of techniques, as appropriate.

Weeks 6–12: refine and practise behaviours.

By week 13: have collected feedback from colleagues in relation to each sub-behaviour.

By week 16: have created a final reflective report of key learning points, evidence and actions for further development.

Actions that were needed to ensure the success of the project were also agreed, which included: 1) get agreement of focus and timescale from own line manager; and 2) practise getting feedback in 'naturally occurring forms' – it was important to Naseem that the authenticity of the interactions was maintained, so he decided to practise ways of getting feedback. Examples included what people say or ask after an interaction which might indicate the message in the communication has been understood. This also involved developing Naseem's own sensory acuity to micro behaviours of colleagues to suggest they feel they have been heard or not (eg what might be seen as a 'genuine' smile) (Dilts and DeLozier, 2000).

Next, Naseem agreed *how* to communicate the outcomes of his learning and the implementation plans of other proposals. This involved communicating the key action plans of other development issues to his line manager. This was to demonstrate the continued commitment of Naseem to his own journey and to maintain management buy-in.

Finally, before the implementation and evaluation of the project, Naseem agreed with the facilitator how the learning in the project would be measured and assessed. Naseem chose the following aspects:

- reflective report of the major insights and behaviour changes during the period;
- evidence to support the claims to learning, such as statements/e-mail extracts;
- simulation/demonstration of some of the new behaviours with the facilitator.

On completing the project, Naseem used the above assessment as part of a Master's qualification in Leadership at the University of Chester. The carefully planned approach and clear assessment strategy enabled academic credit for the experiential learning that had been generated through the real workplace project.

What benefits have been gained?

The leaders within the banking group who participated in the leadership development journey all experienced positive behavioural shifts, according to their intentions. Each had different targets and workplace projects as each was located in different positions and priorities. Naseem also achieved, with convincing evidence, a shift in the specific behaviours he focused on in relation to empathetic leadership. In particular, some of the broader benefits include:

- increased sense of confidence and autonomy in work role;

- greater sense of direction and congruence with values;

- greater work performance from a greater professional flexibility.

Critical reflection with experiential learning in a leadership journey is a powerful combination to enable behavioural change. Yet it can also raise the question of whether someone is ready for the journey – some choose to leave the journey because it can raise difficult issues they are not professionally or emotionally ready to deal with at that moment. The facilitator must be ready for possible disclosures of difficult feelings or situations, and support and signpost as necessary, with the help of the host organization.

Learning points

There were a number of key learning points in this case study:

- Approaching a workplace project is not just about the tools and techniques that will be applied during a project – it is also about how reflection will happen, which is a crucial strategy for experiential learning in projects.

- Planning for the barriers to implementation can affect the overall approach to the project. Conflict handling and management responses/behaviours may also be useful even if they are not intentionally a key part of the learning in the project.

- A feedback questionnaire with customers may be possible on occasion but, with specific behaviours, getting feedback in a 'naturally occurring way' may be more feasible. This could take the form of sensory acuity (paying close attention) to a person's reactions or responses to a newly developed behaviour. This needs to be related to the specific behaviours being developed.

References

Boud, D, Keogh, R and Walker, D (eds) (1985) *Reflection: Turning experience into learning*, Kogan Page, London

Dilts, R B and DeLozier, J (2000) *The Encyclopaedia of Systemic NLP and NLP New Coding*, NLP University Press, Santa Cruz, CA

Schön, D (1992) *The Reflective Practitioner*, 2nd edn, Jossey-Bass, San Francisco, CA

TOOL   Project learning question checklist tool

Tony Wall

What it is and when to use it

This tool is a checklist of questions to use with people undertaking learning projects. It can be used after a leadership assessment, where particular priority areas have been identified and discussed within the action planning process. It is important to do this before the action to begin developing the leadership granular behaviours, as the investigatory work can facilitate major learning points in itself, and be an efficient and low-risk way for talent development.

There are also questions related to the doing of the plan, or reflecting in action. There are additional questions that purposively ask for alternative perspectives or 'who would agree to or dispute'. This encourages people to seek evidence of the claims they are making beyond an internal perception, as evidence is key.

Once acted on, there are questions specifically related to what has been learnt – or the reflecting on action. This is relatively simple but not always conclusive and it is useful to encourage a continuous flow of reflections and encourage the idea that we can always do things different and better. These questions are put to project learners at different points in a learning project's life and can be either in a written form or used orally in debriefing sessions. Not all questions need be answered but they are prompts to encourage insight.

The checklist is not exhaustive and you could develop your own version to focus particularly on the leadership behaviours to be learnt by asking specific questions about, for example, granular behaviours related to empathy.

Project learning questions

Scope

What is the project about?

What is the problem I am/we are aiming to solve?

What is the solution I am/we are putting in place?

What do I need to find out about?

What facts do I need?

What resources do I need?

What are the priorities from the leadership assessment feedback?

Approach

What needs to be done?

What are the alternative ways to do it?

How can it be done?

How will I decide *how to choose* the best approach? What criteria will I use?

Which way is best according to my criteria?

Action plan

Which way have I chosen?

Who do I need to tell?

Who needs to be involved?

What are the tasks that need to be done?

How will the tasks be done? By whom? When?

Pre-action learning check

What has been learnt so far?

What else was interesting?

How could this impact my approach?

In action

How is it going?

Who would agree with my conclusion?

Who would dispute my conclusions?

What evidence do I have?

Am I on schedule?

Is quality being achieved?

Who would agree with my conclusion?

Who would dispute my conclusions?

Do I need to revisit the plan?

Who do I need to tell?

Post-action learning check

What have I learnt so far about what works?

What have I learnt so far about what could be done differently?

What else have I learnt so far?

What else was interesting?

What might I do that is slightly different, to get a different result?

What might I do that is radically different, to get a different result?

How could this impact my next approach?

TOOL   The Meakin Salvage Strategy Tool

Denise Meakin and Tony Wall

What it is and when to use it

This tool can be used in discussions with someone undertaking a learning project. It can be used to focus attention on project learning and also, particularly, when the project learner (or the project team) feels the project has not gone as they wish. It positively encourages the learner to focus on key constructive messages throughout – starting with the name of the tool, SALVAGE – salvaging learning from the project; saving something valuable.

Focusing attention on the learning rather than on other outcomes is particularly important; it emphasizes the importance of learning for moving on and moving forward. (It would be useful to refer to Chapter 6 on feeding back and forwards, and Chapter 7 on coaching.)

The key principles are highlighted in Table 8.3, followed by a template in Table 8.4 that can be used in learning project contexts. The tool can be used in different ways:

1 A checklist to be used by the learner – useful when the learner is confident and self-directed, though a facilitator can help draw attention to the positive angles.

2 A checklist used by the facilitator (a coach may use different questions) – particularly useful when the learner is experiencing something negative.

3 As part of the formal review processes, emphasizing the learning and positive angles.

4 Conversationally – used as a mental checklist of principles in conversations with colleagues and project learners.

5 To explore thoughts using sticky notes in a project team session – rather than 'I', the focus is on 'we'. This is also useful to focus on the learning and positive angles, rather than allowing negative or energy-sapping comments to over-occupy the session.

TABLE 8.3　SALVAGE – key principles

	Key principles
S: Setting the scene	Encourage free discussion where learners simply talk about their ideas, reflecting on their experiences and how these might impact on their future projects.
A: Allow to happen	Use a laissez-faire approach ('allow to happen'). Let the learners drive the pace and decide on the approach for themselves.
L: Live it	Live all experiences and learn from them. Encourage the use of all experiences as learning opportunities, even if they see them as negative.
V: Verify it	Encourage the backing up of assumptions with relevant evidence from their experience, and/or published sources (whenever possible).
A: Accept and Action	Encourage accepting the project stages and put their plan/s into action. This also means that learners should act on the 'findings' of the project.
G: Grow	Encourage learners to grow and learn from the project as a whole. Be confident that new learning has taken place and that limiting beliefs have dissolved, or actions are set to start that process.
E: Evaluate	Encourage positive use of evaluation as a dynamic process during and following each stage of the project and not just on completion.

TABLE 8.4   Meakin SALVAGE tool – template

S: Setting the scene	
A: Allow to happen	
L: Live it	
V: Verify it	
A: Accept and Action	
G: Grow	
E: Evaluate	

Director peer groups for team talent development

09

CHRIS GULLIVER

EXECUTIVE SUMMARY

Working at senior level in any organization can be a very demanding and lonely job. Senior executives have to tackle any challenge that comes their way regardless of past experience, skills or training. Concerns and doubts may also be difficult to explore, especially when experience and capabilities within the organization are limited in some way or there is high sensitivity. Part of the problem may be that, in many organizations, training and development is focused on lower or middle management and continued learning at senior level is neglected, regarded as unnecessary, or positioned as a sign of weakness or inadequacy either by the organization or by the individual. Director peer groups (DPGs) offer a solution to this situation.

With action learning as a core process, DPG programmes have been in use globally for many years. If structured correctly, these are a well-proven model providing continuing development for senior executives. They provide a safe, open and confidential forum for discussion of personal or business issues with peers who provide constructive feedback, and an opportunity to gain knowledge and insights from specialists and experts.

Personal benefits from membership of a DPG include the development of important leadership capabilities such as critical reflection, improved emotional intelligence (EI), insights from other members' experience, improved decision making, increased confidence and a reduced sense of isolation. Organizational benefits include significantly more effective leadership, improved focus especially on strategic issues, updated management thinking and solutions for problems and road-blocks. The keys to optimizing the potential benefits include such things as size and membership mix of each DPG, establishing the best environment for engagement, discussion and learning, the creation of 'ownership' of the DPG, the construction and management of agendas that suit the needs of the members, and good facilitation.

DPGs for team talent development

Personal development is a necessary continuing process no matter what leadership level an individual may reach in an organization. Awareness of the scope and direction of this development may not be generated until some form of formal or informal leadership assessment has taken place. DPGs provide a practical and stimulating continuing learning facility to enable members to follow up on leadership assessments or, alternatively, a means of creating awareness of personal development potential that includes leadership assessment.

DPGs provide an opportunity, sometimes the only one, for members to stand outside their businesses or organizations and look in objectively with the support of other members. It may be the only structured time, in a busy and hectic diary, for some critical and/or constructive reflection on their current situations or their personal behaviours and relationships. This all takes place in a safe and confidential environment where openness and honesty can provide a platform for learning and personal development.

The safety of the environment enables members to be more open about their knowledge and experience gaps than they may feel they can be with their colleagues or staff. This openness and transparency can take the shape of asking for input, advice and support from fellow members and in feeling able to ask what might seem to be simple questions of fellow members or invited topic experts. Again, this enhances learning opportunities.

Significantly improved self-awareness, which can be a key part of a leadership or talent development programme, can be achieved by group participation in psychometric tests and personality profiling. Experience has shown that 360° assessments, such as LEIPA® (see Chapter 5) are especially valuable when they involve working colleagues and/or staff. Real workplace feedback encourages DPG members to take a hard look at their leadership behaviours and how these can be modified and developed to suit varying situations and personalities. Other useful tools for increasing self-awareness include Myers Briggs (see **www.myersbriggs.org**), and Learning Style Preferences (Honey and Mumford, 1992). Participation in a leadership assessment programme such as LEIPA® can stimulate interest in joining a DPG or can be part of a DPG programme for members.

Benefits of DPGs

Personal benefits

Challenging but supportive feedback from fellow members enables individuals to look hard and test their own thinking, behaviour, prejudices and relationships (see Chapter 6 on feeding back/forward). This can sometimes be uncomfortable but very rewarding. The most common challenges relate to people, for example where a working relationship is not as fruitful as it should be. In these cases it is frequently related to the approach and behaviour of the DPG member (see below).

A good facilitator or an invited topic expert might introduce concepts, tools or knowledge that are new to some or all members (see Further Resources section). Members can then practise these new tools and/or concepts so that they can gain understanding and confidence with them before using them in their work environment. A good example is the introduction of coaching skills – a critical leadership capability. This can only be developed with real practice and feedback, so a DPG is an ideal environment.

Providing the group is robust enough in terms of willingness to listen to new ideas (for them) and giving and taking honest feedback, members see significant improvements in their leadership capabilities. These improvements relate to such things as critical reflection, improved self-awareness and EI, improved decision making, improved communication skills (a common weakness emerging from LEIPA® assessments), increased self-confidence and a reduced sense of isolation.

Organizational benefits

In addition to the personal benefits described above, members of DPGs find these spin off into significant organizational benefits.

More effective leadership by DPG members within their organizations encourages and allows the development of their senior teams and a growth in a culture of knowledge sharing and learning. One aspect of this is often a general improvement in strategic focus. Once effectively communicated within the member's organizations, this can energize the management and staff and provide a clearer context for decision making at all levels including an improved ability to react quickly to unexpected crises and roadblocks.

How to set up, structure and run a DPG

As mentioned above, DPGs provide a safe, open and confidential forum for discussion of personal or business issues with peers who are willing to share knowledge and insights, and give constructive feedback where appropriate. Areas of weaker or dated group knowledge can be addressed by inviting topic experts or specialists. However, this will only be optimized if the groups are set up and run effectively and that means some basic structures and processes need to be kept in mind and built in to any programme.

Experience shows that, among other things, group size and mix are critical and that a membership of eight or nine is an optimum size. Beyond 12 there is a risk that there is insufficient 'air-time' for all members to engage in time-limited discussion, the group can splinter into sub-groups and 'hiding' can take place. On the other hand, bearing in mind that it is likely that there will be occasional member absences because of illness or an unexpected business demand, membership should not be lower than six so that there is always sufficient creative resource. Members should be from non-competing organizations that are, ideally, of reasonably similar size, and all have a level of experience that makes it feel like a meeting of 'peers' (although we have experience of groups that functioned well where a European president of a multinational was in the same group as the owner of a small marketing company). Sector-based groups may be inhibited in some discussions by sector history, culture and experience and may not benefit from the diversity of experience that a mix of sectors, and therefore cultures and experience, can provide, especially where there are significant organizational size differentials that may prejudice the willingness to listen to other members' opinions.

It can be difficult to understand how a DPG really works without experiencing one. Attracting new members may be difficult, so start-up groups can be initiated by inviting potential members to a well-facilitated sample meeting at which they can experience a DPG before agreeing to the formation of a new group. Ideally this would be a meeting of no less than eight so that there is a reasonable chance of acquiring enough members to start a new group. In addition to understating the format and process this sample meeting facilitates compatibility – testing between potential members so that they will feel comfortable with the general nature of personalities within the group. An expert session on an already identified topic of common interest will encourage attendance. Members who are interested in joining an established group can be invited to a scheduled group meeting subject to signing a confidentiality letter (see the Tools section at the end of this chapter). Once again, personal compatibility can be tested.

At an early stage of formation new DPG members need to agree their ground rules for membership, which everyone signs up to. This would include such things as attendance expectations and behaviour (an example of ground rules and membership expectations is shown in the Tools section). Meeting frequency and duration also need to be agreed; this may be influenced by members' personal time pressures, availability and working routines and can be amended in the light of experience. However, in our experience a meeting frequency of less than every six weeks can be difficult for members and a full day provides a better opportunity to cover a meaningful agenda.

DPG meeting agendas need to be structured and adapted to meet member preferences. However, members usually like a regular format with guidance and leadership on this from a skilled group facilitator who will sense any need for change (a sample agenda is included in the Tools section). It is always useful to run through the agenda at the start of a meeting to ensure there are no urgent issues or topics that should receive priority or displace planned agenda items. This encourages group ownership of the DPG and optimizes potential value. This agenda shift may arise when, at the start of a meeting, members each give an update on major events or situations that have arisen since the previous meeting.

As mentioned above, action learning is a core process in a DPG issue discussion session. Structuring this discussion, in a way that is understood and accepted by members, is vital so that focus is maintained at the same time as encouraging a well-managed discussion that does not inhibit dialogue and productivity. There are a number of techniques for running these sessions but adapting a one-to-one coaching model has proved successful so that there is a structure and sequence that is understood by DPG members (this is covered in more detail below).

The nature of issue session topics usually changes over time. Initially a series of hard business topics is likely. This will probably then shift to much greater focus on people and relationship issues that may be more difficult to resolve. It is important that all issue discussions are followed up at the next meeting. Members will be interested to hear what action has been taken and share in the evaluation of how well it has worked. It also increases the probability that action will be taken because the issue owner knows he or she will have to report back and explain any deviations and/or prevarication.

Members usually like to hear from invited experts or specialists on topics of interest. It may be difficult to anticipate preferred areas of interest, especially in the early days of a DPG group, so a 'menu' of potential expert topics can be a useful way of establishing momentum (see example in the Tools section). From time-to-time a potential expert topic may become identified during an issue discussion. These expert sessions need to be managed in a way that satisfies members' needs. So apart from reminding the expert about timings and format it is useful to ask him or her to start the session by asking DPG members what they would like to get out of the session and what they already know or have experienced about the topic. This reduces the risk of spending too much time on content that is of low interest to members and increases the probability of valuable take-aways. Other aspects of running a successful DPG are set out below in the Specific action points section.

Using action learning to solve member issues

Action learning is a core process within DPGs for addressing members' issues including individual behaviours and relationship management to improve performance. It is a well-proven and highly regarded concept and method of learning that was introduced by Reg Revans (1980) soon after World War II. It stands in contrast to some traditional teaching methods that focus on presentation of knowledge and skills in that it is a collaborative learning process where a small group of learners, often called an 'action learning set', meets regularly to reflect on real work issues. Its basic philosophy is that the most effective learning takes place when we are faced with a real problem that we are obliged to solve – 'there is no learning without actions (sober and deliberate) and no action without learning' (Revans, 1980).

Action learning works for individuals and teams, so in-company teams or groups can benefit from membership, or sets can comprise individuals from different organizations, such as DPGs. The process enhances the way in which we learn by drawing on actual practice, and using the experience of members to work together to address concerns, problems and challenges that any individual member or a team may be facing. Members receive feedback and new ideas from others who may work in different disciplines, environments and cultures. This sharing enables them to respond effectively to unfamiliar or uncertain situations.

A well-proven process for structuring and managing an issue session is our ToGROWW model, which is adapted from the GROW Model (Whitmore, 2004) and works using the following nomenclature:

To – a clearly defined Topic (issue owner identifies the problem or situation).

G – explain the Goal for this session (issue owner).

R – Reality – describe background and situation – allow questions for clarification.

O – get Opinions of other participants – in turn.

W – other participants suggest courses of action (What you should do) each in turn.

W – Will do (owner – maybe after reflection).

The Topic and Goal may initially appear a bit 'fuzzy' but the Reality discussion is useful in gaining focus. The 'R' part is usually the longest because after the issue owner has provided a summary of the situation there will be a lot of questions for clarification. It is often these questions that raise a number of new thoughts and ideas. In some cases a more important underlying issue can emerge that changes the Goal and possibly the Topic.

In any event, it is often helpful if an issue owner prepares a one-page summary of the ToGR (Topic, Goal and Reality background) part of the session that can be distributed in advance of the DPG meeting. The process of preparing this summary usually clarifies the issue owner's thinking and enables the rest of the group to move faster and get deeper during the discussion session.

Individual and group reflection is an important part of the overall learning process. This can take place both during the group discussion of a problem a member is facing and/or when the consequences of actions taken are brought back to the group for further sharing and learning. Action learning can free up inflexible or traditional thinking and find new solutions for roles and environments that are changing or for complex tasks. This is especially valuable during periods of organizational change or rapidly changing market situations.

One of the key strengths of action learning is that it is both profound and simple, is low cost, and can be incorporated into many group learning vehicles. The effectiveness of action learning can be assessed through the practical results from the learning that have taken place. Key elements of action learning sets include:

- Each person takes part voluntarily.
- All members are regarded as equals (no hierarchy barriers).
- Real problems are being addressed – role playing does not work anywhere near as well.
- Each person is willing to learn from their own activities and from those of others.
- Each person is willing to offer their own experience and knowledge to others.
- Each person has authority to act on the outcomes – this is especially important in organizations where authority may be inhibited or restricted in some way.
- The set feels ownership among its members.
- The action learning process is well-facilitated – either by the members themselves or by an independent facilitator. If it is by one of the members of the group it is important that they are competent in facilitation and only play the facilitator role.

Key aspects of good facilitation of a DPG

Good facilitation is a critical element in ensuring DPG meetings work well and provide value to members, especially as they may be under constant time pressure and will need to justify to themselves, and maybe colleagues, that the time spent at the DPG is worthwhile. Although DPGs may seem like they could be self-facilitating, an external experienced facilitator, with high level skills in listening, questioning, communication and reflection, is preferable. The external facilitator will manage the 'housekeeping' issues, the agenda and its related timings, and the process of the issue and expert sessions. This frees and empowers all members to focus on discussion and learning.

The facilitator is responsible for the overall process and structure, but *not* the content nor the solution, and will be open-minded, tolerant of ambiguity, conscious of group dynamics and will withhold personal opinions. However, the facilitator may have valuable personal experience and knowledge directly relevant to the issue and this input may be requested by the members. In this case, the facilitator should only offer this once all input from members has been shared so that the discussion will not have been unduly influenced.

Process management of the issue discussions is critical but needs to be done in a way that still leaves ownership with the members. Reminding members about the ToGROWW sequence is the start point and this becomes an accepted way of working. A flipchart that sets out key comments can help to retain focus, hold the discussion on topic and goal, stop the discussion becoming side-tracked, and reduce the risk of unfruitful repetition. A separate page can also be used to note or 'park' valuable ideas that are not directly relevant to the topic; they may be valuable to discuss later. The facilitator must manage 'air-time' and ensure that the discussion is not hijacked by more vocal and strong-willed members. The facilitator must keep aware of the level of interest and engagement of each member, watch for non-verbal signals such as posture, facial expression and direction, and invite quieter members to give their views, keeping in mind that quieter people often provide the most valuable input.

Discussions should always start by asking for a volunteer to speak. However, in some situations this could lead to domination by a more experienced member who speaks first and thereby inhibits group thinking. This can be mitigated by asking each member to write down their ideas before speaking. The facilitator can then ask each member in turn, sometimes starting with the quietest or least experienced, to give their thinking to the group. Asking for their views can help their self-confidence. Knowledgeable group members may also be tempted to speak for too long: a good facilitator will firmly but gently ask them to be brief and get to the point so that another quieter member can give some input.

People learn best from insights and a good facilitator supports the group in the generation of these insights by asking open and probing questions that stimulate thinking, building ideas by synthesizing and paraphrasing discussion points, and giving feedback on what seems to be happening. All this can be done with an occasional injection of humour that keeps participants relaxed and thoughtful; these, of course, are classic coaching skills. So coach training is a valuable asset for facilitators. (For those wishing to increase their expertise in coaching and facilitation with a view to successfully running DPGs a very good route would be to do the University of Chester accredited LeaderShape Postgraduate Certificate in 'Coach Mentoring and Facilitation in Organizations'.)

It is important to build and sustain good energy levels in a DPG meeting, especially if it lasts all day. This can be stimulated by such things as an activity based 'ice-breaker' at the beginning of the meeting, regular breaks throughout the day, high-participation exercises, and allowing some 'unscripted' but enthusiastic discussion – and by having fun! Longer-term energy levels are stimulated by the introduction of new members to a group who bring novel sector backgrounds and/or situations. So some modest membership 'churn' as an occasional member leaves or a new member joins should be expected and welcomed. Having said that, our experience is that most members stay for at least three years.

New approaches and alternative tools for addressing sessions may also refresh energy levels. These could include such things as brainstorming and/or force field analysis, 'us and them' teams when exploring and developing competing arguments – for these and other tools see Jay (2000) and De Bono (1985).

A good facilitator will draw attention to behaviour that does not align with agreed group ground rules or is interfering with discussions or meetings. This could include such simple things as timekeeping, telephone/text distraction, interruptions, or potential friction. This also supports the growth in self-awareness.

The facilitator should make sure that key learning points are drawn out at the end of a DPG meeting and that these will be translated into action. The meeting should end up by the facilitator asking each member to write down answers to the following questions:

- What did you like most about today?
- What would you like to do differently?
- What is your main take-away/learning point?
- What action will you be taking and by when?

The responses will be shared and recorded on a flipchart and included in follow up notes that should be circulated within a week of the meeting.

Ideally a DPG will include one-to-one coaching for each member between group sessions. This helps to sustain momentum and learning at the same time as exploring issues that might benefit from being shared within the group.

SPECIFIC ACTION POINTS

The following actions will underpin the successful running of a DPG:

- Preparing and planning – checking in advance that the venue, facilities and food/refreshments are organized and suitable and, if relevant, ensuring all learning material such as hand-outs are available on the day.

- Circulating the agenda to members about a week in advance of the meeting.

- Circulating issue note summaries about a week in advance of the meeting.

- Preparing for exercises and/or skills practice.

- Having reliable audio-visual equipment – check it out in advance.

- Starting and finishing the meeting on time – members will have busy diaries.

- Wrapping up the meeting so that actions are identified and there is feedback on the meeting that can inform and shape the future format, style and agendas.

- Ensuring all participants are engaged and involved in discussions.

- Circulating notes on the meeting to members within a short time after the meeting.

FURTHER RESOURCES

For more on facilitation: Cameron, E (1998) *Facilitation Made Easy: Practical steps to improve meetings and workshops*, Kogan Page, London.

For more on action learning: McGill, I and Beaty, L (1995) *Action Learning: A guide for professional management and educational development*, 2nd edn, Kogan Page, London; Pedler, M (2008) *Action Learning for Managers*, Gower, Farnham.

For more on creative tools and ice breakers: Jay, R (2000) *The Ultimate Book of Business Creativity*, Capstone, Oxford; **www.businessballs.com** – tools and ice breakers; **www.mwls.co.uk**.

For more on Myers Briggs: The Myers Briggs Foundation – **www.myersbriggs.org**.

References

De Bono, E (1985) *Six Thinking Hats*, Little, Brown, New York

Honey, P and Mumford, A (1992) *The Manual of Learning Styles*, Routledge, London

Jay, R (2000) *The Ultimate Book of Business Creativity*, Oxford, Capstone

Revans, R (1980) *Action Learning: New techniques for action learning*, Blond and Briggs, London

Whitmore, J (2004) *Coaching for Performance*, Nicholas Brealey, London

Peer groups to build a team and enable professional consultants to become business coaches

Chris Gulliver

A consulting organization undertook an aid-funded project to provide coaching support to SMEs in an economically disadvantaged area of the United Kingdom. This required them to supply group training for a number of its existing consultants to provide them with higher level skills in coaching and facilitation. The consultants were mature and very experienced people with a mix of business backgrounds, used to working almost independently and unsupervised. Most of the consultants had not worked with each other before and some had never met each other.

The training was in cohorts and shaped around achieving a Postgraduate Certificate in 'Coach Mentoring and Facilitation in Organizations' and took place over a two and a half year period. Each cohort meeting included action learning processes and practice in coaching and facilitation that could be adopted for use with clients. Real working issues faced by the consultants were tackled in these sessions and included a significant sharing of knowledge, experience and know-how that had not happened before. Many of these issues initially looked inwardly at their own organization.

The coaching and facilitation practice was formally assessed and feedback provided at the end of each session. Keeping in mind that good coaching and facilitation are key leadership skills, as well as consulting skills, this feedback frequently identified default behaviour that needed to be controlled. As a result, for each individual their current positioning as leaders and their growth potential became clearer. The most prevalent required behavioural changes that reflected the consultancy background of the cohort. Those that were identified and successfully addressed included the need to listen more and better instead of talking, and the need to have confidence and patience in the ability of the 'owner' (the coachee) of an issue to identify a solution. This required thoughtful open questioning and the need to retain objectivity and focus.

Benefits

These action learning practice sessions proved immensely valuable to them as individuals and as a group. An unexpected outcome was that, for the first time, the consultants felt they were bonding well, knew each other's skills and strengths and were acting like a team. A bonus was that very supportive relationships were established that continued outside the training sessions. This team creation was taken back into the broader consultancy organization and became a formal and informal way of working that had not existed before, and generated significant internal organizational benefits for the client programme.

Members of the cohort took various leadership roles in internal projects and became more open to contributions from colleagues. Better listening meant that the nature of conversations changed. The PGC qualification gained by cohort members increased the level of self-confidence as well as confidence in the techniques being used with clients.

Learning points

Key learning points that were demonstrated during this training programme included:

- Without an assessment process, either through a formal analysis or constructive feedback, the nature and impact of personal behaviour is not fully understood. Working colleagues are ideally placed to provide this feedback.

- The power and benefits of active listening are not fully understood without structured training and practice in a safe environment that can provide a platform and confidence for using it in a working environment.

- Embedded long-term behaviours are often difficult to change, especially when they have not seemed to affect success. Persistence is needed.

- There is no need to show how clever you are if you are helping someone to solve their problems. It is better you show the other person how clever they are – which requires managing one's ego.

- Honesty and transparency with colleagues builds rapport and trust.

CASE STUDY   **Peer groups and the CEO of a scientific instruments small business**

Chris Gulliver

The CEO and controlling shareholder of a specialist scientific instruments SME became a member of a CEO peer group to help him develop some growth momentum in his business. He had no previous formal business training and provided the critical technical expertise within the business. Most of the business comprised international sales of very sophisticated one-off specialist electro-mechanical systems, which often required significant technical input for installation and subsequent support. The CEO had been largely focusing his time on resolving technical challenges and innovating new techniques. Delegation of technical and operational authority and decision making was poor.

Membership of the peer group continued over a number of years during which he shared experiences and challenges with other CEO members. He fully engaged with self-awareness and leadership development activities, including LEIPA®, which made the CEO more conscious of his difficulties in dealing with and developing his top team. Many of his issue sessions covered his working relationships with his major shareholder partner and his key managers. Key behaviours that were surfaced and successfully addressed included the need to improve communication and dialogue with his senior team so that they could take on more responsibility, and the need to reduce the company's reliance on the CEO's technical know-how, which previously had not been formally documented as each product was developed or improved, and therefore needed to be systematically recorded. This is not an uncommon situation and frequently inhibits business growth potential.

Benefits

Participation in the group enabled this CEO to become more aware of how much potential there was for business growth, what it would take to achieve this and to how to realize some personal wealth by eventually selling the business. This included the formalization and standardization of the product range and associated technology, the improved systemization of internal procedures, and the development and implementation of a long-term growth strategy. The latter required him to reduce his excessive focus on operational activity and problem solving so that he could fulfil a more effective strategic leadership role. This required a conscious plan for the development of a senior management team and executive board, supported by a strong middle-management team that could take care of the day-to-day operations and sustain the growth momentum without his regular involvement.

The business tripled in size in five years and established long-term international growth potential. It became very profitable and was sold to a listed company for a premium price.

Learning points

Key learning points from this experience included:

- The formal leadership assessment processes brought to the surface behavioural issues that would otherwise have probably remained unspoken and never properly addressed.

- The CEO was in his late 50s when he joined the group. Age is not a barrier to behavioural change if there is the right attitude and sufficient will to respond to identified leadership needs.

- Moving out of a long-term 'control' position in an organization to one of proper delegation can be very difficult. This can be achieved by taking many small steps rather than dramatic change, thereby matching the scope of delegation to the ability of people to cope with it. Regular communication and dialogue are critical.

TOOL   Conditions of membership and/or ground rules

Chris Gulliver

What they are and when to use them

Conditions of membership, or ground rules, should be agreed by members when a DPG is set up and signed by all members as they join. The purpose is to create a common understanding among members regarding individual and group behaviour. This enables the DPG to regulate itself and address behavioural lapses.

Sample conditions of membership

To gain the maximum value from (name DPG) it is imperative that all members abide by the following principles:

- Participate in *all* scheduled group meetings, subject to extenuating circumstances. Under no condition should a member miss more than two meetings per year.
- Agree a specific schedule with the facilitator for the one-to-one meetings.
- Keep all information received during a group or one-to-one meeting or any other discussion or communication with any members strictly confidential unless it is obviously in the public domain.
- Disclose any potential conflict of interest.
- Not to actively use the group as a means of procuring business.
- Arrive at all meetings in good time and stay until the end of the meeting.
- Not to be disturbed during any meeting unless it is a real emergency.
- Participate fully, be open and honest, and be helpful and supportive to other members.
- Be supportive in the recruitment of new members to the group.
- Host group all-day meetings in rotation with fellow members.
- Give the appropriate notice if unable to continue as a regular member.
- Abide by any other ground rules agreed, from time-to-time, by the group.

I (name) hereby agree to abide by the conditions of membership as described above and confirm that all the information I have provided for membership is true and accurate to the best of my knowledge.

Signature... Date..............................

TOOL   Agenda for a DPG meeting

Chris Gulliver

What it is and when to use it

DPG meeting agendas should be sent to all members around a week in advance of a scheduled meeting. The purpose is to set out and manage expectations on structure, content and timing. The agenda should be briefly reviewed and confirmed at the beginning of each meeting and adjustments made if appropriate to meet member's preferences or current situations. The general shape of the agenda may be adjusted in the light of experience of both the members and the facilitator.

Sample DPG agenda

DPG – Group Meeting Agenda

To be held at (*name venue*) ....

Date: ....

Location: (*address and postcode*) ....

Host: (*name*) ....

Directions: see attachment

Agenda

07.45	Arrival		12.45	Issue sessions:
08.00	Introductions			Member 1
	Major events			Member 2
	One-to-one issues and actions		14.00	Tea break for 15 minutes
09.00	Expert session:		15.30	Admin
	Key Performance Indicators (*expert's name*)			Review of meeting
				Actions members will take away
10.15	Coffee break for 15 minutes			
11.30	Update on host business		16.00	End of meeting
12.00	Lunch (30–45 minutes)			

TOOL   Group issue session topics

Chris Gulliver

What they are and when to use them

Appropriate issue session topics can usually be spotted in advance by a good facilitator either during one-to-one sessions with members or at the beginning of each meeting during the update on major events. They are ideally identified before a meeting so that the 'owner' can draft a brief summary of the topic and the goal for the session with some background detail. This can be circulated to members in advance so that preparatory thinking can take place that saves time at the meeting. The drafting of this brief document also helps to clarify the thinking of the 'owner' and facilitates focus and direction for the discussion that follows.

Example issue session topics

Review of strategic options for the business:

- How to manage staff working from home.

- How to deal with a major customer pressing for substantial cost reductions.

- Defining preferred personal role with prospective new owner.

- How to defend the business from an aggressive and unethical competitor.

- How to handle key distributors during an ownership dispute.

- How to turnaround a failing business division.

- How to motivate the director of a critical part of the business.

- What to do about an acquisition opportunity in Italy.

- How to resolve a major shareholder/shareholding issue.

- What to do about a failing operations director.

- How to sustain staff motivation and morale during an extended period of extreme pressure.

- Identification of behavioural changes needed to improve personal leadership.

TOOL   Key objectives

Chris Gulliver

What they are and when to use them

Experience has shown that DPG members like setting some focus for business and personal objectives that can be regularly reviewed with fellow members.

Example key objectives guidelines for DPG members

Subject: vision, goals and objectives

We believe that setting a vision for one's business and goals for one's personal aspirations is imperative for all business people to maximize their success. The vision and goal should be set at least three years in the future but they may be further in the future if you wish. To achieve this it is necessary to establish annual SMART key objectives to ensure that in each year you are focused on heading towards reaching the vision and goals.

It is advisable that you discuss your business vision and personal goals with your facilitator/coach before the group meeting where they are to be presented. Please think about your longer-term business vision and personal goals before the one-to-one session, then finalize them ready to present at the group meeting. You should also prepare your SMART key objectives for the forthcoming year. The key objectives should include your three most important business objectives and your one or two most important personal objectives.

The following are then presented on a flipchart by each member at the group meeting (preferably the first meeting in the year):

- business vision (at least three years out);
- personal goals (at least three years out);
- three business objectives for the current year;
- one or two personal objectives for the current year.

Note: these should all be in concise bullet-list format.

The facilitator will then collate all this information and prepare a document for review during the year.

It is suggested that the vision, goals and objectives of members be reviewed at group sessions about once every four months.

TOOL   Expert session topics

Chris Gulliver

What they are and when to use them

Topics of shared concern or interest to DPG members can often be identified during member update and issue sessions. An invited expert can explore a topic in depth with members as an aid to their personal leadership effectiveness and development. A session of around two hours is usually sufficient. It is useful for facilitators to be ready with a menu of potential topics (and experts!) to stimulate possible shared interest.

Expert session topics

Examples include:

- 360° appraisal processes;
- leading and directing change;
- how to use coaching techniques to help management teams perform;
- how to establish successful alliances and joint ventures;
- emotional intelligence and leadership styles – including personal assessments;
- employee incentive schemes;
- attaining and managing growth;
- post-acquisition management;
- key performance indicators;
- how to build brands;
- personal communication skills;
- international business development;
- recruiting and retaining the right people;
- how to compete against much larger companies;
- strategic thinking;
- supply chain management;
- successful management of product development.

TOOL **Confidentiality letter for guest attendance at a DPG meeting**

Chris Gulliver

What it is and when to use it

Potential members may wish to attend a 'sample' DPG meeting to understand how a DPG works before committing to membership. All guests should sign a confidentiality letter so that the risk of inhibiting discussion and the passing on of sensitive information is minimized.

Sample confidentiality letter

I have been invited as a guest to a (specify the DPG) group meeting. I understand that during this meeting the members are likely to disclose sensitive and/or confidential matters relating to their businesses, their business relationships and their personal lives. I undertake that:

1 I shall treat any information disclosed during the course of the meeting as confidential and will not disclose such information to anyone outside the meeting without the express written or witnessed permission of the member concerned unless it has already been disclosed.

2 I will not directly or indirectly use any of the information for any purpose.

3 This obligation does not apply to any information:

- that is public knowledge or in the public domain and is generally available at the time of the meeting;

- at such time it should subsequently enter the public domain;

- at such time it should subsequently become available to me from a source that is entitled without restriction to disclose such information to me.

Signed...

Name...

Date...

TOOL   Reflection notes

Chris Gulliver

What are they and when to use them

Good reflection is a very valuable process for identifying deep learning from decisions, experiences or events. Busy executives do not devote enough time to this so a DPG meeting is a useful opportunity for them to practise and realize how beneficial it can be when carried out on a regular basis.

The reflection note process

It involves writing down answers to just four key questions and rarely takes more than 20 minutes. Each member can then share their learning with the group (if they wish). It is very important that question 4 is answered:

1   Exactly what happened and why in that way?

2   How did you behave, think, feel?

3   What were the main learning points?

4   So what will you do differently (is that a SMART goal)?

TOOL   Force field analysis

Chris Gulliver

What it is and when to use it

Force field analysis was developed by Kurt Lewin in 1943 as a tool for looking at all the forces for and against a decision or change. It is a specialized method of weighing pros and cons and defining the challenge.

By carrying out the analysis you can evaluate alternatives, clarify a preferred course of action and/or strengthen the forces supporting a decision or change and reduce the impact of opposition to it.

Why use force field analysis

• It's easy to understand and simple to use.

• It presents the positive and negative sides of a situation so that they can be easily compared.

- It forces people to think about all aspects of making the decision or change.

- It encourages discussion and agreement.

- It can stimulate an honest reflection on the real underlying roots of a problem or dilemma and its solution.

The process

1 Establish the goal, desired situation or dilemma and write it at the top of a flipchart.

2 In two columns:
   - list all forces for change: the pros or driving forces;
   - list all forces against change: the cons or restraining forces.

3 Score each force from 1 to 5 according to their strength.

4 Total up the scores of each column and compare.

5 Look again at each force and consider what actions would strengthen the pros and weaken the cons.

6 Adjust the scores according to the potential impact of these actions.

7 Total up the column scores again and check viability, etc. The driving forces must outweigh the restraining forces for the change or the decision to succeed.

8 Write down the action plan that has emerged.

Driving and restraining forces could include such things as skill levels, motivation, efficiency, capacity, quality, process issues, competition, the market or economy, technology, cost and time pressures.

TOOL   Feedback on a DPG meeting

Chris Gulliver

What it is and when to use it

Feedback on every group meeting is important in building and sustaining format and content that members feel justifies their membership. Each member should complete a feedback form at the end of each meeting and pass it to the group facilitator who will summarize and feedback the average score to the members with the meeting notes. This score can be tracked to identify any trends or unwanted variations.

Example feedback form

Group meeting evaluation questionnaire

Completed by: ....   Group No/Name: ....

Date of meeting: ....

One-to-one coaching session:
Value of the session: mark from 1 to 10, where 1 = very poor/low and
10 = excellent/very high _____

What was the main take-away from the session? ....

....

Expert session:

Name of expert contributor: ....

Subject: ....

Mark the following from 1 to 10, where 1 = very poor/low and 10 = excellent/very high):

Importance of subject to you _____

Quality of subject matter _____

Presentation/facilitation style _____

Level of dialogue (two-way communication – equal air time) _____

Relevance to your business _____

Take-aways to use in your business:..

Issue session:

Value of the session: mark from 1 to 10, where 1 = very poor/low and 10 = excellent/
very high _____

What was the main take-away for you? ....

Overall evaluation:

Value of group membership to you this month: mark from 1 to 10 – where 1 = very
poor/low and 10 = excellent/very high _____

What could be done differently/better? ....

....

Storytelling for talent development

10

LISA ROSSETTI

EXECUTIVE SUMMARY

Those in leadership positions who fail to grasp or use the power of stories risk failure for their companies and for themselves.

(John Kotter, Harvard Business School)

With the explosion of internet-enabled communications and social media, the world has never seemed so connected or able to share its stories at the touch of a button. Yet this move from closed to open communication and from dictate to debate has clearly not resulted in a corresponding increase in engagement in the workplace. Storytelling skills are a vital tool not only to express organizational vision but also to improve workforce engagement and transform morale. Storytelling essentially helps 'get things done' collectively – it must therefore be purposeful and intentional. In these economic times, storytelling skills may be the most effective resource a leader can draw on to motivate his or her team and gain commitment to the collective task.

This chapter identifies key aspects of stories to achieve such outcomes, such as intentionality, emotional content and audience engagement. It then considers key storytelling skills, eg pace and delivery, choice of story, where to find stories and when to use them, as well as storytelling ethics and the steps towards establishing an effective organizational storytelling culture. Creating time and space for stories to emerge in an already busy work environment will require a genuine belief in and understanding of the benefits of storytelling and diverse story approaches. The digital age may assist us in sharing stories in work blogs, and intranets and knowledge via wikis and video conferencing but, to thrive, a storytelling culture relies on internal communications being more open than in organizations characterized by control-and-command leadership where communications are tightly controlled. A vibrant organizational storytelling culture will focus purposefully on 'fostering high-quality interactive human relationships' (Denning, 2010). There is also an ethical side to storytelling; and becoming a storytelling leader requires a profound commitment to one's own development and authenticity, in spirit and deed as well as word.

An appreciation of the power of stories to challenge leaders to assess their beliefs, behaviours and values will ensure that talent assessment benefits from the additional perspective that storytelling can bring:

Stories are the single most powerful tool in a leader's toolkit.

(Howard Gardner)

Storytelling skills and applications

Let us begin with a story...

Sufi folk hero, Mullah Nasrudin, sometimes plays the archetypal Trickster hero, sometimes the enlightened Fool, and sometimes the shrewd Sage. These traditional tales hold the mirror up to our behaviour and challenge our assumptions. Nasrudin tales are still being told today, and can be used in leadership and personal development very effectively.

The lamp and the key

Late one evening a neighbour of Mullah Nasrudin was walking home when he saw the Mullah looking under a lamp post evidently searching for something.

'What's the matter, Nasrudin?' asked the concerned neighbour.

'I have lost my keys,' replied Nasrudin.

'Well, let me help you.' And the kindly neighbour got down on his knees and started searching for Mullah's keys as well.

After some time, having found nothing, the neighbour was quite puzzled. So he stood up and asked 'Are you absolutely certain that you dropped your keys here?'

'Oh, I didn't drop them here,' said Nasrudin.

'Well, where did you drop them then?'

'Over there.' The Mullah pointed across the street to his house that was in darkness.

'So why are you looking for them *here*?' cried out the neighbour, very annoyed.

'Because there is light here,' replied the Mullah.

Once upon a time...

I had to know and understand my own story before I could listen to and help other people with theirs.

(Barack Obama)

Research into using stories and storytelling as assessment tools for leadership development is still relatively thin on the ground. Existing assessment practices that utilize storytelling or narrative structures and methodologies can be discovered in the workplace within competence interviews, 360° exercises, task analysis, performance coaching, and career transition consultancy.

A story emerges in its own right as a valid assessment tool in the competency-based interview. Interviewees are encouraged to tell their story of an achievement or problem-solving occasion. The technique that is taught to structure the interviewee's response follows the well-known STAR approach (Situation, Task, Action and Result). Within this narrative elements of context (and conflict), catalyst and response, change and resolution can be recognized. Storytelling skills can enhance the interviewee's ability to respond clearly with enough personal detail and rich data for assessment of skills, aptitude and personal values.

Another developmental area where storytelling adds value is in cognitive task analysis. This is a technique used to obtain information about how to perform a task from someone with prior experience and competence. The analysis is two-part: the expert explains and the process is recorded step-by-step as a set of instructions. However, the drawback is that the expert may omit certain details (as they have become so common/habitual as to be considered irrelevant or indeed ignored); or they may give the 'by-the-book' or best practice answer (possibly preserving their status as the expert). To find out how experts really perform a task, it is posed as a real-life problem in a narrative format: 'Suppose I ask you to help me with... What would you do?' The expert is thus invited to complete the story and furnish not only all the steps, but the additional perspective of common sense, providing a more emotionally intelligent or relational context as a rationale for his or her actions. Using storytelling brings a valuable extra dimension to understanding not only how people perform at work but *why* they act in the way they do and the crucial relationships that underpin standard procedures and task performance. When leaders and coaches focus on performance improvement, when new teams are formed or when new standard operational procedures are required, storytelling clearly can be an invaluable assessment tool for best practice.

Another opportunity for using storytelling within assessment is to complement the 360° analysis through personal coaching to explore 'the back story', ie the gap between intention (self-assessment) and impact (assessment by others). These assessments are often used at critical stages of leadership development, and manager-to-leader progression. The results of the 360° are shared with the subjects, their manager and increasingly with their coach where performance coaching is indicated. Storytelling can be integrated into coaching interventions in several ways. By suggesting that there is a 'back story' behind 360° feedback, the coachee can explore the difference between intention and impact in a less judgemental way. This is then a useful point for coaches to help clients develop a new story. The client can trial the new story in the safety of the client-coach relationship and finally take ownership of the story and implement it through practising new behaviours in the real world. It is perhaps no coincidence that the words 'author' and 'authority' have a similar root, and this story technique is very powerful in development.

Using personal storytelling to examine and assess clients' patterns of behaviours and 'traps' or assumptions that they make is a powerful technique. Clients are invited to examine their personal story of their leadership, identifying others who also contributed to their achievements and progress, and mapping significant moments in their lives. After recording their insights, they are then invited to construct a new or 'future' story, one which they design to be more authentic, more values-based and which demonstrates commitment to a clear vision. The new personal narrative emerges as a result of deeply reflective self-assessment; it may also be the subject of group assessment (eg rating feasibility, authenticity and commitment) and is the product of highly intentional design. This future story technique can help leaders develop their talent and identify areas for personal growth.

Career transition preparation benefits from a narrative approach too. George Dutch of the Career Management Alliance assists his clients in their career transition through personal story analysis by inviting them to write their life story rather than simply submit a chronological résumé of positions held and qualifications gained. Writing your life story helps you understand your own life in terms of the forces that have defined and changed you over the years. The facts, people and events of your life have formed a seamless web of meaning that help you to answer the questions, 'Who am I?' and 'What am I trying to accomplish with my life?' As a career practitioner, Dutch has developed a methodology which examines aptitudes, skills, talents, strengths, traits and values in order to establish key success factors and map a clear route to successful employment. Says Dutch, in an interview with Kathy Hansen (**www.astoriedcareer.com**): 'Our stories can be mapped. We can identify and define landmarks in the terrain of meaning.'

In group situations, shared and co-created narratives bring together events in a meaningful storyline structure, establishing a coherence that underpins the sense-making process. Collaborative reflection on stories and co-creation of stories, eg in teams, is enormously valuable for individuals and groups to assess their current position, their vision and desire to move forward to shared goals. White (2007) speaks of 'landscapes of action', which stories bring into higher definition. If there is a storyteller there is also a story listener, a witness to the social event; thus stories create valid social roles where perhaps only passivity or reactive modes existed before.

'Listening' to stories is as important for leaders as telling them. In times of pressure and change, stories from colleagues give important information about tacit fears that would not otherwise be discussed. In clinical practice, the use of stories is commonly taught as assessment tools to enhance the ability to listen in a non-judgemental way to clients' values and beliefs (Evans and Severtsen, 2001). Leaders who tune their ears to stories will detect clues about the beliefs and challenges, pressures and aspirations of their employees.

Conversational learning emphasizes business conversations as a social experience built upon interaction. The process of knowledge gathering is through the medium of conversation rather than surveys, questionnaires and fact-finding missions. Creating conversational space has much value as it is integrative rather than divisive (Baker *et al*, 2002). Conversational leadership respects differences and allows team members to share beliefs and create new knowledge. Story listening skills assemble and synthesize these clues into a more accurate map of the commitment within a team or organization and enrich leaders' knowledge of collective understanding. However, teams may be wary about their stories being shared or, worse, overheard if real trust has not been developed between leader and colleagues. Knowledge sharing through stories needs a transparent platform and real integrity of purpose.

Tell me another...

Storytelling is the oldest form of human communication. It is a way to inspire, share values and knowledge, and to connect with others powerfully. To understand how embedded stories and storytelling are in our culture and language, think of all the story-related words we use: legend, myth, anecdote, parable, tale, narrative, case-study, and so on.

There are many definitions of the organizational story, some of which emphasize the social role of storytelling in communicating personal experiences in everyday language and conversation. Gabriel (1991: 481) defines organizational stories as 'poetic reconstructions of events in which the accuracy of the narrative is sacrificed in the interest of fulfilling vital needs and desires, sometimes unconscious ones, shared by organizational participants'. This definition gives plenty of scope to use stories with engagement and wellbeing benefits in the workplace, as well as to paint the vision of future possibilities and collective action. This creative latitude and possibly departure from relying on evidence-based data and hard facts in their corporate presentations may be an unsettling domain for leaders to enter for the first time. However, those who are bold enough to embrace storytelling in their leadership practices will find they enhance their ability to make internal communications relevant and effective. Crucially, storytelling skills empower leaders to be influencers and change agents.

Storytelling is a very powerful personal development tool in business. Through listening to stories and identifying (or disagreeing) with the characters we get the chance to step outside of our everyday world and reflect on what matters to us, on what we contribute and what we share with others. Stories can transform your communication skills and the way you motivate and inspire others. Stories encourage innovative thinking and are highly motivating as they focus on success in your team and common values.

In the 21st century, the medium of stories is being rediscovered as the most effective vehicle for transmitting values and enhancing social relationships. When leaders understand and utilize the value of stories they have a powerful communication tool with which to present complex strategic ideas and to convey their vision meaningfully and memorably. The benefits of storytelling include:

- strengthening relationships and teamwork;
- inspiring people to change;
- fostering creativity and enhancing problem solving;

- improving clear thinking and decision making;
- generating more engagement and better buy-in;
- communicating a new vision quickly;
- discovering and sharing organizational knowledge.

One of the key aspects of storytelling is its power to engage hearts and minds. Why does this occur? The answer lies in the architecture of our brain. Our brain chemistry and nervous systems are measurably affected by those closest to us; this is known as 'limbic resonance'. We have the capacity to synchronize emotionally even at a neural level with others, which has profound implications for personality and lifelong emotional health. Thus the brain's architecture, through our limbic system, provides an inbuilt way to connect with others. Storytelling provides the environment and the medium for this to take place (Lewis *et al*, 2001).

Stories have always been the means by which cultures, tribes and family share their history, norms, values and dreams. Stories provide context and meaning, communicating that elusive sense of belonging to something bigger that has inspired mankind down the ages. This is the secret that the ancient shamans understood when they told powerful myths to provide the collective emotional and social 'glue' for the tribe to ensure its survival.

It is no different in organizations. The role of the visionary storyteller now passes to leaders, whose task it is to engage their workforce proactively in creating a shared vision. Stories provide the context for past, present and future, a story structure we inherently understand. Within this storied context, we are more able to comprehend future possibilities and the part we play.

Leaders should cultivate an awareness of the stories, myths and legends that exist already within their organization. Without this awareness, leaders will miss opportunities to influence the prevalent zeitgeist. The storytelling leader will seek out inspirational stories and establish a legacy of 'legends' for the organization to draw on as a motivational resource. These stories are likely to communicate the trustworthiness of the organization and its commitment to its ideals and values, as well as a belief in a future of possibilities. Communicating these legends is not just a PR exercise; the stories actually work as legends did in the past, to remind people of their shared values and to galvanize commitment to the collective task ahead.

But where can you find stories? Storytelling is happening everywhere, from conversations at the water-cooler to more formal dialogues; you simply need to hone your 'story radar' to hear them. Traditional tales can be found in literature and on the internet or at professional storytelling events. These tales can often be transformational learning tools, useful in mentoring situations, for example. Social media and especially blogs are a rich and accessible library of modern-day stories. Their immediacy and relevance makes them very accessible; but take care that their message illustrates a purposeful point. Anecdotes and stories from personal life experiences, if crafted to convey a message or learning point and delivered appropriately, can also be a very effective means of communicating values. There are also opportunities to learn from stakeholder and client stories so you can review your policies and culture, and promote service improvement.

Leaders who begin to embrace storytelling as a vital developmental tool need also to be story listeners, refining their story awareness. They may also find that they become the story curator for their organization by gathering stories that can be crafted into positive and purposeful organizational legends. Storytelling leaders can also be proactive in creating new stories through engagement with their people at all levels; they can for example leave their desks to 'go walkabout' in corridors, canteens and workplaces, to listen, learn and harvest stories. A highly effective way to create new stories within the workplace is for newly appointed executives to join their workforce and get their hands dirty on the job. These two approaches will spontaneously generate new stories of trust and engagement from staff that will 'go viral' within the organization in a way that corporate mission statements and costly internal publicity campaigns can never achieve.

The storytelling leaders will thus build their own personal 'library' of stories, practise telling and note their impact on story listeners in different situations. Not all stories or metaphors 'land'; beware of spinning stories in a top-down fashion that might be viewed sceptically as insincere propaganda.

Look behind you...

Story ethics and the dark side of storytelling

> *To poison a nation, poison its stories. A demoralized nation tells demoralized stories to itself. Beware of the storytellers who are not fully conscious of the importance of their gifts, and who are irresponsible in the application of their art.*
> (Ben Okri, Nigerian poet and novelist)

As history shows us, rhetoric can be very powerful and storytelling in the hands of the unethical or unscrupulous leader can be used to exert power over others and manipulate them. Anyone using stories should consider the ethics of their intentions. Are there any stories that should not be told? Of course, there may be copyright issues in retelling another's story and there are certainly ethical issues. As we have seen, leaders will need to choose those stories that achieve appropriate business outcomes in order to inspire and motivate us, explain complex strategies in a simple way, engage our hearts as well as minds, call us to action, or provide clear direction.

Leaders' stories should be ethical and intentional, not mud-slinging rants or vacuous gossip and self-promoting ramblings. Never choose stories that induce fear or guilt. These are not only inappropriate, they are counter-productive as they are disempowering; stories that infantilize your work-force will eventually immobilize them. In a nutshell, the storyteller's code is: 'No cynicism, no blame, no swearing!' Understanding the boundaries will ensure that you and your company are ethical and respectful, particularly if you are engaged in third-party storytelling such as telling client or patient stories through digital media. The simplest benchmark of your intentions and ethics in telling a particular story is to ask yourself, 'Who does this serve?' If the story only serves you, then reconsider. If it serves the greater or collective good, then you are being an ethical storyteller.

Should you need to gather and retell real-life stories, whether digitally, in print or orally, consider the following key ethical factors proposed by The Center for Digital Storytelling:

- Protecting emotional wellbeing of the original client storyteller during the process of storytelling; the right to receive emotional support in some circumstances.

- Offering informed choices about content, access, media and distribution, the implications for stories going online.

- Acknowledging ownership, including determining content, distribution and audience.

- Ensuring consent and permission, as well as respecting the right to withdraw consent.

- Respecting the right to choose how the storyteller and their message is represented.

A three-year project, 'Managerial storytelling in practice', led by Dr Reissner (Newcastle Business School) suggests that some leaders and managers are wary of how others may use, possibly misinterpret or even deliberately dis-tort their stories. Using personal stories is certainly powerful but it does require a degree of confidence in one's audience as well as being comfortable with self-disclosure. The overall findings of this research are published as a research monograph entitled *Storytelling in Management Practice: Dynamics and implications* by Routledge (co-authored with Victoria Pagan, 2013).

Once a story is 'released' it may not be controllable, and it may be reinterpreted or misused. In our social media savvy culture, politicians, footballers and celebrities have certainly fallen foul of letting slip the odd incriminating story through careless Tweets and media sound-bites. In some senses stories have a life of their own – Australian Aborigines say that stories are forever hunting for the right teller – and are therefore not controllable. Organizations that have embraced a storytelling culture may embed processes to 'track' stories with a view to analysing their impact and effectiveness of communication rather than for reasons of authoritarian control. Stories that build and maintain culture can be allowed to emerge through the co-creative process of retelling in new contexts. When people are part of the narrative, indeed when they are cast as the 'heroes', they respect the stories.

Leaders must use their skills to build trust and loyalty, and their own judgement to discern the intentionality or even wilfulness of their audience. In the oral tradition, the storyteller relinquishes control of the story and ownership of it; it is offered rather than owned. The listener in any case is reinterpreting and reconstructing the story in his or her own mind. This may result in your story going 'viral', being retold again and again spontaneously and becoming a watchword or motto of the organization. This is something to be desired rather than dreaded, especially if your story conveys a powerful values message for your organization. However, this is not always the case, and distortion or wilful misinterpretation can and does occasionally occur. Resistance to change is a primary reason for distorting the message and thus the story; the strength of the emotion produces a reaction to the story. Another is detecting anything inauthentic on the part of the storyteller as the 'emotional ear' is adept at detecting insincerity. Once your audience has engaged their story listening faculties, any incongruity in your behaviour and beliefs will be emphasized by the story medium.

Another story to tell with caution is when breaking bad news (redundancies, wage cuts, etc); leaders should deliver a 'I know what you're thinking' (Simmons, 2006) story with care. This type of story helps others overcome concerns and fears they may secretly have about change. The task for the storyteller is to be honest and open, and to empathize with the audience. This may be challenging for leaders as it requires a degree of emotional disclosure, revealing one's own concerns and fears rather than retreating behind an executive barricade. For example, if the audience perceives the storyteller as a recipient of bonuses, shielded by privilege from the stark economic realities, then great care has to be taken to construct a story that evokes empathy rather than cynicism. You cannot stop audiences having an emotional response to stories; that is, after all, the point. But you can bear in mind the elements of storytelling that you *can* control: choice of stories, structure, delivery, pace, timing and your own intent and congruence.

Pace plays a significant part in how your story will be received. Too slow, and it can be construed as patronizing, with the audience feeling infantilized and talked down to. Too fast, and you may find your story starts to sound like so much 'spin' and insincere. Controlling pace is a matter of mastering delivery techniques, using pauses – remembering to breathe! Practise your stories, rehearse your delivery. Use a recorder and playback your voice; you may be surprised by your tone and pace. Stories do have their own rhythm and pace that helps the message be assimilated and understood. But beware of assuming the voice of the sage or wise woman: this is fine in performance storytelling, but irritating for colleagues who may perceive you as being patronizing.

Leaders sometimes find themselves in the position of having to warn trusted colleagues, who may also be close friends, about their behaviour. This can be a real challenge to loyalties and leadership. A story can be used to resolve an ethical dilemma where boundaries have become unclear, as you can 'stay safe' within the story and say something indirectly where a direct communication would be difficult. However, be careful when choosing real life stories as examples and ensure you are not betraying any confidences in the telling.

SPECIFIC ACTION POINTS

Using stories in your organization to develop engagement

Stories do not appear in a vacuum; they are a social process. They require the relationship of a storyteller and a story listener and an opportunity to pay attention. Stories do not have to be told by leaders alone; in fact, encouraging your staff to share *their* stories will enhance knowledge-sharing and engagement throughout the organization. Stories do not necessarily need investment in large events but opportunities to share need opening up. With modern technology, organizations have wonderful opportunities to share stories with maximum spread of delivery at relatively low cost. However, empathy and engagement are always enhanced by face-to-face storytelling.

Many practical ways to embed storytelling in organizations already exist but are underutilized as storytelling media. Most require little investment, other than commitment and perhaps a degree of 'suspension of disbelief'. When leaders embrace storytelling as a vital communication tool, they also give permission to their people to do the same.

Stories resonate more than the simple facts; they also provide a barometer of the emotional setting in the group. To assess the capability of a group therefore, it is pertinent to listen to the stories that group is using as it constructs, validates and reinforces its social networks. Equally, allowing time in line-report meetings and in individual personal development reviews for stories to unfold will complement and invigorate traditional approaches to assessment and development.

Here are some simple suggestions for introducing stories into your organization's assessment and development practices:

- Train your leaders to add storytelling techniques to their communication toolkit.
- Use mentoring dialogue as an opportunity to use stories for development purposes.
- Complement your assessment practices, such as performance reviews, with a story approach.
- Create 'story circles' to develop knowledge sharing, and to assess and elicit tacit knowledge.
- Introduce story-based team-building activities and conversations.
- Acknowledge and retell any 'values in action' stories told in your action learning sets.
- Adopt narrative approaches to change management and to communicate strategy.
- Hold World Café events to encourage meaningful conversations and story sharing as a precursor to policy change or project planning.

A story experiment for personal development

You are invited to return to the beginning of this chapter and re-read the story of *The lamp and the key*. Set aside some time to reflect on your insights and learning from this story. The following reflective prompts may help initiate this process of reflection:

- What did you personally learn from this story?
- How might this story help you with an issue you are currently facing in your life or leadership?

- What does this story tell us about habitual thinking or other traps in leadership and organizational problem-solving?
- What leadership lessons could you reframe in a personal story to pass on?

Make a mental note of whenever this story comes to mind and in what context. Notice when situations you encounter remind you of the story in some way. The practical application of the story as a personal development tool to improve reflection and quality of thinking will be enhanced if you tell the story, in your own words, at least three times over the next seven to 10 days. When might this story be helpful to illustrate a point of development to your team or to start a productive conversation?

Group work: tell this story to your team at your next meeting or away day. Use the reflective prompts as a way to stimulate creativity, new thinking and conversations. Allow smaller groups to discuss the story and feedback to the plenary group. Debrief on any new insights. This exercise will also hone your story-listening skills and may help you to assess your team's challenges, emotional state and needs more comprehensively. Recognition that stories offer a way to grow high-quality human relationships (Denning, 2010) will enhance your leadership capability.

FURTHER RESOURCES

Shah (1996) this contains further Nasrudin tales. Idries Shah drew on ancient manuscripts and sources of oral tradition to put together this collection of tales of the folk hero Nasrudin, part sage, part fool. Nasrudin tales hold up a mirror to the foibles of human nature with simple humour. With their 'twist in the tale' endings, they can be appreciated on many levels, from simple entertainment to holding a deeper message.

Hawkins (2005) reworks these classic tales into humorous yet powerful modern stories for organizational and personal transformation. Hawkins has given a modern spin to the stories by casting

Nasrudin as a somewhat eccentric management consultant. The book has an excellent chapter on why the 'mutative humour' in these stories can be so effective in a leadership and business context.

Yiannis Gabriel (University of Bath) writes prolifically on organizational storytelling and is the co-founder and coordinator of the Organizational Storytelling Seminar series, which examines the use of stories in research into different aspects of organizational life, including politics, gender, culture, leadership and emotion (**http://www.organizational-storytelling.org.uk**).

Annette Simmons is a United States-based consultant and director of Group Process Consulting, and author of many books on the impact of storytelling on organizational behaviour and groups, including *The Story Factor* (2006). Her website **www.annettesimmons.com** has many useful storytelling resources, including metaphor maps, six ways to find your story and the six principles for storytelling.

Steve Denning's 2011 magnus opus, *The Leader's Guide to Storytelling* covers the role of narrative in marketing, branding and in innovation. He explains how leaders should perform a story in a business setting and offers a detailed account of why each type of story works and how, with numerous examples from business settings of each type of story. The book also contains practical templates to help leaders construct their own stories. Steve Denning blogs daily at Forbes on leadership and storytelling.

Dr Stefanie Reissner is a lecturer in Organizational Studies at Newcastle University Business School, with a particular interest in narrative methodology and the stories of 'organizational actors' as a rich and insightful source of data. Her research into managerial storytelling was funded by the Economic and Social Research Council, and research findings are published at **www.managerial-storytelling.com**.

Web links

http://astoriedcareer.com/george_dutch_qa.html

http://blogs.forbes.com/stevedenning/

http://www.institute.nhs.uk/delivering_through_improvement/
general/transformational_story_writing.html

www.managerial-storytelling.com

http://www.organizational-storytelling.org.uk/

www.positivelives.co.uk/the-story-cafe/storytelling.html

http://stevedenning.typepad.com/steve_denning/2010/05/how-do-you-
create-a-culture-of-storytelling.html

http://www.storycenter.org

References

Baker, A C, Jensen, P J and Kolb, D A (2002) *Conversational Learning:
An experiential approach to knowledge creation*, Quorum Books, London

Denning, S (2010) What's the role of storytelling in radical management?
The Leader's Guide to Radical Management, http://stevedenning.typepad.com/
steve_denning/2010/05/index.html, posted 18 May 2010

Denning, S (2011) *The Leader's Guide to Storytelling*, Jossey-Bass, San Francisco,
CA

Evans, B C and Severtsen, B M (2001) Storytelling as cultural assessment, *Nursing
Health Care Perspective*, **22** (4), pp 180–83

Gabriel, Y (1991) On organizational stories and myths: why it is easier to slay
a dragon than to kill a myth, *International Sociology*, 6, pp 427–42

Hawkins, P (2005) *The Wise Fool's Guide to Leadership: Short spiritual stories for
organizational and personal transformation*, O Books, New Alresford

Lewis, T, Amini, F and Lannon, R (2001) *A General Theory of Love*, Vintage
Books, London

Reissner, S and Pagan, V (2013) *Storytelling in Management Practice: Dynamics
and implications*, Routledge, London

Shah, I (1996) *Pleasantries of the Incredible Mullah Nasrudin*, Octagon Press,
London

Simmons, A (2006) *The Story Factor*, Basic Books, New York

White, M (2007) *Maps of Narrative Practice*, Norton, New York

CASE STUDY   The role of personal narratives and leadership metaphors in assessment

Lisa Rossetti

This case study examines how creating opportunities to explore personal narratives and metaphors has a valuable role in developing self-assessment skills, particularly among new leaders, and identifies areas for future development. Personal narratives and metaphors are a rich source of 'data with soul', which can be used in coaching or personal diagnostics to discover both underlying leadership values and areas to develop such as engagement and proactive behaviour.

The content is derived from interview material gathered during a project that I carried out in 2009–10 for MISPA, a social enterprise arm of Manchester Metropolitan University (now disbanded). MISPA was responsible for training leaders in the voluntary sector, and also for developing leadership tools and resources.

I conducted semi-structured interviews with course participants to gather their personal stories of their learning experiences during and after MISPA's Inspiring Leaders programme. These narratives were then transcribed and edited into more structured stories, which MISPA published online. Recommendations were also made to MISPA to further develop its leadership talent development programmes for voluntary sector leaders.

To meet MISPA's evaluation needs, the majority of interview questions were based on Kirkpatrick's levels of evaluation (Kirkpatrick and Kirkpatrick, 2006), being a widely accepted methodology for evaluating the impact of training and its benefits to organizations. However, as a coach and storyteller, I was also interested in 'how people make sense of their lives, experiences and structures of the world' (Creswell 1994: 145–6). To elicit sense-making, I asked the interviewees to describe a personal leadership metaphor relevant to their current phase of development. The intention was to explore and understand something of the experiences, challenges and achievements of emergent leaders, viewing this through a narrative-metaphorical lens.

How exploring personal narratives and leadership metaphors develop self-assessment skills

How does the organization use assessments for developing leadership talent? Although MISPA carried out a consistent evaluation process of each programme, it did not have a measure of the impact of its training in the longer term. The interviews captured rich material for MISPA to reflect upon, as well as providing the participants with an opportunity for self-assessment, reflection and sense-making. Crucially, the interviews gave the alumni a formal opportunity for reflecting on their leadership journey from pre-course to present day. Although the interviews were loosely based on Kirkpatrick, the interviewees were encouraged to simply tell their story, using the question framework as a springboard to elicit personal narratives.

Most stories and indeed most conversations incorporate a metaphor; it is a way of understanding something through describing it as something else. This kind of language is often used unconsciously in everyday conversations, but deliberately constructed personal metaphors may offer a new lens through which to understand the experience of being or becoming a leader and perhaps assess other personal development goals. 'Leadership metaphors carry implicit suggestions about values – what is good, what should be done, and how – and may also allow for new insights into the ethics of leadership' (Oberlechner and Mayer-Schonberger, 2003). The personal leadership metaphor was elicited by asking: 'If there was a metaphor that would describe your current personal experience of being a leader in the voluntary sector, what would that [X] be? What is that [X] like?'

I had been warned prior to the project that some people would not be able to construct a metaphor, but most of the people interviewed found this surprisingly easy. The metaphors readily articulated the experience of becoming or being a leader. The metaphors thus provided an illustration of the leadership development phase in which they now found themselves. Many of them said that reflecting on their leadership metaphor was helpful in making sense of their current leadership identity.

The metaphors were consciously constructed and had complex imagery. Examples included being a 'back-seat driver' to convey the experience of leading from behind; leading by example was described as 'being the first one to walk that path'. Another expressed both the challenges and excitement of being a leader dealing with change in this way: 'Being a leader is like riding a bus every day and getting on and off at different bus stops. Not every day is the same. You have different challenges and different things to learn. So you might get off at the same bus stop every day, but you meet different people along the way. So that for me is that whole journey.'

One notable mixed metaphor of being 'a babe in sheep's clothing' came from the oldest of the interviewees who had transitioned from an executive leadership position into the voluntary sector for the first time and was learning to cope with conflicting agendas he encountered in his volunteer team and attitudes of the public at large.

One participant said that before the programme becoming a leader felt like being 'a tram stuck in deep snow trying to get to Mount Everest... I'd say I was a tram that now goes along and picks people up, and drops them back off where they feel they need to be. The tram goes now, all the time; the sun's shining, there's no snow, it's free flowing.' Clearly this was a positive self-assessment of her capability as a leader to engage and empower others within a constantly shifting work environment.

Clearly, allowing participants an opportunity to share their personal narratives and leadership metaphors helped them make sense of their role, its responsibilities and challenges. They were also able to reflect and express those qualities, behaviours and values they personally felt were important to being effective in their leadership. The following extracts from the narratives illustrate valuable insights and learning that emerged from the interviewees' stories.

Sam Malik

Sam Malik is responsible to the Board of Square1, Oldham in north-west England, and to stakeholders such as funders, referral agencies, parents, the young people and artists. He is also responsible for the management of the staff team and for volunteers. Sam reflected that working with a variety of partnerships and agencies he needed to be flexible and adaptable in his style.

'My leadership style [is] like water. Put me in a bowl, put me in a cup, put me in a jar, put me in a jug, I'll fit into any situation that I'm in. So the flexibility, the versatility, the adapting of the situation. So not only am I a water that free flows, I'm a water that will change shape, size, dynamic, everything according to the situation.'

Learning themes emerge from this metaphor which suggest that at this time he is highly skilled in being flexible and adaptable to change. However, further reflection also suggests possible development needs that could be explored such as becoming more proactive rather than reactive, and developing more ability to create change.

The cascading of learning and emphasis on empowering the team, volunteers and stakeholders emerged as consistent values from most narratives. Sam has shared his learning with his senior team. Interpersonal and intrapersonal skills are clearly important and also occur frequently as a theme. Sam's story contained several mentions of improving his people management, ie 'in terms of the relationship management aspect definitely I think I've become a stronger leader... I think what I've managed to improve is my relationship management, you know, how I work, how I deal with staff, volunteers, etc.'

Michelle Dennett

Michelle Dennett is the Operations Manager for Start in Salford, an arts and wellbeing charity in the north-west of England that runs creative activities for people in the Salford community with mental health difficulties or who are at risk of suffering mental health difficulties.

Time for reflection during and post-course is highly valuable for continuing nurturing leaders who are not only skilled but self-aware. Like other course participants, Michelle appreciated the focused learning environment of the course and 'time out' to reflect on her systems and practices, but also on her own personal values and behaviours. The extra dimension of the post-course interview encouraged her to capture some of her insights in a more constructive way: 'Just having time out to reflect on your working practices with other people who were in similar positions to yourself, does allow you to think about how you could do things more efficiently.'

Rahela

At the time of her interview, Rahela had a part-time role as a Family Engagement worker for Black and Ethnic Minority families within the Community Engagement Team for a children's centre in Hollingwood, in the north-west of England. She described herself as a very critical and introspective person who constantly examined her own performance, judgement and abilities, sometimes over-critically. Rahela's challenge was to develop the self-assurance she needed to be a bold leader: 'It's just that looking within yourself, coming out of your comfort zone – I think that's an achievement in itself.'

Rahela's leadership metaphor conveys a sense of purposeful transformation in which she took more control despite the unavoidable elements and could influence her own direction. She illustrated this in terms of changing from a kite into a paraglider: 'Like you really know where you're going. You've got the power and the energy. The kite is trying to fly but it gets caught in the wind. [Now] even if the wind blows, you're not pushed by it. You don't lose your ground.'

Her metaphor suggests that Rahela is someone who is adaptable but also creating change and has moved further forward than the previous example as a proactive leader, something that could be further explored to support her development. During the interview she also identified a clear focus for her leadership in developing young people, and explored her vision to hold a Developing Leaders course in the future for her volunteers.

What benefits have been gained?

For the learning provider, MISPA, a bank of stories was created that provided evidence of the impact of MISPA's Inspiring Leaders programme one year on. This added an extra dimension to its evaluation of the programme. The stories provided evidence of post-course impact, for example whether the graduates of the programme had sustained their motivation and developed their leadership skills in the longer term. The stories and metaphors provided rich data of participants' learning and development. The trainer-participant relationships were close and meaningful throughout the programme, with a genuine interest in their development. These narratives and metaphors provided training staff with very personal feedback, which they found particularly rewarding to read. Overall the organization reported that the insights generated from the interviewees' stories were valuable in understanding the participants' experience, and the recommendations were useful for course improvement.

The participants found the interviews helpful as a more formal opportunity to assess their leadership journey and to revisit and re-examine their experiences on the programme and afterwards, as they implemented new ideas and skills within their organizations. Their narratives confirmed the depth of self-assessment that can occur when post-course reflective opportunities for sharing personal narratives are offered to leaders in development. The exploration of leadership metaphors adds a powerful dimension to this approach.

One participant commented that the interview process offered her a 'formal opportunity to reflect constructively and objectively' on her development, so that she could move on from 'one phase' (her leadership training) to the next. Relating their development stories and leadership metaphors enabled the interviewees to speak and hear their own expressions of growth and confidence in their abilities and to explore their vision of their leadership.

Learning points

Personal narratives and real-life stories provide rich qualitative data not only to assess the effectiveness of leadership development programmes but also to motivate, educate and inspire others. Public, staff and stakeholder organizations can all learn from stories and appreciate the issues that face leaders. Furthermore, stories can be used for research into leadership issues. Some specific learning points that arose out of the case study are outlined below.

Develop sector-specific leadership assessment tools

As a result of conducting the case study, there was an indication that better leadership assessment tools could be developed specifically for voluntary sector leaders as this participant's comments suggest: 'Some kind of assessment [is needed] of an individual's leadership and management skills, and more specifically identifying what needs to be developed.' Participants generally felt that they needed some kind of benchmark of their capability and talent, and one which would be particularly relevant for their sector. We recommend that organizations offering leadership talent development programmes carry out an initial competence assessment of leadership skills with participants prior to their embarking on their development programme.

Optimize opportunities to explore personal narrative

Stories have a powerful role to play in sense-making and this, in turn, enables new leaders to confidently explore and articulate their leadership identity more clearly. Opportunities such as mentoring, coaching, peer coaching and other forums offer advantageous conditions for this type of reflective narrative. Provide opportunities for your emergent and developing leaders to assess their own learning and leadership identity through exploring their personal narrative in a reflective environment.

Provide coach-mentoring support

The learners who participated in the case study did not at that time have mentors or coaches. Some had made informal arrangement to support their development through further contact with MISPA tutors and this was highly appreciated. The nature of the case study interviews and exploration of their personal narratives and leadership metaphors was something fresh and unusual for them, but one they appreciated and found helpful.

Leaders who learn to self-assess their progress become more confident in their abilities. As an added benefit, leaders who are coached understand the importance of empowering and coaching their own workforce. With their coach, leaders can develop a 'vocabulary' of personal metaphors of leadership that strengthens their inner dialogue and enriches their communications with others. In this relationship, both coach and coachee are conversational partners contributing to the meaning-making process and co-production of knowledge.

Offer reflective thinking time

Capitalize on the investment in development by encouraging and providing plenty of opportunities for reflective time through coaching, mentoring or other reflective dialogue. Collaborative witnessing of personal narrative can strengthen groups and teams, but needs to be intentional and within a managed environment, lest stories lapse into indulgent rambling. Sharing personal narratives, enriched with metaphors, is fundamental to the process of social meaning-making. Developing the skills and confidence to share our stories in the context of leadership and team-building enhances team cohesion and motivation.

References

Cresswell, J W (1994) *Research Design: Qualitative and quantitative approaches*, Sage, Thousand Oaks, CA

Kirkpatrick, D L and Kirkpatrick, J D (2006) *Evaluating Training Programs*, 3rd edn, Berrett-Koehler, San Francisco, CA

Oberlechner, T and Mayer-Schonberger, V (2003) *Through Their Own Words: Towards a new understanding of leadership through metaphors*, Center for Public Leadership Working Papers, Spring, pp 159–74, Harvard University, John F Kennedy School of Government, Cambridge, MA

TOOL   Mentoring walks

Lisa Rossetti

What they are and when to use them

The mentoring walk as a leadership development concept originated with former CEO of Oxygen Media, Geraldine Laybourne, who is a programme speaker for the Fortune/US State Department Global Women's Mentoring Partnership. She inspired Vital Voices, a global alumnae-driven mentoring walk initiative, nurturing women's leadership. In her footsteps, I have been using mentoring walks myself and exploring the walks as a simple yet highly effective development tool.

Mentoring walks can be conducted one-to-one, or as a small group with a preferred ratio of one-to-two or one-to-three, mentor to mentee or leader to team members. The mentoring process follows usual mentoring or coaching practice with the mentor managing the focus and time, entering into purposeful dialogue and asking reflective questions in order to develop staff.

There are four key foci to the walks:

1 knowledge sharing;

2 personal development;

3 creative problem solving; and

4 health and fitness.

Mentoring walks are readily incorporated into any weekly work routine. They can be conducted outdoors on an organization's grounds, or a nearby open space such as a city or business park. In inclement weather, walks can be conducted in corridors or other internal spaces.

Benefits

- Provide an innovative approach to leadership and team development.

- Nurture relationships and build trust.

- Develop conversational leaders.

- Provide an opportunity for informal story and knowledge-sharing.

- Encourage reflective learning and thinking, and creative problem solving.

- 'Time to think' contributes to mental wellbeing.

Solvitur ambulando *'It is solved by walking'*

(Saint Augustine)

Mentoring walks are an ideal tool for leaders to nurture positive working relationships and promote knowledge sharing by taking advantage of a process conducive to conversations and stories. Educator Carolyn Baldwin defines conversational leadership as 'the leader's intentional use of conversation as a core process to cultivate the collective intelligence needed to create business and social value' (cited in Brown and Hurley, 2010). Former Chilean Minister of Finance, Fernando Flores affirms that 'an organization's results are determined through webs of human commitments, born in webs of human conversations' (cited in Brown and Hurley, 2010). The mentoring walk is thus a deceptively simple yet highly effective tool to develop conversational or storytelling leaders and hone their engagement skills. Within this context storytelling may be seen as a core process, harnessing the momentum of walking to purposeful and strategic intent, and inviting conversations and stories on critical issues.

There is a long-standing connection between walking and both critical and reflective thinking. Aristotle walked around the Lyceum in ancient Athens, sharing and exploring ideas with his followers, the Peripatetic Philosophers; the medieval cloisters were designed with a similar purpose. When we walk in natural surroundings, we begin to emerge from our protective hermetically sealed 'pods', our cars, offices and the worlds we inhabit inside our Blackberries and iPhones. Falling into an easy pace with a companion seems to harmonize our thought patterns. Our brain waves slow down from Beta waves to the slower Alpha waves we experienced as a child. Our breathing becomes regular; we oxygenate the brain, letting go of tension and stress. We begin to notice things outside of ourselves – and crucially inside of ourselves. The environment in which the walks take place generates a backdrop of images that seem to illustrate the mental maps that are being constructed during the mentoring dialogue and stories. The metaphorical imagination is stimulated and learning anchored to visual images and impressions from the walk.

Mentoring walks can have real business benefits: clearer thinking and decision making emerge as our reflective, problem-solving and creative 'muscles' wake up. We face our working week with renewed enthusiasm. We have better 'conversations' to take back to work, resulting in higher engagement and motivation all round.

Furthermore, the mentoring walk is a pragmatic tool to underpin the new models of leadership where engagement and interpersonal skills are emphasized. The mentoring walk invites executives to step down from their hierarchical perches into a more dynamic conversational process with their employees. In addition, walking together sends out the clear signal that leaders are practising what they preach when they claim to have an open door. The mentoring walk effectively models all the values of smart modern leadership: inclusivity, intimacy, interactivity and transparency. Mentoring walks could be the key to unlocking the 'grid lock' of communication, as well as fostering trust and knowledge sharing throughout organizations.

Reference

Brown, J and Hurley, T (2010) Conversational leadership: thinking together for a change, *Oxford Leadership Journal*, **1**, 2

Improving results through measuring 'return on investment'

11

PHILIP E SWEET

EXECUTIVE SUMMARY

Most people still believe it is not possible to measure definite and un-deniable results that arise from learning and development investments; 20 years ago that was probably true. The advent of modern design, delivery and measurement technologies and methodologies have long since given us the proven means to reliably and consistently measure return on investment (RoI), in all its aspects, not just in money terms.

It is now possible to reliably predict the value a development pro-gramme will have before it commences, to track that the expected outputs and impacts are delivered during its delivery, and to measure the actual results that are delivered from its completion. Real time action-able intelligence about design, delivery, participants and the arena to which learning is applied enable decisions to be made 'in-flight' so that benefits realization is expanded.

Measuring in this way also multiplies the number of people that will deliver results as a consequence of participating in development activities. It has long been known that what is measured affects behav-iour. When this is used deliberately to create a pattern and sequence of communication about what really matters, those who could but otherwise wouldn't take action to apply their learning do so, thereby increasing the resultant dividend.

More than all the above, we also know that we can apply the same to leadership itself. For most, the day they become a leader is the day they cease to make part or all of any front-line contribution they used to make. As a leader then, to justify one's existence, it is important to know that contribution exceeds the cost of one's employ. So, is the ultimate leadership assessment tool that encourages leadership talent development one that enables every leader to consciously measure and know the RoI in all its aspects that they are creating year on year?

Improving results through measuring RoI

Is comfort a crisis?

> Today, the biggest challenge we must meet is the one we present to ourselves. To not become a nation that places entitlement ahead of accomplishment. To not become a country that places comfortable lies ahead of difficult truths. To not become a people that thinks so little of ourselves that we demand no sacrifice from each other.
>
> (Chris Christie, politician, 2012)

What is it that separates the economies and organizations that are emerging, growing and becoming increasingly successful from those that are mature and in danger of declining? You will undoubtedly have your own lexicon of adjectives to explain the difference. For those at the top of their game this may include such words as passion, excellence, clarity of purpose, prosperity, growth and stability. For those who have fallen to their most lowly state, words like unstable, struggle, danger, hunger, strife, poverty and survival are used.

For those that are emerging and growing it is easy to see how there would be motivation to change towards the first set of descriptors and away from the second. For those who make it to the top of their tree there is a real danger. With growing success and prosperity comes the opportunity to attend to all the things you wished you had time for as you were working your way towards your goals. The problem with this is that it can distract everybody's attention from the very things that got you success in the first place and the intentions you had when you set out.

What has all this got to do with measurement you might ask? Well, that journey up the ladder of success is ultimately a journey of development. To make it and continue it successfully requires leadership. The earlier chapters of this book are about how to assess and develop leadership effectiveness. This chapter is about how we know a leader has applied what works by the trail of results he or she has created.

At the development journey's beginning the economic imperatives ensure we use our resources with care and we actively measure what really matters moment by moment. As we get comfortable, the likelihood that we will continue to do this reduces as we increasingly believe we have arrived and systematize our monitoring of results to maintain the good health we assume we have achieved. So is comfort a crisis? Yes: if the route to our success was development and comfort acts against this, then surely it is. For the health, wealth and prosperity of us all, leadership and talent development must surely be continued, and we must measure it to know that this is so.

Disturbing normality

One of the greatest observations of nature and our world is that it is normal. If you get together a collection of anything – people, animals, rocks, plants, planets – and measure them in pretty much any way you like you will find they conform to what is known in statistics as the bell curve or normal distribution. This not only applies to physical attributes but to behaviour as well, including performance and development.

In terms of learning and development, the likelihood of an individual applying what he or she has learnt to create tangible beneficial results for themselves and the organization can be predicted with some simple statistics. An undisturbed group of 20 people, left to their own devices, will perform in accordance with the probabilities described by three standard deviations either side of the norm (Nunnally and Bernstein, 2010). This means that you would expect to see the following:

2 per cent, or less than one person, will definitely apply their learning and deliver some kind of result;

14 per cent, or up to two or three people, will probably apply their learning and deliver some kind of result;

34 per cent, or up to six or seven people, will possibly apply their learning and deliver some kind of result;

34 per cent, or up to six or seven people, will possibly not apply their learning and not deliver some kind of result;

14 per cent, or up to two or three people, will probably not apply their learning and not deliver some kind of result;

2 per cent, or less than one person, will definitely not apply their learning and not deliver any kind of result.

Recent research by the KnowledgeAdvisors (2010) and Brinkerhoff (2003) backs this up by showing that up to 80 per cent of all learning is wasted. Shocking though this is, these figures are pretty much what you would expect from an *undisturbed* natural distribution. It also presents a massive opportunity because there is clearly potential to improve this statistic. If we can systematically disturb or skew this natural distribution in favour of better levels of performance in the same way that occurs in the rapid development phase of a country or organization, clearly we can create much better and sustainable RoI.

Beyond belief

The fundamental purpose of learning and development is to improve the functioning and performance of an organization. Otherwise why invest in it? All the more surprising then is a widespread belief that one can't definitely attribute and measure the results directly arising from learning and development. This is the biggest reason organizations don't measure to see that the intended improved functioning or performance is delivered. To be fair, there might be some basis for this belief.

When work was primarily physical, in agriculture and direct production of goods, it was probably easier to see the connection between learning a thing and knowing whether it was worthwhile, because it would quite quickly turn up in the corner of a field or a workshop. It was pretty easy to see the physical results of more or better produce ready to go out to consumers. As organizations have grown, become more complex and differentiated their roles, it has indeed become more difficult to see this relationship. By the middle of the 20th century this was recognized as a massively important problem that attracted the attention of some of the world's most brilliant minds. Since that time a huge amount of research and testing has been completed to find and prove the methodologies needed to measure results from learning and development. There are four seminal pieces of work that provided the backbone and basis of that emergent capability:

- Gary Becker's Nobel Prize-winning work on human capital theory (Becker, 1994).

- Donald Kirkpatrick's work on the evaluation of learning (Kirkpatrick, 1975).

- Jack Phillips' work on the measurement of RoI from learning (Phillips, 2003).

- Robert Brinkerhoff's development of the success case methodology (Brinkerhoff, 2003).

It is clear that, from the 1960s to the present day, many organizations either didn't know about or didn't properly understand Becker's and Kirkpatrick's work. If you go to their original publications and research it is all there. However, there is a problem from illogical practices. If organizations measure at all (and most don't, and those that do don't go beyond 'happy sheets') they tend to ask participants a series of questions as a progression from bottom to top (ie from participant up to the organization):

1 How much they enjoyed the learning – this elicits descriptions or ratings of a feeling (an abstract notion).

2 Asking about what they had learnt – this elicits a description of internal meaning (again an abstract notion).

3 Asking about behaviour – 10 people's description of what a person does will be similar but different (ie a subjective description).

4 And finally, we ask people what results the above has delivered – most people find it impossible to go from two abstracts and a subjective to a concrete description.

Even professional evaluators have found it hard to get specific tangible proof of results arising from learning using this approach. What is needed is another practical way of providing consistent, believable, validated, defensible, repeatable data on financial and other value created by learning. This has effectively been given by the two other pieces of work already mentioned.

Since the 1970s, Jack and Patti Phillips' work on RoI from learning (2003) has been available to provide the means to measure RoI and easily and quickly isolate the effects of the learning and adjust for confidence levels in the accuracy of the estimates of value created. Regarding 'whole of programme costs' Robert Brinkerhoff's success case study methodology (2003) has been available since the 1990s. This gives us a top-down approach by asking:

- What is really happening?
- What results are being achieved?

- What is the value of the results?
- How can it be improved?

In practice, participants find it easier to start with a factual narrative about the bigger picture, then within that to look for, find and provide concrete evidence of measurable results and value. So, for more than 20 years there has been no foundation for the belief that one can't measure the results and RoI that definitely arise from learning!

The other big belief that gets in the way of measuring the value of learning is that if you perform this task, it will only result in a lengthy and rather vague report that will be massively expensive. Again, there is some basis for this. When the only way of gathering the data was by sending out specialist evaluators to interview everybody involved and affected and to gather the evidence, the bill was often huge: 50 to 250 per cent of a programme's cost is not uncommon. This too is no longer true. With the advent of web/cloud-based tools, automated data collection, analysis and reporting, costs have plummeted. Now, typically, by spending 5 to 10 per cent of the programme costs, these tools will provide real-time actionable data that enables organizations to multiply the value created by learning which, and if done well, will be many times greater than the cost. Otherwise why make the investment? The world's top companies (Microsoft, Cisco, Audi, P&G, Wellpoint, KPMG, Deloittes, PwC, NASA and many other global brands) have been using these tools for decades – no surprise there then!

Development as a prototype

So, what is it about development that makes it so hard to measure? Why can't our regular measurement systems give us what we need? Development by its nature will create something new or improve things. How each person traverses the journey of development is likely to be at least partly unique as each participant will be a different individual. The story of their development journey will also be unique in terms of their:

- wider contribution;
- business impact;
- financial return;
- job impact;
- personal impact; and
- ability to sustain the results.

The narratives and evidence that emerge from this line of enquiry are effectively participant-centred stories. To make the best of the opportunities for improvement, and to maximize the value added, we need to be able to hear them as they are. If we force them to report into the structure of an organization's existing report measurement framework we are likely to compromise new possibilities. Leadership development, in particular, creates prototype possibilities for better and new things to occur. Of course we want to see the value created by the leadership development investment on the organization's bottom line using a bespoke measurement schema, and retaining this, possibly while the learning is progressing, is massively important.

Monitoring to measure

As organizations grow and get more complex one of the problems they have is measuring accurately the way they are performing. Where they have accurate numeric facts and automated data generation, for example transactions through bank accounts or numbers of customer transactions, organizations can usually be quite accurate. For much of the rest they must rely on other forms of reporting, often remote reporting or monitoring.

The problem with this is twofold. First, an organization is never fully sure how the respondents to remote monitoring are reacting to a question, whether they properly understand a monitoring question's original intent, or even if they are responding accurately. Secondly, the act of measurement alters people's behaviour. People generally do what they perceive their leaders ask for. This can lead to what can be described as 'satisficing' – the respondent giving the organization what they believe it wants to hear, even if that means compromising some other aspect of functionality; for example, performance targets leading to compromised customer care or quality. The only way to really know what is happening is to go and observe and measure it directly so that a full appreciation of the reality can be gained – using both quantitative and qualitative descriptors.

While this is too labour-intensive to do for all measurement, managers and leaders at all levels have a responsibility to know what is really happening, and validate and give meaning to the information the organization is receiving. This is particularly important, even though it is rarely done, for assessing the results of development because of its prototype nature. In practice it is quite straightforward to achieve. Narrative and quantitative evidence can be gathered and validated by a third party. The role of the person the respondent/participant reports to is particularly important here.

Confirming the information with a more senior second person (triangulating) gives much greater confidence in its accuracy.

Measurement as behaviour shaping

There are four main factors that we can use to help us achieve results from learning and development:

1 clarity about what the learning is intended to deliver;

2 management and participant behaviour;

3 learning design; and

4 measurement of outputs and outcomes.

For leadership and talent development to be effective and give really great RoI, therefore, these main issues need to be addressed:

- Why is the development being procured? How does it contribute to the organization's current and future priorities? Is it intended to add value by improving performance, quality, reduce risk, increase compliance, etc? Organizations typically spend 3–5 per cent of their revenue budget on learning. To do this without knowing what gain is intended is, at very least, a lost opportunity.

- What is the vision for how the learning will be applied by each participant? What is the expected return on investment and value of that applied learning by each participant? Does that value exceed the whole of the programme costs for each participant (participant remuneration and expenses while learning, plus venue and training provider costs). If not, what would need to change for this to be so?

- How is the learning designed and delivered? Is this done in a way that will create improvement and value for the organization of a value greater than the costs? If this is not so, what would need to be changed? Are the intended outputs and outcomes from the learning aligned to the delivery priorities the organization identified for this learning at the start?

- Are the line managers (the people each participant reports to) fully supporting the application of the learning to realize the intended value (proving, opportunity, resources, time, equipment and help where needed)?

- What is the actual RoI and value delivered within the life of learning programme and longitudinally in the year following its completion?

Just asking these questions shapes the behaviour of the participants, the people they report to, the learning deliverers and the organization in a way that multiplies the results delivered.

The sequence of communication

The key to creating excellent results is to use the measuring RoI tools to create a pattern and sequence of communication that commences before the learning even begins. In fact, an effective measurement process initiates a dialogue prior to procurement and continues after programme completion.

The sequence of communication creates an opportunity for decisions to be made that greatly increase the delivered value of the learning. This is because by using automated data gathering, analysis and reporting, actionable data can be made available in real time. Usually, traditional evaluative information about learning programmes is provided after the event, too late to influence the outcomes and outputs.

With modern web- and cloud-based tools the measurement can be predictive about expectations as well as actual results delivered. The general rule is that if there are no expectations of value being created by the application of the learning, then there will be little value created. The normal distribution will hold sway with only 2–16 per cent of participants delivering only a fraction of the programme cost. In a standard learning evaluation the questions asked are often training- and trainer-centric. In an effective learning RoI measurement schema the questions are participant-centric, about the application of learning, delivered results and bottom line financial value.

Once an effective return on investment measurement process is in place, delivered results would be expected to have a value many times greater than the whole programme costs, often by thousands of per cent. This makes learning and development, especially leadership development, a true 'spend to save' return on investment.

Breaking the grip of mediocrity

Traditional old-style learning design, as it has evolved for larger organizations and in many educational institutions, is as follows: 'There is educational input; from which the participant may or may not learn; if there is learning the participant may or may not acquire an accreditation or qualification.' In this schema there is no direct connection to the application of the learning with the results. To this we give the name the 'learning gap'.

In modern learning design there is clarity about the result to be delivered. This will be the vehicle for the learning and be central to the learning design. Participants will definitely learn a lot from delivering this result because it is live and real and applied to their work (see Chapter 8). If participants wish they can pursue an accreditation or qualification, but many also get benefit from the street credibility of being a high-performing individual, and gain benefit from the enhanced track record, which improves their CV.

In this schema, where the learning gap is removed, it is common for a 400 per cent RoI to be built into the learning design. When this is done, delivered results are often greater than 1,000 per cent, particularly in leadership development programmes. Interestingly, this type of design is much more like the workplace learning that would have predominated in the physical industries mentioned at the beginning of this chapter!

Leadership as development

In the last 25 years research has focused on high-performing organizations. It is increasingly recognized that there are three main phases to organization and leadership development:

Phase 1: Rational leadership. The basic rational business model is
    established to meet demand through the organization of physical,
    human and financial capital.

Phase 2: Transformational leadership. The potential within the people
    of an organization is unleashed through the application of good
    methods and skills and more emotionally intelligent leadership.

Phase 3: Sustainable excellence. The organization has found a way to
    move beyond leader-centric behaviour and systematize the continued
    learning needed to sustain excellent results as a top performing
    organization.

Jim Collins and his colleagues sought out and investigated organizations that outperformed the market by four times or more for at least 15 years (Collins, 2001, 2002). In terms of the normal distribution, what happens is that the above measures motivate and create the conditions for more participants to perform better. Good leaders properly understand that the resources of people can be unleashed through a process of continued systematized leadership in which development success and continuous re-optimization can be built in. The numbers below are typical of the shifts that take place in the best performing leadership development programmes for 20 participants:

16 per cent, or at least three people, will definitely apply their learning and deliver some kind of result;

48 per cent, or up to nine or 10 people, will probably apply their learning and deliver some kind of result;

20 per cent, or up to four people, will possibly apply their learning and deliver some kind of result;

9 per cent, or up to one or two people, will possibly not apply learning and not deliver some kind of result;

5 per cent, or one person, will probably not apply their learning and not deliver some kind of result;

2 per cent, or less than one person, will definitely not apply their learning and not deliver any kind of result.

Our experience is that the leadership development excellence that arises from skilfully measuring return on investment in the way described here might also reasonably be expected to give an improvement in performance that is four to five times greater.

Measuring leadership's contribution

Finally, we now know it is possible to confidently measure the RoI arising from leadership development. So, what about leadership itself? Isn't it by its very nature intended to be developmental? This is surely so if it is to add value. It follows, therefore, that these same tools can be used to measure leadership contribution and return on investment on an annual basis.

SPECIFIC ACTION POINTS

Find out how much your organization is currently investing in learning and development activities and within that:

- how much is being invested in each separate programme;
- how much in each part of the organization;
- how much in each specific grade/profession.

For each element of learning and development investment, clarify what each intervention is intended to create in terms of results for the organization across the six types of return on investment:

1 quality;

2 activity;

3 financial value;

4 job impact;

5 personal impact;

6 satisfaction and sustainability.

Determine whether arrangements are in place to engage the person who a learner reports to (eg, his or her line manager), prior to the learning event/process taking place in clarifying the *expected results* from each individual learner deploying his or her learning in his or her work arena. Is this data collected and reviewed in advance? Check to see whether, and if so how, learners are followed-up post learning event/process to clarify and validate the *actual results* they have delivered using what they have learnt.

Check to see if efficient mechanisms exist to aggregate the data and provide to decision makers the data they need to guide and inform future investment in learning and development and improve the quality, design, delivery and RoI from future learning and development programmes. Are the reporting arrangements to your board/top leaders detailing the monthly/annual contribution of talent development of your human resources on a par with those for your financial resources and your physical resources?

FURTHER RESOURCES

Suggested reading

The undeniable underlying rationale of why leaders need to contribute: Drucker, P (2009) *The Effective Executive*, HarperCollins.

The most comprehensive treatise on the techniques for measuring the effectiveness of learning and development: Barnett, K and Berk, J (2007) *Human Capital Analytics: Measuring and improving learning and talent impact*, Word Association Publishers.

An excellent book from leaders in the field of talent development: Fitz-Enz, J (2010) *The New HR Analytics: Predicting the economic value of your company's human capital investments*, Amacom.

Guidance from the man accredited with producing the core model used for effectively measuring learning and development: Kirkpatrick, D L and Kirkpatrick, J D (2005) *Transferring Learning to Behaviour: Using the four levels to improve performance*, Berrett Koehler.

Two UK views of best practice: Kearns, P (2005) *Training Evaluation and ROI: How to develop value-based training*, Chartered Institute of Personnel and Development, and Bramley, P (1996) *Evaluating Training Effectiveness*, McGraw-Hill.

Core texts for measuring development activities: Phillips, J J, Snead, L and Bothell, T (2002) *The Project Management Scorecard*, Butterworth-Heinemann; Phillips, J J (2000) *The Consultant's Scorecard*, McGraw-Hill; Phillips, J J, Stone, R and Phillips, P P (2001) *The Human Resources Scorecard*, Butterworth-Heinemann; Phillips, J J (ed) (1999) InfoLine Series on Evaluation: *Vol 1 – Level 1 Evaluation: Reaction and Planned Action; Vol 2 – Level 2 Evaluation: Learning; Vol 3 – Level 3: Application; Vol 4 – Level 4 Evaluation: Business Results; Vol 5 – Level 5 Evaluation: ROI In Action: Implementing evaluation systems and processes*, American Society for Training and Development.

A really good view of the higher level issues and the practicalities: Brinkerhoff, R and Apking, A M (2001) *High Impact Learning: Strategies for leveraging performance and business results from training investments (New perspectives in organizational learning, performance, and change)*, Perseus Publishing.

An organizational development perspective: Kearsley, G (1982) *Costs, Benefits and Productivity in Training Systems*, Addison-Wesley.

Ebbinghaus, H (1913) *Memory: A contribution to experimental psychology*: Teacher College, Columbia University, OH

Mattox, I I, Jr (2010) Manager engagement: reducing scrap learning, *Training Industry Quarterly*, Fall

Sweet, P E (2009) *Turning Evaluation on Its Head*, Gold Stamp Publishing, Cardiff

Suggested websites

http://www.knowledgeadvisors.com/: The site of the world's largest provider of learning analytics. An excellent site with access to many up to date research White Papers.

http://www.bersin.com/: Talent development research at its best. Many resources and an excellent source of advice.

http://www.roiinstitute.net/

http://www.kirkpatrickpartners.com/

http://www.thepip.org/: Practical advice and help to design and apply your bespoke learning and development measurement schemas.

References

Becker, G (1994) *Human Capital: A theoretical and empirical analysis, with special reference to education*, 3rd edn, University of Chicago Press, London

Brinkerhoff, R O (2003) *The Success Case Method – Find out quickly what's working and what's not*, Berrett and Koehler, New York

Christie, C (2012) *Election Statement*, Governor of New Jersey

Collins, J (2001) *Good to Great: Why some companies make the leap... and others don't*, Harper Collins, London

Collins, J (2002) *Built to Last: Successful habits of visionary companies*, Harper Collins, London

Kirkpatrick, D L (1975) *Evaluating Training Programs*, American Society for Training and Development, Madison, Wisconsin

KnowledgeAdvisors Research (2010) *Manager Engagement*, KnowledgeAdvisors, Chicago, IL

Nunnally, J and Bernstein, I (2010) *Psychometric Theory*, McGraw-Hill, London

Phillips, J (2003) *Return on Investment in Training and Performance Improvement Programs*, 2nd edn, Butterworth-Heinemann, Woburn, PA

CASE STUDY   Provider and client benefits realization

Philip E Sweet

This case study describes the effect on two organizations of measuring quality, impact and RoI in relation to a coaching programme being delivered over two years to train workplace coaches with the intent they achieve accreditation. This case study was taken direct from the measurement journals of The Performance Improvement Project Ltd (**www.thepip.org**).

Organization 1 – The learning provider: one of the top coaching providers in the UK with an international business whose 'coaching for managers and leaders' programme has been used to set National Standards and provide core learning support materials for a UK and International Coaching Accreditation/Awarding Body. *Organization 2 – The client:* a UK Local Government Authority with more than 4,500 staff that has decided to run a multiple cohort coaching programme spread over two or more years.

The main points of the case study

For the learning provider:

- Improved value for money can be provided to clients without extra cost.

- Learning can be designed to maximize impact and results.

- Proof of value created by its coaching: 1) trebled the volume of new business contracted; 2) increased the share of programmes delivered for its client.

- Pre-eminence as *the* leading highest performance learning provider in its client arena.

For the client:

- Connected learning and development to business deliverables.

- Engaged participants and line managers – improved delivered results.

- Identified and removed internal blockages.

- Significantly improved the bottom line contribution from its learning and development investments.

The impact of measuring quality and RoI of a programme to produce workplace coaches

In most organizations there is a fundamental tension between the need to manage costs and the need to improve quality, productivity and performance. This is particularly pertinent in the learning and development arena.

At times of financial pressure organizations all too easily cut the learning and development budget as an early action. Yet ultimately, development of people is the only means by which behaviour can be changed and the needed improvement achieved. One of the prime reasons for this is that historically it has been argued that it is difficult to measure the definite results from learning and development. However, for more than 20 years this has not been the case. It is possible to design and implement learning programmes in a way that ensures quantifiable and definite results can both be expected and delivered by participants.

Against this backdrop and with a wish to address these issues, a cohort of top performing learning providers and their clients were invited to partner with a learning design and RoI measurement specialist. The aim of the partnership was to spread good practice by:

- Showing learning providers how to add an effective measurement schema to their learning products.

- Using the outputs from the measurement activities to:
  - improve the effectiveness of learning design and delivery;
  - engage with client organizations to enable them to identify and remove their hidden blocks to improvement;
  - ensure the learning and development investment paid for itself many times over.

- Through the learning providers, to show client organizations how they could significantly improve the bottom line contribution from their learning and development investments.

The initiative was started through an invitation-only workshop event to which an initial cohort of top learning providers and clients were invited to form the core of a 'high impact learning' practitioner group. In that session was a 'UK National Training Award Winning' coaching skills provider.

This coaching skills provider understood the importance and potential of the more modern RoI measurement approaches immediately and asked for help to design and apply an effective measurement schema to a coaching programme that was about to be commissioned by a local authority. Their client, a County Council with more than 4,500 staff, had asked the learning provider to develop successive cohorts of mid-grade leaders and managers as successful workplace coaches.

A bespoke measurement schema was prepared for use with the programme and agreed with the learning provider. The initial learning design was as follows:

- Attendance at five one-day experiential workshops in which participants were shown and then asked to use the skills and techniques they would need by practising on other participants.

- The programme was supported with a top quality workbook that participants were expected to complete and use to record their learning journey.

- Participants' skill in practice sessions and their completed workbook were both assessed by the facilitators.

- To gain full accreditation as coaches, participants were expected to complete coaching relationship cycles with two separate individuals. These coaching sessions had to be written up and provided for assessment along with written feedback from the coachees and from the coach's supervisor.

By applying the measurement schema to the first cohort to provide feedback in real time it was soon apparent that:

- Prior to the programme start, neither participants nor their line managers knew quite what to expect from the programme.

- People loved the workshop facilitators – they were clearly excellent and highly engaging.

- The workshops were highly interactive and learning transfer was excellent.

- The workbook was relevant and would provide an excellent reference resource back at work.

- The difficulty with this design was that, although all participants attended the workshops and completed the workbook, very few participants, less than 20 per cent, came back with the write ups of their workplace coaching, and so most participants never achieved their accreditation as workplace coaches.

How does the organization use the real-time outputs from the measurement schema to improve the effectiveness of its leadership talent development? The second time around the learning providers were helped to make a number of changes. Prior to the start of cohort 2, the learning providers went back to the client and asked:

- What were its aspirations for what the programme would deliver? What organization priorities did it want to address? The client wanted to improve overall quality, productivity and performance of the organization while continuing to allow headcount to fall through natural wastage and staff turnover.

- The client was asked to arrange for participants' line managers to be contacted and made aware of the aspirations for the programme, which were to be delivered by enabling participants to use workplace coaching to lead and manage their people more effectively.

- It was made clear that participants were expected to attend all workshops and to complete the full accreditation as a workplace coach within six months of completing the five workshops. Failure to do this would result in a recharge of the whole of the programme costs to the budget code of their own department.

- Line managers and participants were asked to fully engage with all the parts of the programme measurement instruments that were sent to them.

Prior to the start of the first workshop line managers were asked to work with participants to:

- Clarify priority learning needs for the individual.

- Clarify the quantitative and qualitative improvements expected from that individual deploying his or her learning in the workplace and to estimate the financial value of those expectations. That estimate was discounted by the percentage they felt those expectations would have been achieved in the next 12 months without the programme and further discounted by the extent to which they felt less than totally confident in their estimate.

- Identify the support (time, money, manager help and resources) that participants would need during and post-programme to deploy their learning and deliver or exceed those expectations.

The five workshops were measured for quality, impact and learning effectiveness as before and to ensure that expected outputs and outcomes were achieved along the way. Post-programme longitudinal tracking was used to measure gross and net results that each participant achieved in his or her workplace in the year after the programme. These results were validated by line managers.

What benefits have been gained?

The benefits flowing from this type of in-flight assessment are:

- The organization knows, before the programme starts, the expected minimum net RoI likely to arise from the programme. This can be set against the anticipated whole of programme costs (travel, venue costs, learning provider fees and value of participant salary for the days they are engaged in the learning process) to confirm value for money.

- If the net RoI is negative the programme can either be redesigned or stopped.

- The percentage of accredited workplace coaches emerging from each cohort was increased to more than 80 per cent; a 400+ per cent increase in results delivered.

- The RoI for the programme was hugely improved.

- The immediate and ongoing value of continuing to ensure important learning is applied was recognized.

Client learning points

- Lack of support and understanding from line managers (including senior ones) was hindering change.

- The client now insists that managers sign up before participants attend (with a claw-back clause!)

- The client now holds mini launches for each instance of its key training programmes.

- The client measured other programmes and found that 44 per cent of its training is in need of serious redesign.

- The potential and real value assigned to learning by the organization and its leaders was hugely increased. The possibility that learning programmes that were well designed, well delivered and expertly measured and adjusted in flight could deliver bottom line results of far higher value than the costs, was made a viable and attainable possibility.

- The results delivered in alignment with the organization's core priorities were a matter for reporting to top leaders/the board.

- Expert assistance is required to learn how to design and deploy an effective bespoke measurement schema to a programme. A six-level return on investment produces the best results (see section: 'specific action points').

TOOL   The diligent dozen

Philip E Sweet

What it is and when to use

This tool, developed by The Performance Improvement Project Ltd, is for use prior to the start, throughout the life and after the end of any new or existing development programme or activity. It enables the user to put in place the sequence of communication that disturbs the normal distribution of participant behaviour in favour of higher levels of performance. It also enables the user to gain insights into the conditions necessary for the organization to sustain those increased levels of performance through:

- Identifying blockages to delivery so that they can be removed.

- Discovering what systematized dialogue and stimulation are needed to shape employees' and managers' behaviour in favour of higher performing choices.

- Creating the means to deliver the real-time learning required to support those higher-performing choices in the best way possible.

TABLE 11.1   The diligent dozen

Step 1	Be clear about why the learning and development is being commissioned and what areas of individual, team and organization performance it is intended to improve and by how much over what timescale.
Step 2	Set up expectations for the training that identifies and describes something the trainee delivers as a product of the training, whatever it is.
Step 3	Calculate the definite value of expected results in money terms.
Step 4	Get crystal clear about what one thing you can measure to know this is definitely being delivered.
Step 5	Isolate the effects of the training from other factors that may cause some of this result and adjust the amount of the result you ascribe to the training.

TABLE 11.1   *continued*

Step 6	Check to see that the trainee and their line manager understand what is to be delivered as a result of the learning and have put in place the necessary time, resources and support to consolidate learning and achievement.
Step 7	Design and deliver the training in a way that prompts, supports and motivates the participant to learn and deliver the agreed results and more. Behaviour flows to wherever the reinforcement is!
Step 8	Proceed when the intended results have a monetary value that is greater than the whole of programme costs – if not, redesign the pre-frame and the training until this is achieved.
Step 9	Build in at every stage during and after the training the means to measure and track the six types of return on investment: 1 Wider contribution 2 Business impact 3 Financial return 4 Job impact 5 Personal impact 6 Ability to sustain the results
Step 10	Measure and validate the results and return on investment and feed back to senior managers/ commissioners.
Step 11	Spread these design principles to all other coaching, mentoring, training and organization development programmes in the organization so that performance can be massively improved.
Step 12	Get professional help to learn how to do this well if you are unfamiliar with preparing bespoke behaviour shaping measurement schemas for development programmes.

ABOUT THE AUTHORS

Chapter authors

Danielle Grant is a Director of LeaderShape, a Fellow of the Higher Education Academy and Honorary Lecturer at the University of Chester. Following a successful blue-chip commercial career, she is now an accredited executive coach-mentor working with emotional intelligence and the neuroscience of learning to enable transpersonal insights for senior executives.

Chris Gulliver is a founder Director of LeaderShape, a Fellow of the Higher Education Academy and the Institute of Consulting. Following wide experience in senior management positions in industry he has worked for many years with chief executives and their top teams, either individually or in peer groups, to enhance leadership performance.

John Knights, chairman of LeaderShape, is an experienced senior executive coach and facilitator, and an expert in emotional intelligence, transpersonal leadership and neuro-leadership. He has been a senior executive in major international corporations, a serial entrepreneur and lecturer at Oxford University. He is author of *The Invisible Elephant and The Pyramid Treasure* and has written for *HR Magazine.*

Denise Meakin is a senior lecturer and leadership accreditation specialist at the Centre for Work Related Studies, University of Chester. She leads a unique work-based learning facilitation programme recognized by the UK's Higher Education Academy. She speaks and writes internationally on how businesses and universities collaborate to enhance learning impact.

Etukudo Odungide is a management consultant with an interest in leadership and personnel development. He holds a Master's Degree in Management with Human Resources and is an experienced analyst of leadership data and published works. He uses this expertise to evaluate training needs and offer bespoke solutions in organizational growth.

Lisa Rossetti an executive and leadership coach, writer and story practitioner. She currently works within health and social care settings for service improvement, CPD, recovery and wellbeing. Lisa writes about applied storytelling, creative writing and journaling for health and academic publications, including the NHS publication, *Words for Wellbeing.*

Philip E Sweet is Director and Lead Consultant at The Performance Improvement Project Ltd. He uses human systems engineering, leadership and organization development to enable individuals, teams and organizations to improve performance and become all that they are capable of being. He speaks and writes internationally on measurement and performance improvement.

Tony Wall is a senior lecturer and researcher in personal and organizational transformation at the Centre for Work Related Studies, University of Chester. He uses applied psychologies to facilitate behavioural change and impact in business, government and education. He speaks and writes internationally on transforming practice for performance.

Case study authors

Kate Julian is a senior lecturer in the Department of Corporate Business and Enterprise at the University of Chester. She has a broad business background including supply chain development and engineering R&D. For the past 12 years she has specialized in learning and development in the private sector and in higher education.

Nadine Perrins is Chief Pensions Service Manager for the West Midlands Pension Fund. She was previously Head of Human Resources in Local Government specializing in employment law, organizational change and recruitment utilizing profiling and competency frameworks. She has a particular interest in developing leadership capability within organizations from grass-roots level to senior management.

Greg Young is an experienced Chief Executive, coach/mentor, facilitator and adviser on leadership development in organizations. He specializes in board behavioural development and facilitation and is a Fellow of the Royal Society of Arts. Developing expertise includes utilizing new technologies to aid self-development in a leadership context.

INDEX

NB 'action points', 'further resources' and 'references' have their own subject entries page numbers in *italic* indicate figures or tables